En

METROPOLITAN ANTHONY
OF SOUROZH

Translated from the Russian by
Tatiana Wolff

DARTON · LONGMAN + TODD

First published in Russia in 1999
under the title *O Vstreche* by the Christian Life Foundation,
edited and compiled by E. L. Maidanovitch.
This translation published in 2005 by
Darton, Longman and Todd Ltd
1 Spencer Court
140–142 Wandsworth High Street
London SW18 4JJ

The publishers gratefully acknowledge the assistance
in the preparation of this book of the publishing house
of the Russian Orthodox Diocese of Sourozh:

St Stephen's Press, 31 Warnborough Road, Oxford OX2 6JA

ISBN 0 232 52600 1

A catalogue record for this book is available from the British Library.

Designed and produced by Sandie Boccacci
Phototypeset in 11/13.75pt Times
Printed and bound in Great Britain by
Page Bros, Norwich, Norfolk

Contents

❧ ❧

Church and Society

Spirituality and Pastoral Care

Introduction: Metropolitan Anthony
and the Diocese of Sourozh

❧ ❧

The Diocese of Sourozh, the Russian Patriarchal Diocese in Great Britain, remains Metropolitan Anthony's primary legacy, and now, under the leadership of Basil, Bishop of Sergievo, it seeks to continue his work. In this introduction, Bishop Basil places the work of Metropolitan Anthony and the texts published in this book in their historical context.

In this collection, Metropolitan Anthony's 'word', his particular proclamation of the Word of God, is made available to the English-speaking world. For his original audience in Russia, they had particular significance in the context of his life and his work for the Russian Church in Western Europe.

Metropolitan Anthony was born Andrei Borisovich Bloom on 19 June 1914 in Lausanne, Switzerland, of Russian parents. His early childhood was spent in Persia, where his father was part of the Russian Imperial diplomatic mission, but when the Russian Embassy there was handed over to the Bolsheviks after the Revolution, the family was forced into emigration. Travelling westwards, they found themselves in France in 1923, where Andrei grew up, eventually training as a doctor at the Sorbonne in Paris. In 1931 he was given permission to serve at the altar in the Podvorie of the Three Holy Doctors, at that time the only parish in Paris belonging to the Moscow Patriarchate. In 1939, before being sent to the front in the French army, the young doctor took secret monastic vows.

These were confirmed in 1943, when he took the name Anthony after one of the founders of the Monastery of the Caves in Kiev. In 1948 he was ordained priest and sent to London to serve as Orthodox chaplain to the Fellowship of Alban and Sergius, and in 1950 was appointed rector of the Moscow Patriarchal parish in London, which moved to its present location in the Church of the Dormition and All Saints, Ennismore Gardens, in 1956.

In 1957, Father Anthony was consecrated Bishop of Sergievo to serve as an assistant bishop to the Exarch of the Moscow Patriarchate in Western Europe. Then, in 1962, by a decision of the Holy Synod in Moscow, a diocese of the Russian Church was formed in the British Isles and he was put in charge, as Archbishop of Sourozh. From that time on he devoted himself primarily to the task of building up the Diocese of Sourozh, which has always remained faithful to the Russian Church, while opening itself to people of all nationalities. Most recently it has welcomed the great numbers of new arrivals from Russia and the Former Soviet Union who have come to Britain since the fall of Communism.

The Place of the Diocese of Sourozh in the Twentieth-century History of the Russian Church

The Diaspora: A Child of the Revolution

The Diocese of Sourozh is a child of the Russian Revolution: not in the sense that the Revolution gave birth to it, but that its existence can only be understood as an aftermath of the Revolution. The flight of two or three million Russians from the 'Brave New World' brought into existence by the Communists led to the formation of Russian communities all over the world: in Western Europe, North America, South America and Australia.

These communities, however, though made up largely of Orthodox Christians belonging to the Patriarchate of Moscow,

INTRODUCTION

found themselves unable to live together in a single Russian Orthodox Church. Often it is said that the reasons for this were political: those of the 'left' chose to stay with the Patriarchate of Moscow; those of a 'liberal' persuasion left the Patriarchate to form the 'Metropolia' in North America and the 'rue Daru' jurisdiction under the Ecumenical Patriarchate in France and Western Europe, while those on the right, the 'monarchists', formed the Church in Exile, the Russian Orthodox Church Outside Russia (ROCOR).

No doubt political factors explain a great deal of what happened, but there were other factors concerned with what the émigrés thought about how the Church should face the challenge of emigration. Those who stayed with the Patriarchate – and they were very few – were committed to obedience to the canonical authority of the Church, no matter what difficulties this meant in practice. They were unwilling to separate from the Patriarchate of Moscow even though it was clear to everyone that the Church in Russia was being violently persecuted by an atheistic regime that controlled its outward life and was even able to force the Church to say (at least in public) that the regime was treating it properly. Over and over again one heard representatives of the Patriarchate say: 'There is no persecution.' There was persecution, of course, but those who remained faithful to the Moscow Patriarchate said to themselves – and to others: 'We cannot abandon the Russian Church in its time of greatest need. We will stand shoulder to shoulder with the martyrs and confessors.'

Those who guided the formation of the 'Metropolia' in North America and the 'Paris jurisdiction' under the Ecumenical Patriarchate had a different reaction to the situation in Russia. Both groups felt unable to accept the constraints that membership of the Patriarchate entailed. For them exile was also an opportunity, a chance to bring Orthodox Christianity to the West, and to put into effect the changes introduced into Church life by the Moscow Council of

1917–18. This council, the first to be held in Russia for more than two hundred and fifty years, was specifically intended to bring Church life into the twentieth century. It introduced far-reaching reforms, the most significant of which was undoubtedly the introduction of the laity into the heart of the administration of the Church. The Council itself was attended by elected lay representatives who contributed greatly to its deliberations.

The Moscow Council of 1917–18 took the momentous step of restoring the office of Patriarch, which had been abolished by Peter the Great in the early eighteenth century. Metropolitan Tikhon (Beliavin) of Moscow, who had spent a number of years in charge of the parishes in North America, was chosen by lot from among the three candidates elected by the delegates to the Council. Diocesan Assemblies were introduced through-out the Church, parish councils were established, the system of Church Courts was reformed, and – perhaps most important of all – provision was made for the election of bishops by the dioceses themselves.

In the aftermath of the Revolution, however, it proved impossible to introduce these changes in Russia. The office of Patriarch could not be abolished by the Communists because its restoration was so popular, as was the Patriarch himself, but the rest of the changes were a dead letter. The Church in Russia had entered upon a period of persecution more systematically violent than any the Christian Church had ever known. In such circumstances believers understandably held on to what they already knew in the hope of preserving at least something for the future.

The work of the Council was carried forward, however, out-side Russia, largely by the 'Metropolia' in North America and 'Paris' jurisdiction in Western Europe. The reforms that were impossible in Russia were gradually put into effect in the emigration in the belief that they not only reflected the deep will of the Russian Church itself, but also would enable the émigré communities to strengthen their Church life, relate more readily to their new situation and thus bring the Orthodox faith to the countries in which they now found themselves. It was a distinctly missionary attitude that saw in exile an opportunity and not just a loss.

The general attitude of the third group, the Russian Orthodox Church Outside Russia, where the reforms of 1917–18 were also introduced, was strangely similar to that of most Orthodox inside Russia: what mattered was to preserve what once had been and live in the hope that God would bring about better times.

The interaction of these three political and ecclesiological trends led to the establishment of three parallel Russian jurisdictions wherever there were enough Russian émigrés to make this possible. All three exist in Western Europe, in North and South America, and in Australia – almost everywhere, that is, except in Britain.

The Situation in Britain

In Britain, though there was once a 'Paris jurisdiction' parish in London, it no longer exists. And this is in spite of the fact that many – if not most – of the Russians who settled in Britain had close ties with Paris. What is the reason for this anomaly? The original Russian community in London in the 1920s and 1930s belonged at first to the jurisdiction headed by Metropolitan Evlogii, to whom Patriarch Tikhon had entrusted the Russian émigré communities in Western Europe. This community then split, part of it joining the Church in Exile and the rest remaining with Metropolitan Evlogii when he left the Moscow jurisdiction to place himself and his parishes under the Patriarchate of Constantinople. From that time there have been two Russian parishes in London. For a long time they used the same Anglican church, St Philip's, Buckingham Palace Road, on alternate Sundays. When St Philip's was torn down to make room for Victoria Coach Station in the 1950s, the Church of

England offered All Saints Church, Ennismore Gardens, London SW7, to the community that would later form the nucleus of the Diocese of Sourozh.

At the end of the Second World War, in the general euphoria that followed the victory over Nazi Germany, Metropolitan Evlogii and the parishes under him returned to the Mother Church, again becoming part of the Moscow Patriarchate. After his death in 1946, however, most of the parishes in Western Europe soon rejoined the Ecumenical Patriarchate – but in Britain the London community chose to remain with Moscow. It was to this Patriarchal community that Father Anthony was appointed in 1948 on the death of its rector, Father Vladimir Theokritoff.

Father Anthony, later Bishop, Archbishop and finally Metropolitan Anthony, made it quite clear that the openness to the Western situation and freedom from interference by the captive Mother Church offered by the 'Paris' jurisdiction were also available in his parish and later in his diocese. In his understanding – shared with the leadership of the 'Metropolia' in North America and the 'Paris' jurisdiction – the émigré communities had been given the opportunity to carry forward outside Russia the reforms introduced by the Council of 1917–18 – in his case, within the Moscow Patriarchate. In practice this meant the gradual introduction of lay participation in the practicalities of Church life. This in turn meant the increasing participation of non-Russians who were attracted to the Church, as laity and eventually as priests.

This increased involvement of non-Russians corresponded to the tacit if not openly avowed policy of the Patriarchal Church itself. In the 1970s the Russian bishop in Dusseldorf was a Belgian, Archbishop Alexis (van der Mensbruge), in Paris a Frenchman, Bishop Pierre (l'Huillier), and in Holland a Dutchman, Archbishop Jacobus (Akkersdijk).

At the same time the official position of the Patriarchate was that the communities of the worldwide Orthodox diaspora should gradually be freed from the tutelage of their Mother Churches and allowed to form local territorially-based Churches. This position was expressed in documents sent to the preparatory Commission for the Holy and Great Council in the 1970s. These were never published in full, but Archbishop Paul of Finland, who, though head of an autonomous Church under the Ecumenical Patriarchate, supported the position of the Russian Church, referred to them at length in an article published at New Valamo (Finland) in 1979 and reprinted in the first issue of the diocesan journal, *Sourozh*, in August 1980.[1] Already in 1970 the Patriarchate of Moscow had put its policy into effect by granting autocephaly, or the right to choose its own head without reference to another Orthodox Church, to what had been the 'Metropolia', which then became what is known as the Orthodox Church in America (OCA). What is more, both the 'Metropolia' and its successor, the OCA, were multi-national jurisdictions, containing Russian, Carpatho-Russian, Polish, Romanian, Bulgarian and Albanian parishes. This body, it was hoped, would eventually be the catalyst for the formation of a local American Orthodox Church embracing all Orthodox whatever their national origin.

It is this open aspect of the Russian tradition that was espoused by Metropolitan Anthony and which he tried to incarnate in the Diocese of Sourozh. It is essentially a worldwide vision realised so far as possible in a small but representative community in the particular cultural and historical context provided by Britain.

The Moscow Council of 1917–18 deliberately tried to reintroduce into Church life what was best in the ancient canonical tradition of the Eastern Church. It could be said that it was the most important council held in the Orthodox Church since the seventeenth century. In the Russian context of its day it was itself revolutionary and, as far as the other Orthodox Churches are concerned, was far ahead of its time. The principles of Church life it sought to introduce are now being adopted by the other Orthodox Churches, thereby confirming their importance and validity. Clergy-laity councils are now a feature not only of the life of the Russian Church in the emigration, but also of the Greek and Antiochian archdioceses in North America, and of the Romanian dioceses in Romania and Western Europe and the Church of the Czech Republic and Slovakia. In fact, they are being introduced wherever the Church is alive and well.

It was against this background that Metropolitan Anthony visited Russia over a period of more than thirty years. For Russia he represented the voice of the 'free' Church, a position consolidated over the years as a result of the many broadcasts he made on the Russian service of the BBC. When Communism collapsed in Russia in 1991, it became possible for the first time to publish his talks and sermons there for general distribution and to date, more than a million copies of books and pamphlets by Metropolitan Anthony have been printed for sale in Russia.

The immediacy and freshness of his approach to Christianity is apparent in these texts, as is his openness to other faiths and to the contemporary world. These aspects of his thought, together with his strongly 'evangelical' proclamation of the Orthodox faith, were what impressed those who heard him speak on the radio or in person in the Russian language, and are no less relevant for us in the West today.

+ Basil, Bishop of Sergievo

Chapter 1

❧❧

Encounter

A talk given in Moscow in 1968. Printed in the journal *Novyi Mir* (1992, No. 2).

The theme of encounter is one which is at present entering more and more into people's consciousness, and is often experienced more acutely than it was in the past. It has become universal because there are now opportunities for people to meet those whom before the First World War, say, they never even wanted to meet. Young people in the West are more and more conscious of the fact that they are not members of isolated ethnic or state groups, but simply people, and that the world which they now want to build is a human world, and not a national or a class world or one belonging to one culture or another. And so in connection with all these experiences the theme of meeting has surfaced in a new way in the consciousness of very many people, and when a theme surfaces in this way, then everything that one sees and everything that one reads, one sees and reads in its light.

If you examine the Gospels anew, read them with new eyes, if you look at how they are constructed, you will see that apart from encounter there is nothing else in the

Gospels. Every tale is an encounter. It is the encounter of Christ with the Apostles, of the Apostles with other people, of other people with Christ, of people in Christ's presence with other people without Christ, apart from Christ, against Christ, and so on. The whole of the Gospel story is constructed precisely in this way. These are concrete, living encounters, each of which has an universal significance in the sense that, of course, there were a thousand times more encounters, but in the Gospels are singled out only those stories which have as far as possible an absolute, all-embracing significance. They are the kinds of encounters or situations in which, as in a mirror, many people can see themselves, and not merely unique events which are not applicable to anybody else. And so this theme of encounter seems to me very important, because of course the encounter continues. The encounter with God continues, the encounter between people continues, and the encounter of people before God and of people outside God continues. And all of this is the theme of the Gospels.

We can, I think, separate out two or three themes, two or three events. Firstly there is the encounter with Christ or, if you prefer, with God in Christ. That is the encounter which we constantly see. It runs like a red thread through the whole of the Gospels. There is the encounter of the disciples with Him who will become first their teacher, their mentor, and then their God. This encounter happens in various ways, and maybe it is worth pausing a little on this subject.

A typical encounter is shown to us at the beginning of St John's Gospel. The people gathered around the Baptist. Together with the Baptist were standing two of his disciples, Andrew and John. Christ, at that time unknown to anybody, approaches the Jordan. He is, as yet, only Jesus of Nazareth in the public mind. And John bears witness: 'Behold the

Lamb of God, who takes away the sin of the world' (John 1:29).

This is the first event. Two of John's disciples – precisely because they understood the words of their teacher, because they had grasped that John had come as the Forerunner, as an anticipatory figure, and after him was coming someone greater than he himself, because they are through and through John's disciples – abandon their teacher. This is a tragic moment, for to go away from one's teacher for the very reason that you have understood that he must diminish, so that the other who has now come, can grow, that he must become as nothing so that the other can grow to his full height – that is very difficult.

This was the primary situation: those people who were prepared leave, tearing themselves away from what was the most precious for them, to follow Jesus simply because John had said: 'This is He.' Christ turns round and asks what they want from Him, and they answer, 'We want to see where you live' – and they spend the whole day with Him.

That is how the encounter face to face took place, where Christ lived. And it is hardly the case that they wanted simply to see in which hut Christ was living. They wanted to see the place where He lived, that place where everything breathed of Him, that place which bore some mark of His presence. They found Him there, and their first action was to call their friends and relations. Andrew called for his brother Peter, John called for his brother James, and both called for their friend Philip. Philip called for his friend Nathaniel. And thus was formed the first chain of relationships. This first encounter begins to blossom into a whole tree of inter-relationships, all based on encounter. If Peter had not been Andrew's brother, or James the brother of John, if they had not met and become friends of Philip, or had not met and become friends of Nathaniel, they would not have formed this circle and would not have come to this fundamental encounter with Christ.

And so they come, and they discover Him, each of them discovering Him in his own way. One of them brings a special testimony, and that is Nathaniel. When he approaches Christ, the Saviour says: 'Behold an Israelite indeed, in whom is no guile!' (John 1:47). Nathaniel asks, 'How do you know this?' And there follows a strange response: 'I saw thee under the fig tree.' What is the connection? In the life of St Nathaniel it is said that he was one of those who lived in expectation of the coming of the Messiah. The moment he was called for by Philip, he prayed and cried out for this coming, and Christ's words were absolutely plain to him, which is why he says: 'Rabbi, thou art the Son of God; thou art the King of Israel' – for only God could know what was taking place between him and God at that moment.

That was the first series of encounters. One has to constantly underline and be aware of how important were these fundamental, simple human relationships of kinship – simple, human, healthy, country friendships – and how important and valuable all our human relationships are, what a decisive influence they can have in the basic events of our lives. We have to nurture, with care and deep thought and in their entirety, all the relationships which we have, because each relationship defines a situation which might blossom into a miracle – the miracle of an encounter with God.

Then something else happens. If Christ had been a political leader, He would immediately have taken advantage of the inspiration, the joy, and the devotion of His disciples in order to call them to action: 'Go, call others, bring others!' Which others? Those people with whom we have no relationship? Those people with whom there has not yet been an encounter on the grounds of simple human love or friendship? Christ does not do this. Christ sends them home. They go back to Galilee, and Christ goes into the wilderness. They meet about two months later: the Saviour had been in the wilderness for forty days, and He also spent some time on the journey back to Galilee. At this point something happens of which, it appears, one of the Old Testament prophets has spoken: God calls us once, and He calls us twice. The first time Christ called these people, He stood before them, and they saw something, and He let them go in peace: 'Go.' The second time, the encounter was different. Two months had passed. They had had time to cool down. The astonishing impression made by John's sermon, the encounter with Christ by the Jordan, the talks at His house, the beginnings of being His disciples – all this had receded somewhat. And now Christ walks past the lake where His disciples are mending their nets. He does nothing to remind them of what has happened. He does nothing to re-awaken the emotions which have perhaps died down. Now that which had been an inspiration has become a clear and peaceful memory, Christ approaches and says to them, 'Follow Me.'

If everything that had happened before had lodged in their souls as an authentic, reliable memory of something completely real, they would go after Him. If, on the other hand, what happened had become indistinct, and had begun to acquire hazy outlines, if they had the impression that it was a momentary inspiration which disintegrated on contact with the real life they lived, they would not get up. Christ does not need people who have been inspired. He needs people who live calmly, with a crystal-clear, deep conviction, people whom the Holy Ghost can inspire, but who do not live according to their human raptures. One cannot build on that. And they follow Him.

That is one encounter. Another which you will remember is that of the Apostle Paul on the road to Damascus, when he came face to face with the One who had died, and of whom his disciples – according to Paul's conviction, falsely – preached that He was resurrected. Paul was on his way to expose and unmask this in Damascus. And suddenly He who had died was standing alive in front of him, in heavenly glory. That is a different kind of encounter. You have only to read the Gospels to find many of the same kind.

And so I would like to make one general comment. When we read the Gospels, we must remember that every story is presented to us absolutely concretely: we could have been a part of that crowd. What was it that happened then? Christ engaged in a conversation with somebody, or somebody asked Him a question and He replied. In that crowd there were people for whom both the question and the answer had meaning; and then everything that was said aloud between Christ and that person was absorbed by those few people (or maybe by many), for whom this was an answer to a living, concrete, meaningful question. There were probably many others for whom the question itself did not exist, and therefore the answer did not exist either. And we have to be very careful not to imagine that everything that is said in the Gospels relates directly to us, simply because it is told in a particular story about Christ. Yes, it does relate to us, but not necessarily immediately, and not necessarily totally. It relates to any person, but in different ways and at different times.

There is a criterion here, which we also find in the Gospels. Do you recall the travellers on the way to Emmaus? Christ approaches them, they start a conversation, and when Christ reveals Himself to them at the breaking of bread and then vanishes out of their sight, they say to each other: 'Did not our hearts burn within us while He talked with us on the road?' (Luke 24:32). When we read the Gospels and some phrase, some image or story, so strikes our souls that our hearts begin to burn, that our minds are enlightened, that our whole will urges us to follow that word, we can say with conviction: 'Christ said this to me during a conversation with others. What was said to me personally I must take in fully, to the end, and treat as an encounter with Christ, in which He spoke to me with words of command, of entreaty, of counsel, of plea, and I must act accordingly.'

There are many such encounters, either with Christ Himself – the rich young man, the centurion, the lepers, all sorts of people – or between people who met each other near Christ, because the crowd around Christ was a colourful one and very varied, where people who did not know each other at all met, and sometimes never parted again. So gradually a group of people built up of the twelve Apostles and of seventy disciples. The group surrounding Him continued to grow wider all the time.

But an encounter with Christ also plays another role. Christ came to bring 'not peace but a sword' (Matt. 10:34), to divide and not only to unite. Christ came as a stumbling-block: some accepted Him, others rejected him. Because of the encounter with Him, some turned away from God; others, because of the encounter, came to God. Some saw a new inconceivable revelation of God: a God who was helpless, vulnerable, humble, as if defeated, and saw that only in this truly lay God's glory. Others, having seen God or, rather, having heard a sermon concerning what God is like, turned away, because they did not wish to have such a God.

There is one encounter of which I want to tell you, though it is not in the Gospels, for I think it throws light on a whole range of problems. The Desert Fathers said: 'He who has seen his own brother, has seen his God.' Often, when we meet a person who is suffering and worn out, we become capable, even in a small measure, of seeing God through him. But I want to tell you of something else: sometimes the face of suffering is ugly: the face of suffering repels us. However, that, too, can bring us to a complicated encounter specifically with Christ, and to an understanding of something relating both to Man and to Christ. After Paris was liberated,[1] they began to search for and ferret out those people who had collaborated with the Germans, who had betrayed and sold people to death and to torture. There was such a man in the district in which I lived and he had played a terrifying role in the fate of many people. He was found and caught. I was going out of the house and there was a crowd coming, dragging this man along. They had dressed him up in the clothes of a clown, shaved off the hair from half his head, he was covered with slops, and there were marks on him where he had been hit; and he walked, surrounded by the crowd, along those streets in which he had practised betrayal. This man was undoubtedly evil, indubitably a criminal: his trial and its verdict were just. After a little while I found myself in the Metro, waiting for a train to come – and suddenly it became completely clear to me that that was exactly how people had seen Christ, when He was taken to His Crucifixion.

We see in Christ a divine martyr, but thousands of people saw something else in Him. In their opinion, this man agitated the people, and was a political danger. Because of Him, the Romans might come and occupy the whole country. He was also a troublemaker in the religious sphere, and preached a blasphemous picture of God. He was taken, He was judged, He was beaten, and finally He was condemned to death. It is exactly the same picture: there is no difference. The difference starts where our faith in Christ appears, and when we see Him with new eyes. But it was possible to see Him plainly then, in Jerusalem – beaten, exhausted, a man being led under guard to his execution, which He had deserved.

This is a completely different kind of encounter: an encounter of man with man, but in the light of Christ or under the shadow of the Cross. A Christian cannot simply recognise the Parisian collaborator as a criminal who is going to his deserved execution, because he is, as it were, projected against the background of another man called Jesus from Nazareth, whom others regarded in exactly the same way, and who also died.

The encounters of which I have just spoken – Gospel encounters, dramatic encounters – are given to us, are put before us as we go on our way. There is no escape anywhere from them, but life does not consist of dramatic encounters: it consists in the fact that we are constantly, hour by hour, meeting people – and we do not see them, we do not hear them. We walk past. We have not met now in a dramatic way, but we have met, we have looked into each other's eyes, we are open to each other, we want to meet each other. But does this happen often? How many times does a momentary encounter take place which is absolutely empty, purely physical, or a collision, in which two people collide with each other and then part. We walk past someone anonymous as a passing shadow: he is nobody, he had no personality, he had no existence, there was nothing because he did not even enter into physical contact with us, and so it means that he does not exist. And yet the whole stress of the Gospel message concerning encounter, the whole stress of the Apostles' encounter, lies in the fact that any encounter may or may not lead to salvation for the one or the other. There are many kinds of encounter: superficial ones, deep ones, true ones, false ones, leading to salvation, or not leading to salvation – but they all start with the fact that anyone who is conscious of the Gospel or simply has a keen, living, human understanding, must learn to see that another person exists. And this rarely happens, very rarely.

Think of yourself: how many people have crossed your path when you most needed it, when you were in sorrow? We do not see people. Very often we can describe them, but only their exterior; we perceive a physical shell – and only that. We do not even notice what lights up a person. We look at a lamp and assess what it is made of, what the artist put into it, but the fact that it is alight hardly even interests us – or we do not notice that it is not alight.

This is the first thing: we have to develop in ourselves the ability to encounter every person that we meet, to see every person, to listen to every person, and besides that to acknowledge that he has the right to exist – and this happens very rarely. Mostly our relationships with each other and with those around us are the same as our relationship to the circumstances of our own lives. We are at the centre, and around us there move – or do not move – phenomena. Objects do not move, but animals and people move – and often that is the only difference. We know that such and such a person is useful to us, and such and such is not useful. Unpleasant things emanate from such a one, and from another one none do. If I want warmth or friendship, I will go to this person as I would to a stove, in order to warm myself, or to a baker's for bread – and that is all there is to it and nothing else. That, I would have said, is the constant attitude of each of us to a certain number of people. It means we do not acknowledge that they all have objective existences. We are gracious, charitable and friendly towards them – all these of course in the best circumstances. But what does that mean? It means that we pay the same attention to the 'menials' that surround us as we do when we polish a cupboard or a table: on occasion we can bestow on someone a smile, or a kind word. If we are in any way constant in this, we might even be regarded as good friends – but all the same there is no friendship, because we are treating these people as objects around us. Yet these are not objects but people, and every one of them has the right to be himself, and not only a part of my life. One has to learn this. This can be so difficult, I would say, and often so unpleasant, that it is necessary to learn it. It is much more convenient to recognise in a person only that side which is turned to us with a smile. But the trouble for our own vanity is that there is another side, that a person exists not only when he is with us or near us. He has a whole life outside us.

We often say that equality lies in giving something or other to another person. Equality does not start here. It starts when we acknowledge that this person exists absolutely outside ourselves, that he has a right to exist absolutely separately and even over against oneself. He has the right to be himself, however inconvenient, distressing or deadly for oneself this may prove to be. If we do not achieve this measure of equality, we do not accept him and we are just throwing out scraps. There is the bestowal of certain rewards, certain gifts, but it is not a relationship with someone. A relationship means, firstly, to acknowledge a person's right to live his own life, to develop the ability to stand back and look at a person not as he relates to oneself, but for himself: what is he like, what is he? – and to realise (which we do not like doing), that if we did not exist in the world, he would still exist or could exist, and that our existence is not a great blessing for him, bestowed on him by God.

Secondly, we must know how to look, which is another thing we do not know how to do. We all know how to look in front of us and to take in something, but what do we see? We see two kinds of things: those which attract us, which suit us, or we see those which repel us; a person is either attractive to us or not. But these two extremes, or two aspects of a person, in no way sum up all that he is. He does not consist of the fact that there are in him things which I like and things I do not like, things which are dangerous or which are beneficial to me. But to see a person not in relationship to oneself, one has to know how to renounce oneself.

There is an English writer, Charles Williams, the author of a number of religious-philosophical novels. In one of them, *All Hallows Eve*,[2] he describes the posthumous fate of a young woman, suddenly killed by a plane crashing as she is crossing a bridge. At one point in the story this young woman is standing on the bank of the river Thames looking at the water. When she was alive, all her bodily being experienced revulsion at the thought that one could touch and could drink this dirty, greasy, heavy, leaden water, in which floats everything that is thrown out and discarded by the city. Her body previously stood as a shield between her and her ability simply to look and to see. Now, bodiless, she stands and looks, and the first thing that she sees are the dark, dirty, heavy waters which are flowing past her. And as she can no longer experience revulsion towards them with her body, she sees them as they are. They are something outside her, and do not relate to her. And further, this is a reality which fully corresponds with what has to be. That is what the waters of a river which flows through a big town have to be like. She experiences the total relationship of everything. And at that moment, when she suddenly acknowledges this, she begins to see something clearly. Through this first layer of murkiness, she begins to see layer after layer of water which is cleaner and more transparent, and gradually, somewhere at the very depths of the Thames, she sees a stream of pure, clean water. Then, at the very heart of this stream, she suddenly sees Water, that Water of which Christ spoke to the Samaritan woman at the well (John 4:7–15).

What had happened? She had become able to look at the water of the Thames without reference to anything, simply to look and to see it, not in relation to herself but in relation to itself. At that moment she became capable of seeing the light through the darkness. We usually behave in the opposite way. We see the light, and, when we look deeper into it, we see darkness and everything grows murky. Here the reverse happens, and throughout our lives we have to learn this in our attitude to people: the moment we give up on making judgements, we start to be capable of seeing into the depths and of discovering there, in the depths, more rays of light, and not the opposite.

That is as far as seeing is concerned. We also have to learn to listen. This is also difficult, because to listen means to consent to the contents of what the other person says becoming part of us without picking and choosing: to listen to a person without discarding what is not congenial to oneself, or what is offensive or difficult to accept. To listen properly means to become a participant, and to accept into oneself everything that that person will pour out, and to live through a shared experience in a kind of communion. In certain respects we do that easily. For example, people who love music give themselves over to it, lay themselves open to it, so that the stream of someone else's experience should become theirs, through the music. But that is much harder to do when a person speaks in prose, and talks of things which are in themselves unattractive or wounding. For this, one has to begin with a small part and later come to a total communication – which can tear one apart.

And that is how encounters take place. They are very varied. There are life-giving encounters, there are lacerating and murderous encounters. But however they are, in each real encounter one is given the opportunity to see something divine in a person, something which is not darkness, but is the true self of that person. Otherwise an encounter has not taken place.

In this respect the Orthodox marriage service is very interesting. At the beginning, in the first prayer of the ceremony, Isaac and Rebecca are mentioned. This is not by chance, and not because of the Church's love of remembering characters from the Old Testament, but because Isaac and Rebecca as man and wife found themselves in a totally exceptional situation: they were given to each other by God. You remember that when Isaac, the son of Abraham, grew up, his father wanted to find a wife for him and sent a servant to Mesopotamia, to find, through a sign from God, somebody who would be a God-given bride; and how the Lord showed the servant Rebecca. This gift of God also reveals itself to us in another way, not necessarily in a particular, visible sign, but in a manner which no one can confuse with anything else – in love. Love shows itself thus: we see something in a person which nobody else has seen. A person who was passing by unnoticed, abandoned, rejected, a stranger – simply one of the mass of humanity – is suddenly noticed by us, becomes significant and unique, and in this way becomes permanently meaningful. You should know, no less than I do, how this happens. In your midst there is someone whom nobody notices, who exists at best as part of a group, if not somewhere on the fringe – and suddenly someone looks at him and sees him, and then this person acquires real existence.

One of the Greek Fathers expressed this wonderfully. He says that until a young man falls in love, he is surrounded by young men and girls. When he has spotted his betrothed, he is surrounded only by people, because she has become the only one, while the others are only people. They do not belong to the same category of mutual relationships. And this happens not through virtue, nor as a reward for certain qualities. You know yourselves that our friendships, our love, do not come as a result of thinking about another person: he is so clever, so kind, so handsome, or so something or other, and, taken all in all, he has many good points, and therefore he is going to be my friend, fiancé, or whatever.

The marriage service also speaks of this. In the second prayer it says: 'O Lord our God, who hast espoused the Church as a pure Virgin from among the nations ...'[3] Christ in all languages and for all people has betrothed the Church to Himself as a pure Bride. If we think about how much reality there is in this, we can in no way say that about Old Testament Israel, and we can in no way say that about ourselves. But we can say it, not because the Church, or a single person are thus perceived and respected, but because a person who is loved becomes more than he ever was before. He has acquired the quality of eternity. Gabriel Marcel,[4] a French Existentialist, says that to say to someone, 'I love you' is the same as to say to him or to her: 'You will never die.' Because the moment that a person has been recognised, he is already supported by love. And not only within earthly time, but in eternity.

Often in the world, while we are not loved, while we are strangers to each other, we try to exist in a limited way, that is within ourselves, asserting ourselves in contrast to others, or by stressing how different we are. We exist specifically by asserting our existence: 'I am not you, and I exist.' But the moment that love is born, something happens which is in a sense destructive and frightening. To love means to cease to see oneself as the centre and the purpose of living. To love means to see another person and to say: 'He is more precious to me than I am myself. This means that I am prepared not to exist, as far as it is necessary in order that he should exist.' To sum up: to fall in love means to die completely for oneself, so that one forgets oneself – only the other person exists, for whom we live. Then, already there is no awareness of self, no wish to claim one's rights. There is no wish to exist apart from the other person. There is only the striving towards him, so that he should exist in the fullness of his being. And at the moment when a person is marked out by somebody's love, he no longer needs to assert his existence. He no longer needs to become different from others, because he has become unique; and being unique he is beyond comparison, he is simply unrepeatable, he is incomparable. That is what our encounters should lead to. That is what the meeting between God and each one of us is. For God, each one of us is unique, unrepeatable, incomparable. Each one of us is dear enough to Him for Christ to take on Himself Incarnation and the Cross. Each one of us has full significance, and with that, the fullness of freedom, because Christ does not possess anyone. He gave Himself through His love. He is at one with us, but His love is freedom. This freedom is again born of encounter, because the Lord has accepted us as we are, because He believes in us unconditionally, because He is ready to be at one with us to the end, and because this communion is mutual.

But here comes the moment of faith. In various places in the marriage service, it is said that we ask God for those who are getting married to have a strong faith. Faith in what? Obviously, faith in God – but not only that: faith in each other, because the first impression which existed when two people looked at each other and saw each other, can fade. Time passes. Many things happen – other encounters, other people, other circumstances – all of which can cause that clear and bright vision, which came first, to fade.

And here we must say, 'No, what I once saw was more true, more certain, than the fact that now I no longer see it.' This is very important. Because the uniqueness of this marital encounter, this encounter of love, is absolute, and it has got to be defended from blindness, from the intoxication which overcomes us, from the inability to take in once again a person with the initial vividness of this vision. It often happens that we have looked at a person and begun to see clearly the light of eternity in him. And then we look more and more closely, and we see more and more of his superficial layers. And, having started with a vision of the inner, mysterious man, we end by seeing his 'ego', his powers of thought, his emotional and other gifts, and that obscures for us what was and is in the depths, and will always remain there.

Methodius of Olympus[5] writes that when a man loves another, he looks at him and says: 'He is my *alter ego*, another me.' And as soon as he ceases to love him, he says, 'Here is *ego*, and you, my friend, are *alter*.' He no longer uses the word 'friend', but in general it works out like this: first, two were one, because each said the same to the other, and then there was a split and the two individuals parted.

And here it seems to me all the teachings of the Church about the uniqueness of brotherly love are colossally important, that if a person loves another he must never afterwards deceive himself and think: 'I made a mistake', as what was revealed at that moment cannot be erased. You cannot bring back what was revealed by any artificial vision, but you can live by your faith. If you have been blinded at a given moment, you have to say: 'I am blind, but I have seen the only light of which I can say "this is my *alter ego*".' Everything else – all the '*alters*' around – are simply other types and forms of relationships. And here the question is not one of gritting one's teeth and saying, 'I will die, but I will remain true to my first love' – but lies in the fact that we must say: 'I live by my faith. What was once shown to me is paradise, is a vision of eternity, and I will not let anything deceive me. I will put nobody and nothing on the same level with that. This is my bride, and those are people.' I want to say that they *are* people, and not tables, chairs or dogs. It does not mean that, since you are people, you do not exist for me. But it means that this person is unique, and those are others. One relationship is absolutely exceptional, although every other relationship, as far as encounters are concerned, is also unique in its own way. And here the question arises not of discipline or asceticism, but of the triumph of joyful, all-conquering faith.

The Human Vocation

Chapter 2

❧ ❧

We Have to Bring Faith to the World – Faith not only in God, but also in Man

This interview took place with Michael Epstein in London in April 1989. It was published in the collection *Man and Ecology* (Moscow, Knowledge, 1990) under the title: 'The Ecology of the Spirit' and in the journal *Literary Review* (1991, No. 2). It is printed here with a few editorial emendations.

Metropolitan Anthony, the relationship between religion and culture has become much more complex; culture has, in fact, abandoned the basis on which it had stood and should stand from time immemorial. People coming to Orthodoxy abandon culture, come to despise and neglect their worldly studies – in learning, in art and so forth.

It seems to me that the divorce between culture and religion is largely the result of the fact that religion or, more correctly, people who practise one religion or another (and often the Christian religion) have drastically narrowed their outlook on things. In fact our attitude to all that is created and to all history, culture, and learning should be the same as God's approach – that is, a deeply rational and loving one. St Maximus the Confessor already in the sixth century spoke of the fact that Man is created from two elements: the spiritual, which ties him to God, and the physical, which ties him to everything that is created in the world, and that Man's task is to spiritualise the whole of the created world, and to bring it to God, so that in the words of the Apostle Paul, 'God may be all in all' (1 Cor. 15:28).[1]

Historically, it seems to me, we have in large measure forgotten this vocation of ours. On the one hand there is religion – that is, faith, theology, people's ascetic and mystical paths – and on the other hand it is as though the world remains outside religious thought. To say that the world is steeped in sin, that we should not be 'of this world',[2] does not mean that we are not responsible for everything that makes up God's created world. And there is no aspect of this world which cannot be holy in our eyes and rendered spiritual by a person with faith.

I graduated in the Natural Sciences, and became a doctor on completing my medical studies. I studied physics, chemistry, biology and medicine, and I saw them as an aspect of theology, of the understanding of what God has created, in which He is revealed, and which He loves – because God created nothing through power, but created everything with love. And it seems to me that the Renaissance in the West, or asceticism in the Orthodox world in particular, which drew people away from everything worldly, away from universal political, social and cultural thought, is most unfortunate. Culture should be permeated with our religious experience, and should be made meaningful by it. And it seems to me that now it is time to reappraise both our own position and that of a culture starved of the Divine, that is, of the secularised world.

On our own part we should repent of the fact that we have allowed the whole world, millions of people, to lose God –

in that we proved not to be Christians to the end, that nobody meeting us sees Christ in our eyes; our image does not reflect the shining glory of a godly life. And for this the Church as a whole, and every Christian, should repent before God.

Concerning Russia, is not the colossal falling away from faith explained in the words of Leskov, that Russia was christened, but was never enlightened? And who but Christians must answer for this enlightenment or its lack? On the other hand, look at the culture of the West, including Russia, and the whole world which rose as it were on the yeast of the Christian faith – can we not take a look at this world and re-evaluate it, estimate it anew, taking note of how much there is in it from the Gospels? The whole of the world, however godless it may be, grew out of Gospel teaching. And what is preached or proclaimed by so many secular thinkers and politicians is in fact rooted in the Gospels. For example, only the Gospels established the absolute importance, the absolute value of the individual person. The Ancient world was not aware of this.

I think also that we have to take a totally new look at our attitude to the fallen world. Firstly we have to recognise our responsibility for that falling away, and secondly begin to see clearly with the eyes of faith and love that everlasting truth of the Gospels, that shining image of God, which is reflected in certain faces and proves to be the strength of society.

It is easier for us, obviously, to leave the world and form our own closed society. But such a closed society is, in my opinion, the negation of our calling. Because Christ came to save the fallen. He came to save sinners and not the righteous. He came to bring peace to mankind, who were at enmity with God. I once spoke with Patriarch Alexis,[3] and asked him how he would define the Church. He answered,

'The Church is the body of Christ, crucified to save the world.' I knew him fairly well and he was of course thinking of the fact that the Church is not only a body of people who are praying for the salvation of the world: we must go out into the world. Christ said to us that we are the light – that we must go into the darkness; that we are the salt, which prevents decay[4] – we have to go there, where decay is setting in: all this provided we possess faith, that is total assurance of the existence of God.

The level of awareness of God in Man depends on the fact that we are all called to become, as the Apostle Peter says, 'partakers of the divine nature' (2 Peter 1:4). It is this faith – faith not only in God but also in Man – that we have to bring into the world. We must bring to the world the certainty that God did not create us in vain, that He believes in every one of us, that He has deep hope in everyone, that He loves every person even unto death on the Cross; and therefore there is no person, however distanced he may be from God in his own eyes, who would not be infinitely close to God, who loved us so much that on the cross he was filled with horror of our godlessness and cried out: 'My God, my God, why hast thou forsaken me?' (Matt. 27:46). He died our death, experienced our godlessness, and no one can estimate the tragedy of the agnostic or the atheist in the way Christ at that time experienced it. He was in communion with everything that represented creation, leaving aside sin, but taking on Himself all the tragic consequences of sin. And therefore we are inseparable from the world, we exist because of the world. And this seems to me a very important point at this time.

Concerning the attitude of people who meet Christ and find faith when they are already mature (I to a certain extent belong to this group of people), of course the first thing one aims for is to forget everything else and be solely with Christ, solely at prayer, solely reading the Gospels, solely immersed in that miracle which has opened up to us. But here we must remember what happened to the Apostles Peter, James and John, whom Christ took with Him to Mount Tabor at the Transfiguration.[5] There they saw Christ in glory. But His appearing in glory was not when He was speaking with Moses and Elias of his departure from the world through crucifixion. The full glory of God is His love on the Cross. And when Peter said to Him on Mount Tabor, 'It is good for us to be here,' Christ took them into the valley, and there they met the dumb child and his grieving father who only partly believed, and the disciples were unable to heal the child. He purposely brought them down from the mountain of the Transfiguration, where the disciples wanted to stay forever, into the heart of human grief.

We can, of course, understand this descent to the depths better than aspiring to the heights of culture. But we must know how to read: how to decipher works of art, to read literature, to immerse ourselves in the ways of God through history – both in the personal history of an individual and in the history of a people. There is nothing human that should be alien to a Christian (these are not my words but those of Tertullian).[6] I now have quite a wide experience of people who have found God and who turn to God, and I always remember the words of St Isaac the Syrian: 'If you see a novice rising into the sky grab him by the feet and throw him down, because the higher he flies the more he will hurt himself when he falls ...'[7] This is very, very important to remember. Soberness, forbearance: that is, not to be greedy either in prayer, or in reading, or in anything. It is the readiness, as one of the ancient writers has said, to leave God for God's sake, that is to leave off praying and communion, in order to be of service to someone near to you. St John Climacus says: if you find yourself in contemplative prayer and hear that your neighbour in the adjoining cell is asking for a cup of water, leave your prayers and give him the water, because prayer is your personal matter, and that cup of water is God's work.[8]

Tell me, can an Orthodox person learn from other cultures and other faiths? Is there anything spiritually helpful in an Orthodox person exploring things that are holy, for example, to Catholics or to Protestants, or to Hinduism or to Buddhism, either through culture or directly through reading the relevant theological literature? What do you consider to be more helpful at this time: isolationism or, on the contrary, an open strategy of personal spiritual self-improvement in maturity?

There is, of course, the obvious danger in that an inexperienced person, who has little knowledge of religion or who is intellectually unprepared, can fall under the sway of much more developed, sophisticated minds than his own and then be drawn onto some false paths. I am thinking at the moment more of Catholicism than of Protestantism, because I think there is much more untruth in Catholicism, and much less truth in Protestantism. In Protestantism there is much that is lacking, whereas in Catholicism there is much that is distorted. But to read and ponder and compare everything with Orthodox teaching could be a very useful exercise in that if one does that, while continuing to pray, and continuing to live the life of the Church, one continues to meet God by every available route, that is in silence, in prayer, in reading, in the sacraments, and thus we can gradually perceive more clearly and more clearly the beauty, the depth, and the truth of Orthodoxy.

As far as the non-Christian religions are concerned, I think that nobody can *invent* God and therefore every religion which speaks about God, speaks from within some immediate experience of the divine. This experience may be very incomplete, but it is still a real experience. It may be partly distorted by its very incompleteness, because nature does not tolerate a vacuum; but at the same time there is some direct knowledge, knowledge through experience, to which we can relate or which could open up something for us. The Greek word *Theos* – God – has two roots. One root speaks of Him as the Creator, and the other root makes one think of Him as the one before whom one bows the knee. The German word *Gott* or the English *God* – from an early Germanic root – means 'Him before whom every knee shall bow'.[9] I do not think there is a single person in the world who has not at some time fallen on his knees before the Living God, whose presence he was suddenly aware of – or who has not met the Living God. How he will later express his experience, what forms he will give it, how he will later interpret it: this is where differences and mistakes may arise, but the root experience, it seems to me, is always real.

Of course one can say that a person can become the object of a demonic temptation. But here there is a criterion by which to judge. St Seraphim of Sarov[10] spoke of the fact that if an inner experience is linked with light from the mind, warmth from the heart, joy, a feeling of deep humility and gratitude, then one can think that this is an experience of God. The Devil is cold: when we are under his influence we enter into darkness, coldness, arrogance and so on. If a person experiences the former, he can say that he has touched the hem of Christ's garment. I do not say that he has been in full communion with God, but his experience belongs to that which is proper to God. Of course, every time that God draws near to a person, a dark force also draws near, wanting to tear him away. As soon as you start to pray, temptations appear; as soon as you seek an integral spiritual life, immediately certain difficulties arise – both from without and from within: that is the law of everything.

Maybe I will say this to my own disgrace, but I have understood a very great deal about Christianity and about Orthodoxy through reading and consorting with non-Christians, simply with secular people, with non-believers, who were, if one can put it this way, 'human beings', that is in whom I saw real people, able to love, to make sacrifices, to feel compassion, to show mercy, to be capable of every-thing which is spoken about in the parable of the sheep and the goats. In that parable there is not a single word said to suggest that people will be judged according to whether they had a belief in God; the question will be only: were you a human being or were you less than human? If you were a human being, God's path is open to you; if you were not human, then do not presume to see heaven. And so it seems to me that everywhere one can find much that is of value – not opening oneself to everything, but looking into everything. As the Apostle Paul says: 'Prove all things: hold fast that which is good' (1 Thess. 5:21). But if we do not *experience*, that is if we do not look into things, observe them, try to understand that which is outside ourselves, we will, of course, become so narrow that we will cease to be an embodiment of Orthodoxy. Because Orthodoxy is as broad as God Himself. If it does not match up to God's stature, then it is just one of the religions: it is not an experience of God.

Tell me, why does God not give consciously expressed faith to people who are responsive and virtuous by their natural inclinations? Is virtue possible without faith?

I cannot answer this. If I could, I would be known throughout the Orthodox world as a wise man. But one can point out some salient points. Firstly there is not a single person in whom there may not be a hidden but living image of God which continues to live and be active. There is not a single person who is not an icon and in whom this iconic likeness to the Living God does not operate.

From this it follows that a great deal of what we call human is in fact a facet of the divine. When you read the Gospels, you meet not only the Living God but a true, the only true, Human Being in the person of Christ: a Human Being in the full sense of the word. And therefore every human being – in so far as he is a human being – is already a part of this mystery of Christ.

There is another thing (but it is my interpretation and therefore I am not sure of the objectivity of this idea): humanity does not consist of separate individuals. Each one of us is born not as a new creation, but as an heir to all previous generations. This is confirmed by the fact that in the Gospels – both in Matthew and in Luke – we are given Christ's genealogy. If a genealogy has any meaning for Him, it has a meaning for us too. He appears as the inheritor of all members of the human race from Adam to the Blessed Virgin, Mother of God. Among all those generations there are saintly people and there are those whom we would call ordinary sinners – imperfect people – and there are out-and-out sinners, for example the lascivious Rahab – an obvious example – and she appears as an ancestress of the Saviour Jesus Christ.

Can we imagine what makes them part of this stream of people, which finally ends with the Incarnation of the Son of God? It seems to me that both the sinners and the virtuous strove with all their might (either successfully or, in our view, completely unsuccessfully) to live life to the full as they understood it, that is they strove for closeness to God. They lived for the sake of God. In the Jewish race this is, of course, clearer than among pagans, because the whole of the Jewish race was headed in that direction. And it seems to me that each generation inherits from all the previous ones. In particular from our parents and closest ancestors we inherit characteristics of the mind, of the heart, of the will and of the body – and problems, both solved and unsolved. That is if the parents have solved some problem between themselves they will pass on to the children a humanity which is more refined, and freed of this 'accursed question',[11] to use Dostoevsky's words. If they cannot solve it, the following generation will sooner or later be faced with it. I have met people who said to me, 'I am seized by one or another temptation, I am faced by one or another problem, which is absolutely foreign to me. Where does it come from?' And, digging into their past, I have managed several times to find in their forefathers and their parents the same unresolved problem: it presented itself to this person, who solved it just because he knew that it was inherited and that in solving the problem, he was doing it for his grandmother, for his grandfather, for his great-grandfather and for his parents.

About twenty years ago a very interesting experiment was undertaken in America.[12] A doctor involved in research experimented on himself with medicines, which, it appeared, removed the barrier between the conscious, the semiconscious and the unconscious. He describes it in a very interesting way. He increased the dosage under a colleague's control. At first he felt as he normally did, but then he found depths in himself that he did not know existed. He went further, and suddenly various images surfaced: images of his ancestors, images of people who by their manner of dress and speech belonged to one or another previous epoch, who were of his flesh and blood, who as it were lived in his soul and whose fate was determined by his own.

There is no reason for you to believe what I am saying, but for me it is very clear and very convincing. And therefore the fact that a person has not found faith does not mean that he is not preparing the ground for faith to come to one of his descendants, and through this descendant he will himself be justified before God, because he will have proved to be the ground on which this faith could grow. This may be my fantasy, but I am not sure that it is merely a fantasy. I am sure, for instance, that the lascivious Rahab was justified in Christ.

This is one explanation, although there are others. St Paul says: 'Faith cometh by hearing, and hearing by the word of God' (Rom. 10:17): not only from hearing with the ears, but also from a person whom you meet. Are not we, the believers, guilty of the fact that the people around us, in meeting us do not meet Christ? Do we dare to reproach the unbeliever because, looking at us, he cannot believe in Christ? The Apostle Paul also said: 'For the name of God is blasphemed ... through you' (Rom. 2:24). People would like to believe, but think: 'Lord! If these are Christ's disciples, then why should we join them?' And *we* are responsible for this, and we condemn ourselves, when we say, 'These people do not believe, in spite of what we say.' My spiritual father once said to me, 'No one can turn away from the fallen world and approach God if he does not see on the face or in the eyes of just one man the light of eternal life.' If people were now to meet Seraphim of Sarov, Sergius of Radonezh,[13] John of Kronstadt[14] (one could name any number of saints), they would stop, look and say: 'What is there in this man that I have never seen before?' C. S. Lewis says in one of his books: 'Every unbeliever meeting a believer should stop and exclaim: "A statue has become a living human being, a stone statue has come to life!"'[15] But can this be said about us? The answer to the question 'Why do they not believe?' is very simple: it is because they have not met in any of us the revelation of a person who has met God.

Bishop, there is another question. One meets Christians, or at any rate people who call themselves that, who in some manner identify Christianity, or at any rate Orthodoxy, with the Russian idea, with the Russian faith, who are convinced that the Russian people possess a messianic destiny, in the sense that they carry God's truth to all other peoples. Is this possible after a limited messianism – that is within the limits of a certain historical period, which is spoken of in the Old Testament?

I think one can return to the thought of the Russian chronicler Nestor.[16] He says that every nation possesses some individual, distinctive characteristics, which must contribute to the total harmony of all Christian peoples: that all Christian peoples should be like voices in a choir or like musical notes. Each of them should sound with its own sound, each with the utmost purity, but at the same time they should all merge into a single harmony, into one single, complex, rich sound. By this Christ's meaning becomes universal. He does not appear either as a Jew, or a Russian, or a German, or as anyone in particular. He is neither white, nor black, nor yellow: He is Man with a capital M. It is perfectly right that the Chinese and black peoples paint Christ in their national image. There is an English Christ, there is a German Christ, a Russian icon, a Greek icon and so on. We cannot say that any nation in its ontological essence is the only one.

One can say that historically one or another nation, at one or another time, was destined to play a particular part. For example, there was a time when Orthodoxy blossomed in Byzantium: now we cannot say that. Present-day Constantinople[17] is not ancient Byzantium. One can say that in the Russian people there are certain spiritual characteristics which may cause them to be more all-embracing. But that is by chance, and maybe confined to a certain era.

I speak from my own experience here. Russian Orthodoxy can be understood by Western people and is accessible to the West in a way that Greek Orthodoxy is not. That is because Greek Orthodoxy is so ethnically defined, is so Greek, that it does not reach Western people. Two Orthodox Englishmen, a bishop and an archimandrite in the Greek Church, were speaking in my presence after a service in the Greek Cathedral, and one of them said, 'If there was only Greek Orthodoxy, none of us would become Orthodox ... Russian Orthodoxy opens itself to people in the West, as neither Greek nor Arabic Orthodoxy have done.'

In my youth I belonged to a purely Russian Orthodox milieu, where we did not even think of using foreign languages or of including non-Russians in our midst. But now, during the last ten years, Orthodoxy has become the faith of very many Western people. This is firstly because after the first emigration[18] there were many mixed marriages with people of various nationalities, and now there is a fourth generation of children and young people. They no longer know the Russian language; they are not rooted in Russian culture in the same way as people now in the Soviet Union or those in pre-revolutionary Russia. They are simply English, German, or French, or whatever you will. But they are Orthodox. Besides that we have several hundred converts simply from the local population: in Britain we have English people, in France there are French people, there are Germans – people who by blood have nothing in common with Russian reality, but who found God, the Gospels, Christ, faith, the Church, a new life – in Orthodoxy. And to say that these people are 'second class' Orthodox is impossible: they are as Orthodox as the most culturally rooted Russians.

The good thing about Orthodoxy in the West, it seems to me, lies in the fact that we do not count as an ethnic Church. We are the bearers of Russian spiritual culture, with its particular characteristics: the experience of God as having the utmost beauty, truth, and life, embodied in the Divine Liturgy – in its absolute reverence. The wholeness and the simplicity of our theology, our openness to universal thinking, the compassion which was born of great suffering – all these qualities open Orthodoxy to other people. Therefore I am certain that the Russian people are bound to speak the living word of Orthodoxy, especially having passed through the crucible of more than seventy years' persecution, horror and striving, through darkness and light. They can speak more convincingly than those Orthodox peoples who did not go through such tragedy, who did not acquire their faith anew, consciously, personally, maturely, as adults. But this is not because we are Russian, but because that has been our fate.

I say 'our'. Of course in the Soviet Union people have experienced a thousandfold more than, let us say, my generation in the West – but even my generation experienced something. We did not swim through the history of these last seventy years without wounds, without pain, without deep unhappiness. And therefore I believe that the Russian people can be God-bearers. But that is not always visible; and sometimes is totally invisible. There were epochs when other nations were God-bearers; and we must be very careful because it is very easy to fall through pride, feeling, somehow, that we are the elect.

Do you consider that that falling away of masses of people from the Church, which happened in our recent history, is a sign of being chosen, or of sin?

This can be interpreted in various ways. As I have already said: Russia was christened, but was not enlightened. There was a great deal of very dark faith, and a great deal of superstition – and there was also much that was golden in the Russian people. But the Church was, of course, responsible for the lack of enlightenment, the darkness, and the superstition. I say 'the Church' not as the Body of Christ, but the Church as it exists in particular: you and I and all of us, and those who lived before us, and who were given the power to teach people and taught no-one or taught them badly.

That is one thing. On the other hand, 'The time is come that judgement must begin at the house of God' (1 Peter 4:17). I remember that in my youth this phrase was used as proof that the Russian Church was the Church which stood above all other Churches. I think that is a very optimistic interpretation. It might have been very comforting to think so, but it was not the case.

But in reality God passed a terrible judgement on the Russian Church – and not only on the Church but also on the people. The ways of God are unfathomable. We cannot know the ways of God, we cannot know why certain things happen, but we can know where they lead. We do know that as a result of all the tragedies there came about a certain *renaissance*, a new perception of the Gospels, of Christ, of

God, of the Church as something that lives and is completely new. And that is God's great mercy.

Chapter 3

❧ ❧

We Have Something to Say
about Man

This text is based on a talk given by the Metropolitan Anthony in Moscow in the House of the Artist on 15 October 1989. It has been filled out with extracts from previous talks, and was published in the journal *Chrysostom* (1992, No. 1).

In ancient times, and even not so long ago, the question of our faith in God was absolutely central throughout the world: it was *the* question. During the last ten years this question has evolved into one concerning faith in Man. It has become a question of whether or not we believe in Man at all. It seems to me that this is a very important contemporary theme both in our native Russia and in the West. What, then, does faith in Man consist of?

The atheist will say that contemporary man has no need of God, because Man has replaced Him, with all the richness of his mind, with the complexity of his personality, with all the possible activities open to him, and with his knowledge, all of which seem inexhaustible. The believer, for his part, will say that he believes in Man but not in that empirical manifestation which presents itself to us in history. He believes in a different Man, who obviously includes the latter within himself but who considerably transcends him.

Man, for a non-believer, is the final outcome of the evolutionary process. For Christians the conception of Man is somewhat different. For us, Man in the full meaning of this word can be understood only as the Lord Jesus Christ, that is as God and Man, as a man who has not only a worldly dimension but also a heavenly dimension. Man in the atheist world exists in two dimensions: time and space. Man as seen by a Christian has an additional dimension – a divine one. Christ shows us his extraordinary depth, his extraordinary size. Just think: if indeed, as we believe, God could become Man in the full meaning of that word, and at the same time that Man Jesus Christ did not become a superman – He did not become a different kind of being, unlike other people – then His humanity tells us that Man has such depth and such breadth within himself that he can contain the Godhead. Archbishop Michael Ramsey[1] once said that Man has such depth and such breadth that nothing that is created and earthly can contain him – that there is within Man an abyss, into which one can drop all knowledge, all love, all human feelings, all creation, and they will fall into the depths and will never reach the bottom: that this infinite abyss can only be filled by God Himself. Here you have two images, two views on Man.

But at the same time, both the believer and the unbeliever are equally concerned with the same creature, with Man, and Man becomes as it were the single point of contact between the complete atheist and the conscious believer. This meeting can be a polemical one if we each approach it with the desire to destroy the other's outlook; or it can be a very deep and thoughtful one, which can enrich both parties. When that happens, it is a wonderful thing. One of the most tragic things in the world is when two people or two groups of people cannot meet, not only because they have no common language, but because there is not even a point of contact, so, like two parallel lines, they go each their own way, to two opposite points of infinity.

This is our first task, which in our time, both in the West and in the East, must be regarded with particular seriousness. At present passions have died down to a large extent. We can view each other with a certain measure of friendliness and with the wish to understand each other, not with the desire to destroy each other or even immediately to convince each other of something, because the first stage must consist of listening to and observing each other.

You will certainly have noticed how, when two people talk to each other, they rarely listen to each other. For the most part, while one is speaking the other is preparing his answer. He is selecting from what he is hearing anything to which he can say, 'But I know better, and I can tell you something even more extraordinary' – and he breaks in. It is very rare for us to listen to one another with an open mind and with the passionate desire to understand the other person, especially when what he is saying is something alien to us.

We do not react in the same way when we are engaged in scientific research. In science – in physics, chemistry or biology – we look into the reality of various phenomena without preconceptions: reality is more important to us than our preconception of it. In the sphere of ideology (and here I include religious convictions which have been poorly formulated) it seems to us important to be right, and objective reality is not as important as for us to hold on to our own impressions. Anything different is very difficult to achieve: it is not at all easy to learn to listen with the intention of hearing; it is very difficult to look with the intention of seeing.

Many years ago I was a doctor and often saw how friends visited the sick. Somebody comes to see a person who is dying and is afraid to start talking about death to the dying person – and equally afraid lest the dying person should start talking about it. So the visitor carefully asks, 'Well, how are you feeling today?' And the dying person, who is gravely ill, sees the fear in the eyes of the visitor, sees that he is afraid, and that he does not want to hear the truth, and answers evasively or simply lies, 'Well, better than yesterday.' And the visitor who was afraid to hear the truth, grasps at those words and says, 'Oh, I am so pleased that you are better!', and shortens the visit so that the truth should not come out.

Maybe you have never experienced this, but I have seen it so often. I was a doctor for fifteen years, five of which were during the war, and I saw a large number of dying people. I saw this terrible situation when a person is left on his own, because others do no want to hear, they do not want to see, because they are themselves afraid of death. A distancing from oneself is necessary, a readiness to look into another person, not only to hear his words, but to note the intonation, the sound of this weakened, unsteady voice, to see the eyes which say the opposite of what the lips have said, and not to be afraid, but gently and lovingly to say, 'Do not deceive me. Do not deceive yourself. I know that this is not the case. Let us speak to each other, let us break down this circle of silence, destroy this wall which causes you to be lonely, and also makes me hopelessly lonely. It estranges us, so that our mutual love cannot bring us together again.'

You may say that between ideological antagonists there often is no such love. That is no better – it is actually more frightening. There is no comfort in saying that I cannot talk to a man who is my ideological adversary because *a priori* I have already excluded him from the sphere of love. Have I really already condemned him with a final judgement? Is it possible that neither on earth nor in eternity is there any room for him where I hope to be? This is a frightening thought! But that is what we do when we refuse to meet someone. Obviously there are periods when circumstances do not allow for conversation, or argument, or dialogue, but there are no circumstances where people cannot at least try and grope their way towards trying to understand each other, no circumstances where people who are honest cannot try to listen to another person and to understand how he can feel and think as he does.

And we have got something to say. We have something to say which might inspire and not destroy another person. We are not talking about giving an unbeliever a view of Man which would destroy his view. We are talking about saying something which shows the unbeliever that Man is infinitely greater and deeper than he had thought, and that he himself is much more important than he had thought himself to be. There is no point in speaking *against* another person. As soon as you begin to contradict someone, he will, obviously, defend himself, because everyone fears being destroyed, everyone fears having no support.

In the 1920s, at a time when it was still possible to do so, Vladimir Martsinkovsky,[2] one of the sub-deacons of Patriarch Tikhon,[3] used to take part in debates. In one of his articles he wrote some wonderful words: 'Never speak against the man who is opposing you. Speak in higher terms, beyond opposition, so that he can hear and grow beyond himself, and marvel at what he could become if only he could rise above the level he is at.' One can speak in such a way with any man.

And what can we say about Man? We can accept a person as he is, having the experience of any godless person, any atheist, anyone who has not met God, and who is not godless through conviction but lives simply in the material world, and we can talk to him of the depths that we know exist in Man.

There is a story of the Elder Silouan[4] which tells how he discussed missionary activities with one of the Russian bishops, who lived in the Far East. The bishop was very direct, very confident and very fanatical. Silouan asked him: 'How do you go about convincing and converting to Christianity the people who surround you?' He replied, 'I go to a Buddhist temple and address all those present, telling them that all those statues they see – those are idols, simply stone and wood, nothing more. Give them up, break them up, come to believe in the true God!' Silouan said to him, 'And what happens to you then?' The missionary replied, 'These insensitive, crazy people throw me out of the temple and beat me up!' Silouan said, 'Do you know that you could achieve better results if you would go to the temple, look at the degree of reverence with which these people pray, how they honour their faith, and then call a few of them to sit on the steps outside and say to them, "Tell me about your faith." And whenever what they said gave you the occasion for it, you could say to them, "What you have just said is so splendid! If you could just add the following thought, how it would blossom out in absolute beauty!" And thus you would have inserted into their world view, first here and then there, some thought from the Gospel or from the Orthodox faith. You would not convert them at once but you would have enriched them with that which Christ brought to the earth.'

We could act similarly when we are dealing with people who see in Man only an earthly being. We would open up to them those depths of which they know nothing. But here we encounter another difficulty.

I remember my spiritual father once said to me, 'Nobody can renounce the world and seek the Kingdom of God if he has not seen the glow of eternal life in the eyes or on the face of at least one person.' Some of you have read the Gospels and recall the tale of how Christ cured the man blind from birth. This man had never seen the world that surrounded him. He had never seen a human face, and at the moment that Christ cured him, the first thing that he saw was Christ's face – a face which was the incarnation of God and the eyes of God's mercy and love. But who will dare to assert (of any of us, but primarily of himself) that, meeting us, another person could say: 'I can see in his face and I see in his eyes the shining of a life of which I have no conception! Light is pouring from him, which he calls eternity, and for which I have no name!'

Yet this does happen. It happens when one meets certain people that one stops, benumbed. One stops because behind that face there is a ripening of something which one has never seen before. This is what could happen if this beauty, this light, flowed from us. We obviously cannot seek for this with the idea of converting others; but if we were to seek our own rootedness in God, then sooner or later it would happen in some measure or other.

The other question is this. We often regard someone who disagrees with us as an enemy and as a result we do not see him: we see only the enemy within him. I remember a meeting in London at which Pastor Niemoller spoke,[5] who was the head of the Evangelical Church in Germany under the Nazis. He gave a talk to German pastors in London. I was invited but he did not know that I was there, and therefore he spoke without any reference to my presence. He spoke of his experiences when Hitler was in power, and said that his most tragic memory and the thing for which he blamed himself, was that during the whole of that time he had never thought that the Fascists, the enemies of Christianity and of his Church, were not enemies but lost sheep of Christ's flock, and he was responsible for them: that he should have gone to them. These were children of God who had lost their way – and he forgot about them or, rather, he treated them only as enemies. And he added a wonderful thing. He said, 'The Russian Church never separated herself from those who persecuted her.' This thought illustrated the words of Patriarch Alexis [I],[6] whom I once asked how he would define the Church, and he said to me, 'The Church is the Body of Christ, crucified for the salvation of those who torture it.' That is a completely different approach, which is of course not at all practical, nor political, nor aggressive.

And we have something else to learn: we have to learn to grow to the stature of our Christian humanity which we have not achieved. We remain at our personal level, in spite of the colossal gifts which we receive. For when we receive the Holy Mysteries in Communion, the Body of Christ merges with our humanity – and we do not notice it, we do not change because of it. It passes through us and goes somewhere else. And at the same time it happens that even without the Mysteries, the presence of God reaches a man. I want to give you an example. About fifteen to twenty years ago an Englishman came to our church in London. He was simply an unbeliever, but he had been asked to bring a parcel for one of the congregation. He took great care to time his arrival so as to be late for the service – to come after it was over and everybody would be leaving. But God decided otherwise, and he arrived at the church while the service was still on. He was upset and sat down at the back to wait for the end. And this is what he later told me. He sat down and began to wait for 'all this' to end. At first he was impatient, but then he began to calm down and suddenly he felt that in this church there was some richness, the presence of some thing. He began to explain it to himself: that he was intoxicated by the incense, that it was the effect of the melodious singing, that it was caused by the flickering of the candles, that it was from the collective hysteria of the faithful – he understood it all, of course, and still he became curious, and he asked my permission to come to the church when there was nobody there, to see what would happen then.

He came, sat for two hours in the empty church and then said to me, 'You know this Presence is still here. There is no singing, no incense, no flickering candles, no faithful, but the Presence is here.' He began to come to church, both when there was nobody there and when a service was taking place, and after a while he said to me, 'You know, I have been coming quite a long time, because I thought, "All right, let us suppose that it is God, but what do I need of your God if He simply lives in this church and nobody is any the better for it. If this is a passive God, who does not change people, I do not need Him."' And then it appeared that when he looked at the faithful praying and especially at those who were taking communion, he saw on their faces, just for a second, some kind of glow which he had never seen any-where before. He said to me, 'I do not know whether they become better people, but they are changed, as if they were, so to speak, a different form of creation. And I have to become different. I would like you to teach me and baptise me.' I prepared him and eventually baptised him.

That is an example of how God can work, quite apart from the Sacraments, simply by His presence and by the fact that He exists. But we, too, must learn to see God's image clearly through another person. I remember a priest in

France who once said to me that when God looks at us, He does not see our non-existent good works or our non-existent successes: He sees in the depth of our being, often hidden among trumpery and dirt and darkness, His own image, glowing like light in darkness. And that is what we have to learn. We have to learn to look at our adversary, at our enemy, and forget that he is an enemy, that he is an adversary, and see the image of God in him, an icon: a damaged icon, an icon which at times one is barely able to recognise – and because it is so damaged, because it is so befouled, one must pity it more than if it was in glory. An icon in glory – yes, we honour it, but an icon which has been trampled on, shot at, an icon which was trodden into the ground – with what reverence we should treat it. This is a holy thing, which has been defiled by human malice; similarly we must know a man who does not know he is an icon.

Do we know this? – hardly. At any rate it is rarely seen in our attitudes to each other, not only in respect of those who think differently from us, but even towards our close friends. We forget it. We only see that a person is difficult: we rarely remember that he is blessed.

This is the problem for us now, as much in the West (though of course there is a vast difference in approach and situation) as in the East. It is a central, real problem that we must believe in Man with the same sort of faith that we believe in God – a faith as absolute, as determined, and as passionate. And we have to learn to nurture God's image in man, a holy thing which we are called to bring back to life and to honour, just as a restorer is called to bring back to honour an icon that has been spoiled, trampled on, shot through. It starts with ourselves, but it must also be addressed to others: both to other Christians, whom we judge so readily, and to our nearest and dearest, as well as to people who think differently from us.

Answers to Questions

Please would you comment on the words of the Holy Fathers: love the sinner, but hate the sin; love your enemies, that is your personal ones, but not enemies of God and the Church.

I recognise the first part as the words of the Church Fathers, the second part, was said to me in his time by the present head of the Russian Orthodox Church Abroad:[7] he practised exactly that.

If we regard sin as a misfortune, as an illness, obviously one has to love the sinner as we love a man who is ill and hate his illness. And this in fact completes my answer. If a man falls ill with any disease, we can hate the illness, we can rack our soul with the thought that a man has become a victim of such a disease; but we cannot hate him, even if he was at fault. Even if the illness is a result of his debauchery, none the less one is sorry for the man, because he was not created for this and was not called to it.

As regards hatred of the enemies of God and of enemies of the Church – that is a very risky way of wording the question. It is risky because it is very easy to see all one's own enemies as enemies of the Church and of God. In arguments and in political differences it is so easy to think that I am on God's side and that anyone who disagrees with me is on the other side.

Is there not a danger of substitution: to value love of kindness more than love of God?

Of course, but one would be deceiving oneself, because to

say: 'I love God but kindness is secondary' could prove to be a superficial approach. It is easy to become a false mystic instead of being a real Christian. The third question concerns the definition by the Apostle Paul of the synagogue as Satanic. That was written at a time when there was sharp opposition between the young, growing Christian community and the synagogue, the Old Testament place of worship. 'Satan' is a Hebrew word and means 'the enemy'. So what they were talking about was not 'the demonic' in our understanding of it, but the fact that that community was against everything which the Apostles taught. That is why we have to spurn any sense of hatred or repulsion in these words. We have to be very careful when we read certain texts.

The Synod[8] was handed a letter from a group of clergy and of laity concerning the conciliar nature of the Church.[9] What was the reaction to this document?
The document as such was not read in full, but even without it the conciliar question was discussed attentively and very responsibly. The whole Synod, which consisted of bishops (that is, if one can express oneself in this way, of people who are usually the least conciliar, because they are used to giving orders and not to consulting with others – I being one of them, can boldly speak with such impertinence), was conscious of the fact that yes, one of the unhappy features of the life of the Russian Church is that we have lost the ability to consult each other, to listen to each other and to express ourselves with complete frankness and truthfulness. It goes without saying that there is also an awareness of why this has happened.

We have also lost the ability to listen to the idea of another person – not only to his words – and sometimes to read into them more than he can express. After all not every-body is an outstanding orator and can express with great clarity and precision the ideas which arise within him. The conciliar idea must penetrate the whole Church, but it must firstly be assimilated by the laity in an unorganised form. That is, lay people should discuss among themselves their Church life and their secular life. They must learn to speak among themselves and not to argue – which is a very Russian trait. Secondly, when instead of a casual argument around the tea-table people meet at a parish council meeting (even if tea is being served there!), they have to learn to listen and to speak with the aim not only of understanding each other, but also of taking into account what the Church represents: of what it is we are seeking to build. Are we building a practical human community, which can consist of believers, unbelievers and anyone else, or are we building a Church? Further, parish councils must come together in Diocesan Assemblies, with the same approach. At all levels (and here a two-fold training is required) people have to learn to be serious, truthful, able to be understood by others, but also – and this is very important – they should under-stand that they are building a Church, and not simply a public body. In England we have worked hard at this, and spent five years drafting Statutes for the Diocese of Sourozh.[10]

First we studied dogma concerning the nature of the Church, then the ancient canons of the Church, then the decisions of the 1917–18 Council,[11] then the statutes of local Churches, and finally worked out a statute which expresses the life of a Church in action. That is what we have to aim for. And for that no particular theological learn-ing is required, because every one of us, if we are believers, if the Gospels live in us, if Christ lives in us, should be in a position to say something and make our own contribution, according to our involvement with the Church. If someone lacks the words for this, he can bring a prayer. If he lacks the words for a prayer, he can contribute a reverent attitude to the task in hand; and that is how ecclesiastical conciliarity can be built up.

Similarly it must be built up among the bishops, and I have of late been astonished by how much it has grown. I have attended Episcopal Councils in the past – I remember very vividly the Councils of 1971 and 1988 – and I can see how, step by step, this conciliarity, this wish for mutual understanding, mutual involvement, mutual contribution of knowledge and experience, has grown; and I think that all this will bear fruit. There is one difficulty: the Church has been deprived for a very long time of the experience of really existing. We have to learn, and to learn it now, immediately, is impossible: it comes gradually through trial and error. We discovered this in England, when I first began to establish councils of priests, and then of parishes, and then a Diocesan Council composed of clergy and laity. We had to work a very long time at this in order to work out a common understanding and a united heart: but it is necessary to work at it, and it will be achieved.

Your Grace, when the Lord had brought you to the age of maturity you probably had to face the question as to which Church to belong to. Why did you choose the Moscow juris-diction just when the Russian Orthodox Church was passing through a very difficult time?

I shall begin, maybe, at an earlier stage and will say that out of all the possibilities I chose Orthodoxy – not only because I was christened as an Orthodox, and so it was natural to gravitate towards it, but also because I was astonished by the precise and, for me, extraordinary harmony between the simplicity, completeness, transparency and freedom of the Gospels and that of Orthodoxy. I saw in both the same quality; they were harmonious, as two sounds which can flow into one. My experience of other Churches which I had visited at that time, had given me the impression that they were narrower, more restricted, or in some other way did not resemble what I had experienced when I read the Gospels. Of course this is a subjective assessment: that does not mean that it is invalid, but it was what brought me personally to the Orthodox Church.

As far as the Moscow Patriarchate is concerned, we were at that time a very small group of people in the West, who took this decision on a very simple basis: so long as the Church does not preach heresy, one does not separate oneself from it. That is the Church's approach. Also, a Church which finds herself in a tragic position must not be abandoned by her children. This was not simply a different or irrelevant approach to the situation. We, of course, could do nothing for the Russian Church at home. There were about fifty of us in Western Europe: we were of no importance. But we felt that in this way we became witnesses that the Russian Church is a Church that is holy, our own Church and Christ's – and that was enough.

In this first group, as far as I remember (I was about seventeen at the time) there were people of very widely differing political and social approaches, and this played no part in the matter. People came to the Patriarchal Church not because they had a particular social or political conviction. They came because it was the Russian Church, it had not betrayed Christ in any way and we wanted to stand by it and be part of it. We had the feeling that it was holding us and was carrying us in its arms (and this feeling exists to this day).

Rather more than forty years have passed since that time. There are different people now, and the situation has altered. In America, in the United States, there are now about five million Orthodox, of which a very small number are native Russians, that is, born in Russia. With such a large number of Orthodox on the one hand and with such a tiny percentage of Russians on the other, it is very natural that the Church,[12] which began as a Russian Church, has now become an American one. But it became an autocephalous Church, the true lawful American Church, not by breaking away or renouncing anything. It became an *independent* Church, just as, for example, a daughter grows up, marries and begins to build up her family. It is a completely different situation.

At the time of the Russian schisms in the twenties and thirties, there was no question for me of forming a local Church in France, disassociated from the Russian Church, either because it was regarded as a 'non-Church' or because it was easier to live without it. I could not accept either of these reasons. Regarding the Russian Church as a 'non-Church' went very far. About twenty years ago[13] I spoke with the head of the Russian Church Abroad in London and asked him, 'What do you think of me? What am I for you?' and he answered, 'If I did not wish to offend you, I would have said to you: "You are simply not a priest", but I will say frankly to you what I think: you are a priest of Satan, because you have accepted ordination from the Moscow Patriarchate.' One must understand how far the renunciation went. And when people from outside ask us why we are so divided, why we do not mix with each other, or why we do not have a greater unity with one or other group of people, I say to them, 'Just try to create unity in such a situation.' If he had said to me that he considered me to be a bad man, I would not have argued. I know myself better that he knows me, and I agree with him. But to say that I am not a priest or that I am a priest of Satan, that is that the Sacraments that I administer are at best nothing, but more likely blasphemous, and that what I preach is antichristian, that I cannot admit because I have my own conscience, and I check very carefully what I say. I can be wrong in something – that is another matter, but I am not preaching a different Gospel from that of Christ.

There is another way of seeing things, to say: 'Let them [the Russian Orthodox Church in Russia] live their life, and we will build ours without interference.' I, and not only I but many of us, felt this to be a brutal and ugly attitude, because as I have already said we could do nothing for the Russian Church at home in the USSR, but to break away would have been to declare to everyone, 'Leave her. She is a doubtful institution. Something is wrong with her.' That is how it would have been understood. And no one had the right to do this.

I consider that those who, in the 1920s and 1930s left the Patriarchal Church in this manner betrayed in some way a truth, both ecclesiological and human. Those people who condemned any of our hierarchs – either Metropolitan Sergius[14] or anyone else – as misguided in their Church politics, could have said, 'We are not in agreement with what he is doing, but we cannot condemn him and we do not renounce him. Whether he is right or not can best be judged by the people in Russia, but certainly not by us, who are abroad. If I am insufficiently honest or truthful, this is my fault and not the fault of the Russian Church. If I make mis-takes, then they are my mistakes, they have not been foisted on me by anyone.' When the Civil War came to an end [1921], there were approximately five million Russians outside Russia. If those five million had formed one Church, our witness would have had significance. But when in the Patriarchal Church there remained about fifty people in the Holy Trinity parish in Paris, about thirty people in Berlin, and six people in Nice – yes, bearing witness was indeed very difficult. But that witness was concerned with a radical approach to the Church, and was not an expression of political accommodation. There were deep differences among the people involved: there were monarchists, there was Berdyaev,[15] there was Mother Maria,[16] there were ordinary people with varying views – but we were completely united in our love for our native Church and steadfast in the conviction that while the Russian Church does not preach heresy, we belong to her.

Do your words mean that the Russian Church, which is active in our atheistic society, symbolises the body of Christ crucified to save those who tortured Him, and must remain silent and acquiescent, and not call people to think deeply and to proclaim the truth in deeds as well as words, and bestow the light of Christ on both believers and non-believers? How is it possible to continue existing with a Marxist-Leninist ideology in government?

I think that in Russia the relationship between society and the Church is much more acute than it is in other countries in the West; because there is there just one Party and it 'preaches' atheism. But in the new situation [i.e. Gorbachev's *glasnost*], with the emergence of a careful, thoughtful attitude, the presence of two incompatible ideologies could bring about dialogue. As I said earlier, if we learned to look at our opponent not as an enemy, but as a man bearing God's image, which he has not discovered or realised in himself, if we could learn to speak not against him but beyond him, if we were prepared to teach by our example, to teach that we are a different kind of people whom he would wish to imitate, then we might achieve something in this respect. The Russian Church is in fact now doing a great deal to open new churches and to make possible that which before was impossible. From my experience of other circumstances (for example, I worked for more than three years in the French Resistance movement during the German occupation) I think that it is very important today to do everything that is *possible* rather than attempting the impossible. But if we do today what is possible now, however exhausting it is, then tomorrow that which we could not do yesterday will become possible. I certainly do not want to say that everything will become perfect, but from what I have seen and heard in a large number of conversations with various people, it seems to me that much more is being achieved than appears on the surface.

We already hear it being said, both here and in the West, that Orthodoxy in Russia is again becoming a State religion. What is your view?

I think that, thank God, there is a long way to go before this happens. It is a different matter that the State now believes that it is possible to be a Christian, or, in the widest sense, a believer (for example a Muslim or a Buddhist) and at the same time a faithful son of one's motherland. But every time that whatever Church presents itself as having an overwhelming majority of believers, the relationship of that Church with the State becomes obviously much closer and more complicated. The Church – and this applies both in the East and in the West – should not become a part of the political or social system. It should remain loyal to the end to its native land – that is, to wish for the greatest good for that country – but at the same time make society aware of the fact that there is another dimension to life besides the socio-political one: that there is depth to life.

Please say more about the life of the Russian Church in Exile[17] in the West. Were they guilty, and to what degree, in what happened in Russia in the 1920s and 30s?

Being a member of the Russian Church in Exile was a label which stuck to a group of Russian Orthodox bishops and their clergy and people who in the 1920s renounced the Moscow Patriarchate, and formed their own Church organisation, and who, to this day, consider us unacceptable. There are various groups among them, who are more or less extreme. I have already mentioned the reaction to me many years ago of their priest in London. That is one extreme, and one has to take it into account. Another group is much more moderate, and regards us differently. They consider that they themselves cannot belong to the Moscow Patriarchate, fearing that the Soviet authorities will influence them through the Church, but they regard us, as a Church, with respect. For example they advise pilgrims or tourists who come from Russia to mix with us and have dialogue with us. And there are any number of variations.

In 1925 there occurred a very unhappy event during the Synod of Sremski Karlovats where bishops, priests and laymen had gathered, among whom there was a very strong working group of political activists who appealed to the then League of Nations for military intervention in the Soviet Union in order to restore the monarchy. This had tragic repercussions, because the Church in the Soviet Union was put under attack: 'That is what your hierarchy, your lay people and your priests are doing – they are calling on foreigners to invade our country in order to restore those State structures which they themselves support …' That was a most unfortunate and destructive event, which played a part in exacerbating the relationship between the State powers and the Church. I do not want to say that this was the cause of everything that followed, but it served as a pretext, and as proof of what someone had once said to Bishop Basil of Brussels:[18] 'Everyone of you is like a radish – red outside and white inside …' I want to say one more thing: one should not judge too simply or too bitterly. Those Russians who left Russia in 1919 and in the following years left Russia under extremely tragic circumstances, having lost everything. I am not speaking of property, but of family, of their native land, even of the right to call themselves Russians – because by Soviet decree we lost our citizenship. Therefore it is not surprising that that generation was filled with pain; and you know what effect pain can have. A wild beast that you injure can tear you apart. People who are frightened and whose souls have suffered can become embittered.

Therefore, although I never belonged to this group, and always since the age of seventeen belonged to the Moscow Patriarchate, when our parishes drew away from all divisions, I could not regard the *Karlovchanie*[19] without a feeling of deep sympathy. Now, for instance, in London we give pastoral care to many old *Karlovchanie* whom their own clergy cannot care for, because their senior priest is ninety years old, and his helpers do not speak Russian. And while their parishioners are healthy, alive and in good heart, they go to their own church, but when their life crumbles they phone us up and say, 'Help!' Now there is but a thin line between them and us, but there was so much pain, which explains both the bitterness and the fear.

Whose will, God's or the Devil's, almost destroyed Holy Russia? After all, Russia was called Holy Russia, and in Moscow there were forty times forty churches, it was filled with grace, which emanated from the believers.

Every country chooses some epithet by which it defines itself; but that epithet does not necessarily describe what actually exists: it expresses the country's ideal or that to which it strives. Thus France called itself *La France très-chrétienne*, the Germans insisted on *Deutsche Treue*, that is German loyalty; Russia always spoke of Holy Russia. But to what extent it was holy and to what extent in a state of struggle, whether she was truly striving, but not achieving her conscious calling, we can see through Russian history: there both holiness and horror are not uncommonly merged together. One short, clear and vivid picture of what took place is found in Leskov's tale 'The Exorcism' (*'Chertogon'*),[20] in which we see a man who is both a believer and devout, but who is overcome by 'the devil knows what', not as a term of abuse but literally so. He raves and rages and then, having sown his wild oats, just as suddenly returns to God and to his previous state. This is in general very characteristic of Russian history, and this tendency runs through it like a red thread.

As far as God's will and Man's will are concerned: in ancient times the Church Fathers said that history is defined by three wills: God's will, the devil's will and Man's will. And they pointed out that the will of God is all-powerful and always positive – and limited itself by means of Man's freedom. The devil's will is always wicked and far from being all-powerful, but it can work in the world, having come to control Man's will, working by way of deceit and violence. And Man's will is like a pendulum, swinging between God's will, which calls it, and the devil's will, which tempts it. On God's side freedom remains, on the devil's side there is no freedom. And history is shaped in the world as if by Man's decisions; but in fact it is shaped only inasmuch as Man's will has, in any given circumstances, joined God's will or the devil's will, the energies of God or the energies of darkness.

In the history of the people of Israel this is at certain moments very interesting, and clearly seen. For example, for generations the leaders of Israel were saintly people, whom God Himself had chosen and put in command of His people. These were the patriarchs, judges, and prophets. Then, in the First Book of Samuel, the Hebrew people ask the aged Samuel to choose them a king in order that they should be like other nations. That is, so that there should be no risk that God would direct them, that they should be protected against the arbitrary nature of God's will. Samuel refuses, but the people insist, and, addressing himself to God, Samuel receives an answer to his prayer: 'Give them a King: they have not rejected you, they have rejected Me' (cf. 1 Sam. 8:7). And by Man's will a king was chosen: the most tragic of the whole of human history – Saul. This man was placed in the position, where only God's chosen could stand, whereas he was the people's choice. And Saul went mad in this position. Here we see how two wills met, and Man's will tilted the whole fate of Israel towards the world: 'Let us be like everyone else'. The other question: 'What happens to an individual personality at such a point?' is too big to answer in a few minutes, but in human history there are such moments of the terrible, colossal responsibility of Man, because Man introduces into the fate of the universe either God's will or the devil's will.

Further: when a man has done this, God does not remain unconcerned. God fights for this universe, and this is sometimes very terrifying for us, because as soon as we give ourselves over to Satan, as soon as we become earthly in the flesh, He destroys everything that exists on earth: the flesh, happiness, security, because what matters is salvation and eternity. This is not because God's acts are not directed towards our happiness, but because our happiness sometimes proves poisonous and intoxicated. In ancient days they said that tragedy enters our life in a place of peaceful security, which is the broad road leading down to the depths of hell, which Christ had spoken about. That is at the moment all that I can say in reply.

What can you say about the ecumenical movement, about its positive and negative characteristics and also of your attitude to it?
I worked hard for a very long time within the ecumenical movement, and I have a two-fold attitude to it. On the one hand, the ecumenical movement has a very positive side. It has allowed Christians, that is people who sincerely and seriously believe in Christ, and often live a Christian life with all their soul and with total conviction, to meet, to discover all that they have in common, to discover all that separates them, and in spite of that not to upbraid but to respect each other and to exchange experiences, and not just negative ones. They can exchange views, not only in a polemical sense, but to discover that for centuries the separation of each group of Christians (because it insisted on one thing or another, maybe in an unbalanced way) meant that it had thought through and experienced one thing or another more deeply and more thoroughly than others. In this sense their meeting enriched all the denominations at least through mutual respect and love.

The negative side lies in the fact that the majority of participants in the ecumenical movement, who belong to the

Protestant world, think of the unification of the Churches on a minimalist basis, whereas the Orthodox Church cannot speak about a minimalist basis. We can speak only about an integral acceptance of the Gospels – not of any form of accommodation of evangelical teaching to contemporary attitudes, which would change with every new contemporary view.

But, in one way or another, much that was positive was achieved. One very important decision was taken in Lund[21] many decades ago: that Christians should do jointly everything which their conscience allows them to do together, and not do together only that which their conscience does not allow them to do together. This opened up the possibility of doing a great deal together in the spheres of charity, help for the needy, medical assistance, and in the sphere of education and so on – things which are not within the sphere of confession of faith but are universal. For instance the Protestant Churches provide the Orthodox world both with the Holy Scripture and with prayer books, without any provisos and without any changes in the text of those writings. This is a brotherly attitude.

As I said, however, we cannot go beyond a certain line, but even when we judge other denominations very severely, we have to remember that if we call any denomination heretical, we simultaneously affirm by this that it remains Christian nonetheless. For in order to be a heretic, one has to be a Christian. We are not saying that a Buddhist, a Muslim or a Pagan is a heretic: he is simply a Pagan, a Muslim or a Buddhist. We have to remember that an ecumenical meeting takes place within a very complex Christian family. One of our bishops, who in his time was a Catholic and became Orthodox, Bishop Alexis van der Menhsbrugghe,[22] used to say that he saw it in this way: a

THE HUMAN VOCATION

candle is burning; the Orthodox Church is the flame, but the light and warmth of that flame spreads further, and that is to those denominations in which there still remains both the warmth and the light of Christianity, even though they no longer burn with the same flame in all its purity.

How do you react to Father Seraphim Rose?
Negatively as far as two-thirds are concerned – for one third positively, but with indifference. I have the impression that he is apocalyptic and very narrow in his views, and I am not pleased when my parishioners read him with relish. He has no sense of moderation: he is enthusiastic, he sees things in an apocalyptic light, and, I would say, totally unrealistically. That is my opinion, and I express it forcefully for the very reason that it is my personal attitude.

*Forgive a tactless question: is there anything heretical in Florensky?*23
That is not a tactless question, but it is not addressed to the right person. For one thing, I have not read the whole of Florensky. For another, I am allergic to Florensky. What I have read I have not absorbed. He arouses in me a feeling of such sickly sweet sentimentality, which I cannot bear; therefore it is better to ask someone else.

Do two different kinds of icon serve to the same degree as a means to salvation, if one of them is painted according to the ancient canons and the other is simply a print?
There exist two completely different approaches among believers. Some, and maybe all iconographers, consider that an icon must not only be painted according to the canons but must be permeated with reverence and prayer and blessed in church, and that an icon which is reproduced in an artificial

way is lacking something. I am made infinitely happy by the fact that, contrary to the judgement of experienced iconographers, there are in Russia so many miracle-working icons which any experienced iconographer would call bad icons, but God bestows His grace not necessarily on perfect examples of the iconographer's art. Just as through us, imperfect creatures that we are, grace is transmitted to others, so also God brings grace to people through imperfect human creations. I do not doubt that a paper icon, that has been torn, stuck together, attached to a board or to sticky paper, which represents the Saviour, the Mother of God or one of the saints, is holy in the fullest sense of this word (just as each one of us is made in the image of God, however much we are made ugly by sin and imperfection). And an icon, I am deeply convinced, becomes holy not because it has been painted in one way or another, but because it has been taken, placed on the holy altar, and sprinkled with holy water (in ancient times icons were anointed with oil just as Christians are anointed after Baptism) – and that it then enters into the mystery of the Church and of grace. I have now expressed something of which I am deeply convinced. I do not claim to be right, but I treasure with reverence paper icons which came to me from my mother or from people that I have loved, and I see no difference in them in this respect. But I am not so ignorant as not to understand that an icon painted according to the canons is not only a focus for grace, but is a source of radiance. It is also a source of instruction – but that is a different subject.

Do you think that an iconographer who paints icons today creates icons which carry the same spiritual content as ancient iconography? Is there such a thing as creative iconography? I know that in the West there

are attempts in this direction, for example Uspensky.[24]
You see I am not an expert, I know very little. I received my
knowledge of icons from Uspensky himself with whom I
was in the same parish for twenty years. I think that art is
always possible, but one can never *invent* an icon. The equi-
librium of which Uspensky spoke to me can be formulated
as follows: one cannot copy in a slavish way, but also one
cannot make anything up. An icon is the expression of the
religious experience of the Church, which becomes embodied in a certain creative personality. But it is impossible
to copy slavishly another's religious experience; you cannot
become another person to that extent, and in fact that would
be even undesirable. On the other hand, you cannot make up
a religious experience, so that one cannot sit down and say,
'Well yes, they painted in this way – but are there not any
new ways?' For this it is necessary that there should be a
new religious experience – that is a Church experience and
not a private one, not saying, 'I imagine God in this way.'
Therefore one can say that a certain period – let us say that
of Rublev[25] – brought the icon to a state of extraordinary
perfection. But I think (and this is my opinion and not that
of the Church or of Uspensky) that at some time a new form
of expression will arise, a different style of expressing the
same truths. The Byzantine icon, it seems to me, answered
extraordinarily well a question which it had put to itself, but
whether there are any other ways of doing it, I do not know.

There is an analogy which I can handle more easily than
iconography. We have a Byzantine Liturgy in its perfection,
but there was a time, when Western Orthodox liturgies
existed, equally Orthodox though different in form, because
they were born in a different culture and from among
different people. Therefore I admit the theoretical possibility
that the same could happen to iconography, although at the

present nothing similar has happened. The attempt to achieve some sort of novelty belongs to the sphere of fantasy, and not to the sphere of religious experience.

If one compares an icon to a picture, each has its own advantage, depending on what you are talking about and what you want to say. A picture gives a representation of something which our world today contains: both good and evil, light and darkness, struggle – both victory and defeat, the aggregate of everything, including failure, and creativity, and ambiguity. In this sense the scope of a picture is wider than that of an icon, because an icon excludes a whole lot of things. An icon is not trying to paint a picture of the emergence of evil. Rather, when evil exists in an icon, it comes related to good (for example the dragon on the icon of St George), but this personified evil, which clearly exists, does not permeate the image to the extent that ambiguity can permeate a picture. There is a great deal that is excluded from an icon. On the other hand godly, eternal and absolute dimensions exist in it. In this sense it gives us more than a picture does. But I do not think that it is fair to say: 'either/or'. If you carry a picture into a church in place of an icon you are making a mistake, because it is not in its right place, but a picture has its place as an insight into the reality of things. And when I speak about a picture, the same can be said of all forms of art.

But attempts to stay within the canon also, it seems, do not lead to the preservation of authentic iconography. What results is something anaemic, a reproduction, but not an icon. There is a problem which can face a painter who is a believer. An icon greatly surpasses in depth and scope all works of secular painting, and at the same time it remains inaccessible as a path for today.

You see, it seems to me (and I am speaking at random, not through any experience or knowledge) that as far as the canon and classical icons are concerned the position is the same as in music. A person learns from great creations and develops his taste, his perception and his technique up to the point when, having taken everything in, he unintentionally begins to create – not with the aim of composing music different from that of Beethoven or Mozart, but simply because he has taken everything in that he could receive from the past, and from the depth of this past something new grows. It seems to me that when young artists (I am thinking now of the West) attempt to paint icons which would be 'contemporary', they are acting as people who, not having studied music, not having experienced the strictest discipline of past creations, want to create something new.

We have a whole number of iconographers, the most talented of which was Father Gregory Krug[26] (this is Uspensky's opinion, so I can say it quite confidently) and then Leonid Uspensky, and then their pupils, some of whom paint very good reproductions while others start to create; in other words, their icons come to life. The wife of our choirmaster Father Michael[27] studied with Uspensky and has herself taught iconography to a whole lot of young people. Two of them, I would say, began to paint icons which amaze one very much – they are alive. They are painted according to the canon but from the depth of experience: they are not attempts simply to copy something.

In Ancient Russia it was considered that to be an iconographer is to follow an aesthetic, morally contemplative road. And too many people now in the West who are not Orthodox, take to icon painting and paint them in their spare time. That is, they paint portraits and paintings and icons and consider that Orthodox art, both Russian and that of other Orthodox countries, has had its day because it is not rooted in their culture. But unfortunately the culture of Western countries broke away from the Orthodox view of the world and of experience so long ago that one cannot create icons from the culture which arose in the Renaissance. We have a self-taught Spaniard, who began to paint icons and now has even opened up a school. My first meeting with him was not a great success. He came to me and said, 'I am being given the chance to buy two icons, and I do not know whether they are worth buying. Could you tell me what you think of them?' I glanced at them and said, 'Throw them away – they are rubbish!' He stood up and said, 'Excuse me, they are my work!' I answered, 'You yourself are at fault, you should not have deceived me.' They really were nonsensical. He draws well, and applies paint well, but overall they were painted in a parrot fashion, and one could not pray in front of such an object, because what he had made up were his 'improvements' on the models he had chosen. He thought at that time (I do not know what he thinks now, because he did not come back to me a second time) that Rublev, Theophan[28] and so on were primitive and that we had developed since their time. But there are people who paint from within a prayerful tradition, and not just according to technique.

What do you think of the relationship between Christianity and culture?
I am not a particularly cultured person or set on culture, but it seems to me that one cannot simply set culture aside and it is unrealistic to question it, because all aspects of our spiritual life are to a large extent conditioned by culture.

Let us say that the form of our divine service is conditioned by Byzantine culture. If we want to set culture aside altogether, then we have to serve God in spirit and truth, but without form. But even then we would adopt some type of form, because our language is also rooted in culture. We speak in a certain language which expresses the genius of the people to which we belong: in it is lodged the history of the people and the history of the language, and we cannot leave that. Speaking of icons again: two streams merge in them. On the one hand, there are eternal truths which we want to express, on the other hand the dynamism of a given culture. Take for example Ethiopian, or Byzantine, or Russian icons of the periods before the Mongol invasions and those after them – they are completely different, not because they are expressing differing truths but because their form is determined by their historical context and experience. That is why it seems to me one cannot just ignore culture: it exists. Even when you talk of very simple things in simple Russian language, the words are embedded in their cultural context. For example, when a Russian preaches a sermon, it is intelligible to the extent that he uses words which are so rooted in the past of a given people and in their present circumstances that they evoke a deep response. So I do not know how one can get away from culture – there is nowhere to go from it. But to replace spirituality by culture, which now very often happens in the West, and I cannot say does not happen here – that is a substitution of something false for something real.

Is it then acceptable for a believer to study art?
Remember what Gregory Palamas[29] clearly says: that he sees God's image in what a man has been given – to be a creator in God's image. It seems to me that in art a man must be an artist and express that which his inspiration teaches him according to his ability, but the moment an artist tries to

make of his work an illustration of his faith, it usually becomes a pot-boiler. Take Tolstoy for example.[30] When he is writing a novel it can be marvellous; but as soon as he sets out on his thoughts – help! Because instead of the free flow of inspiration he begins to adapt things to a certain system. I think that an artist has to have the courage in whatever sphere of activity to act as an artist. If he is saturated in his faith he does not have to collate it with his inspiration, because they are not only intertwined, they form a unity. I do not think that one can, for example, expect from an artist who is Orthodox that he will paint Orthodox icons, write Orthodox plays or compose Orthodox music, if he is not an Orthodox iconographer, writer or composer. If one is to speak of something more primitive, then in the book of Jesus, Son of Sirach, Ecclesiasticus, it speaks of doctors, and it says clearly there that God created the doctor, bestowed on him intelligence, skill and talent and a line is clearly drawn to indicate that all is given by God. But how we use it – that depends on us.[31]

Chapter 4

❧ ❦

Certain Categories of Our Existence in Creation

These addresses were given to the Moscow Theological Academy on 1 December 1966, one of the first occasions that the Metropolitan spoke to students of theology in Russia. It was printed in the journal *The Church and Time* (1991, No. 2) published by the Department of External Church Relations of the Moscow Patriarchate.

I: The Human Vocation

I want to say to you first of all with what joy I came to you – not only to the Troitskaya-Sergieva Lavra but especially to the seminary and academy, with the joy of a new meeting, when one can see people who are dear to one face to face. And I have brought you a greeting from the West, from our priests and from our lay-people, who pray for the well-being of the schools here and among whom there are many who hope sometime also to become pupils and students of the seminary or the academy.

The theme of my talk is rather hard to express. Formally and not very descriptively I could call it, 'Of certain categories of our existence in creation', but having said that

I would probably only have frightened you with complicated words and would not have conveyed what this theme means to me, and why I should like to talk about it with you.

Creation and our relationship with God

The creation of Man and the world is very often taken simply as an objective fact. It appears doubtful for some people and absolute for others. For some people of our time the whole theme of creation raises problems and arouses doubts, but I have very rarely met people who have thought through the theme of creation from the point of view of a living religious experience: from the point of view of what creation opens up in our relationship with God, and how it defines very deep and precious facts about the relationship of created beings to God and their relationships between themselves.

To start with I want to draw your attention to two things. Firstly, we are not simply created, objectively, as though we were objects. We are created straight away, even before we begin to exist, in some sort of relationship with God. God has made us because He wants us, in the warmest and deepest meaning of the word 'wants'. We are not necessary to God in order for Him to be God. There is no necessity to call us out from non-existence. He would be as fully a self-sufficient being, with the same fullness of exultant, joyful life, whether we existed or not. He has created us for our sakes, not for His own. And in the harmony which existed before time began, which called us into being, there already exists God's love for us in all its fullness. In his autobiography, Archpriest Avvakum[1] speaks of this harmony before time began. God says to His Son, 'My Son, let us create Man!' and the Son replies, 'Yes, Father!' Then, revealing the future mystery, the Father says, 'Yes, but Man will sin and fall away from his calling, and his glory, and You will have to redeem him on the Cross.' And the Son says, 'So be it.'

There is something very important here. It is important that God, in creating Man, knew what would happen – and still He created him. He knew what would happen to Man: He knew that death, suffering, and the infinite sorrow of the Fall would come to him. And He also knew that His love for Man has within it the shadow of the Cross, that in love there is the joy of giving and the joy of receiving, and there is the triumphant, tragic joy of the Cross.

So God creates Man against this background. Before Man is created he is already loved by God's love on the Cross, and not just by a love which is joyful and full of light. When Man comes from non-being into being, he encounters God's love: he is loved and he is desired.

As I have already said, the creation of the world and in particular of Man is not a necessity for God. It is an act of regal, creative freedom. And the fact that we are not necessary to God is the basis of a relative but nonetheless genuine originality in our being. If we were necessary to God, if without us, without creation, God would not possess the fullness of being that He has – we would be only a pathetic shadow in that shining glory; we would be like fire-flies in bright sunlight. It is true we would burn with some sort of light, but in comparison to unfading Light, the shining of the Sun of truth, the midday light of Godhead, we would be limited and insignificant. It is precisely because we are not necessary to God that we have some sort of individuality. We are placed before the Face of God with some sort of independence. There can be a dialogue between us and Him.

God spoke, and the prophets replied. A man prays, and God responds. This is possible only because we are different from God, because we do not merge with Him, because Man's final vocation is to become 'a partaker of the divine nature' (2 Peter 1:4) – which is not a given quality, but precisely a vocation which can be attained by gradually growing into it.

The Scriptures teach us that we are created out of nothing: from non-existence we are called into existence. In this lies, on the one hand, our infinite poverty – and on the other, our infinitely joyful wealth. Poverty because we do not possess anything, because we are not rooted in anything (I am now talking not only of Man but of the whole of creation). We are not rooted in God: we are deeply different from Him. Neither are we rooted in anything that existed before us. According to the words of Metropolitan Philaret of Moscow,[2] we hang between two abysses: between the abyss of non-existence and the divine abyss, only because of God's word and will. In fact we are totally groundless, and we can obtain roots only if we become totally ourselves and akin to God, communicants of God's nature, living members of Christ's Body, temples of the Holy Spirit, the Father's children through communion – that is, all of us together in the Church, and each one of us a living member of this Church. Each one of us but not separately, because it is exactly here that one cannot use the world 'separately'. There is no separation between us. There is an all-conquering unity in Christ and the Spirit, so that 'our life is hid with Christ in God' (Col. 3:3).

That is our calling. While we stand before the Face of God, we are called to exist. Before us lie vast expanses, and we possess nothing. That is the beginning of the Kingdom of God. Call to mind the first commandment of the

Beatitudes: 'Blessed are the poor in spirit: for theirs is the Kingdom of Heaven' (Matt. 5:3). What sort of poverty is this, which makes us members, citizens, children of the Heavenly Kingdom? Of course it is not the simple, bare, and, for many, bitter fact of our total, infinite wretchedness and dependence. Spiritual poverty does not lie in this: it is the poverty which can be spiritual or can be terrible wretchedness. Remember the words of John Chrysostom, who teaches us that it is not the man who has nothing that is poor, but the man who wants to have that which he has not got.[3] One can have nothing and not be poor; one can be rich from the point of view of everyone who looks at our lives, and feels oneself to be a wretched pauper. We are rich only, then, when we absorb everything which is given to us in life as God's gift and the richness of God's love.

There is a story, which is quoted by Martin Buber[4] which tells how in the eighteenth century there lived a rabbi in Poland. He lived in extreme, desperate poverty, and every day he gave thanks to God for all his generous gifts. Once somebody asked, 'How can you thank God day after day, when you know, and know for sure, know in your flesh and in your soul, that He has not given you anything – how can you lie in prayer?' The rabbi looked at him smiling and said, 'You do not understand the crux of the matter! God looked at my soul and He saw that in order that I should grow to my full stature, I need poverty, hunger, cold and abandonment; and in this way He enriched me infinitely.'

This is a marvellous story, because we see in it a man who is able to believe God and love Him, and to understand God's wisdom through love, which is incomprehensible to the mind of the flesh. We see how this man in his utter wretchedness was rich – was, in a certain sense, already in the Kingdom of God.

This Kingdom of God opens to us if we understand that we radically and absolutely do not possess anything. We are, after all, called out of a state of non-existence. We have no roots in anything, neither in God nor in anything created which preceded our creation. The life which we possess is also God's gift. We cannot create it, we cannot defend it, we cannot preserve it or keep hold of it. Our body is not in our power. It is enough for a small vein to break in our head for the greatest mind to fade and for a person to become less than an animal. It happens that sorrow and need stand before us and with all our strength we would like to feel compassion, but our heart lies in our bosom like a stone. We cannot arouse in ourselves a living feeling if it is not given to us from above. As for our will – it is unnecessary to speak of it – what can we make of ourselves? We have no power over ourselves: laziness, depression, tiredness, the circumstances of life – these are enough to break down even the strongest will. If we look around further: human relationships, kinship, friendship, love, the achievements of life, comfort, security – we have all that, and we have nothing, because we cannot hold on to anything.

How would we not grasp at all this that flows between our fingers? Everything that we possess can be taken away in an instant. And if we will think about this we will already receive some conception of our poverty, but it will be far from complete. Such a conception does not bring Man into the Kingdom of God. He can fall into despair, fear, uncertainty, but still not attain that stability which is characteristic of the Kingdom of God, nor the joy of the Gospels. In order to enter into that joy, one has to understand something else.

We must notice first of all that with all our definitive poverty we are not in fact all that unfortunate. We do not possess either life or being, nothing in fact – and yet we have all these things. It is only philosophically speaking that we do not have them. We are alive, we move, we love, we think, we rejoice, we suffer, to speak of nothing else. But here one has to understand, to understand with both our hearts and our minds, that everything that we have is a sign of God's love at every moment, and at every hour of our lives. If we could take possession of something, it would become ours, but we would lose our link with God which exists precisely because everything that we have is not ours but God's. All that we possess is God's love made concrete, His living care for us.

If we understand this, then indeed God's Kingdom opens up before us, because we find ourselves in this Kingdom, where above everyone and everything is God Himself, Who reigns eternally. He gives gifts in various ways. There are obvious blessings, and there are secret blessings, and the story of the rabbi relates to the secret blessings, blessings which few of us are capable of understanding.

That is our basic situation in relationship to God. That is what, in non-philosophical terms, is the active life, a living, simple human experience of existence: the fact that we are created out of nothing, called into existence out of non-existence. Within this lies our loving relationship with God, our immeasurable, wonderful richness in God. Let us remember the words in the Gospels, that the rich man will lose everything that 'is not rich toward God' (Luke 12:21). That is exactly the way we *can* be rich: and we *are* rich exactly in this way. And this relationship is not a mechanical one, but a living, dynamic and moral one, having an inner, living and spiritual content. Because the very fact that we stand before God, face to face in absolute dependence, and at the same time are endowed with the terrible power of repudiating God, of denying God, of losing God, opens up before us the theme of our freedom.

Freedom and obedience

I would like to say a few words about freedom and about obedience. There is a definition of freedom in Khomiakov,[5] based on philological deduction. He points out that by analysing the Slavonic roots of this word we see that in Russian understanding to be free means to be oneself. Each one of us wants to be himself, and mostly we imagine that that is what we are. In fact Man cannot be himself if he does not outgrow himself. Remember the story from the Acts of the Apostles, how the Apostle Paul found an altar dedicated 'To the Unknown God' (Acts 17:23). Is it possible that in our own times (and of course this story might be interpreted differently at other times) this 'unknown God' might in fact be Man?

Man could be placed on this altar – but in a very different way. If we see Man only as a complicated combination of matter, energy, of transient processes connected with the flesh, and place him on a throne, or on an altar, we are creating an idol which comes under a general condemnation in the Psalms: 'Eyes have they, but they see not: They have ears, but they hear not ... They have hands, but they feel not ...' (Psalm 115:5–7). That is how Man has appeared to many since the eighteenth century. Such a man is an idol, and to this idol, as to any idol, sacrifices are made, both bloody and otherwise. But that is not Man. That is a deceitful image, and a lie concerning him; to use ascetic language, it is a source of temptation.

But only we – believers – can put a Man on an altar, believers who have known Christ as the Incarnation of the Word of God, as God and Man. He is truly painted on icons.

He truly belongs on the Holy Throne in the Mystery of Body and Blood. He truly sits next to God the Father: 'The Man Jesus Christ' (Rom. 5:15).

Perhaps it is appropriate here to remember once again John Chrysostom. He puts the question: Where should we look for the authentic image of Man? And he answers that we should not look for him in royal apartments or on earthly thrones, but should lift our eyes to the Throne of God, and on the right hand side of God the Father we can see a human image. Here we see some answer to many of the current perplexities concerning Man's place, Man's meaning. We see that the image of Man, as he appears without God, is too small. We can make an enormous idol of him, but there will never be any greatness in him. Only our belief in Man, the Son of God, who became Man, opens up to us the amazing depths of humanity, and of what a man can be.

In this respect the freedom to be oneself opens up before us vertiginous heights and depths. We have to understand that we have a great deal to say to the world about Man, even before we begin to talk to the world about God. The small man that you suggest I might become does not satisfy me 'for the heart of man is deep' (Psalm 64:6) and only the Holy Spirit can fill that temple. It is very important to remember this, because if we not only lower ourselves in a worldly sense but also lose sight of the scope of our calling, then there will be nowhere for us to go. We will also begin to pray to idols: we will worship size and not greatness.

But the word 'freedom' becomes even richer if you bring in other languages. The Latin word *libertas* is a legal term from Ancient Rome. It legally defines the social position of a child who was born of free parents and not of slaves, and has himself inherited freedom. It says that is he is socially absolute, and has the right of self-determination. But if you think a bit about this concept and not only about the word, you will see that the entire upbringing of this child is balanced between two extremes. On the one hand he is taught to be free. On the other, his parents strive to safeguard this freedom by teaching him the utmost self-control and power over himself. His education must teach him never to submit to anything outside himself without the agreement both of his reason and of his soul. He is taught to become the kind of man who is never affected by outward circumstances or inner passion, a man who is not passive by orientation, who is not an object under pressure. They try to make him a man who is always the master of his own life – and one can be a master of one's own life right up to death. Remember Christ's words: 'Nobody takes it from me, but I lay it down of my own accord' (John 10:18). That is a complete and absolute power over oneself. But to achieve this one has to conquer within oneself all the powers of spiritual stagnation, all impotence, all inertia and all impulses of body and soul which are incompatible with such power over oneself.

And here we encounter the concept of obedience, discipline. Discipline is also a Latin word. It means something not quite the same as we usually understand it. When we speak of discipline we think of being put into iron handcuffs. But 'discipline' comes from the word *discipulus* – 'pupil'. It is not simply a factual description but an inner condition of one who has become a pupil, who wants to learn and is prepared to abandon his own habits, his own thoughts, his own judgements and feelings in order to merge with a greater mind, with a deeper heart, and with a more absolute will. Only through this association with a great man does one become free from the lesser one, from oneself, such as one is at present.

In Roman law the father of a family provided such a

standard. He knew what sort of man he should be and how to grow to that stature. And severely and firmly he led his son along this path. God also leads us into sonship by this method. Recall the words of the Angel to Hermas,[6] 'Fear not, Hermas [notice the words 'Fear not'], the Lord will not leave you, until He has shattered your heart, or your bones!' God does not tolerate slaves – He does not need them. God wants people to be His children, to be with His only-begotten Son true sons and daughters of His Kingdom. Remember the parable: the Prodigal Son is about to say, after he has confessed to his guilt, that he is ready to be a hired servant in his father's house. He has prepared his confession, but his father only allows him to say the first half: 'Father, I have sinned against heaven and in thy sight, and am no more worthy to be called thy son' (Luke 5:21) – and his father cuts him off at this point: 'Yes, you can be an *un*worthy son, but you can never be a worthy hired servant in my house.' One cannot let go the fact of being a son: God's gifts are inalienable. In this way God leads us into being His sons, that we should become the children of His Kingdom through obedience and through freedom.

And finally, how this understanding of our relationship to God opens up to us is found in the word 'freedom' in English and in German. 'Freedom' in German is *Freiheit*, and both words derive from a more ancient Sanskrit word, which meant 'beloved'. He is free who is loved absolutely and who is capable of responding to love with absolute love. He has become a child of the Kingdom: he has become himself in the full meaning of this word.

All this rests on the fact that what so often seems to us either a fact of history or a philosophical question is based on the premise that we are created by God, that we are called from non-being into being by His creative and life-giving word. And it also rests on the fact that God desires us, even though He does not need us. That is the only reason that we are able to stand face to face with the Living God, and this becomes not only our calling, but an actual fact, not as something that is given but as a calling to become that which Christ is by nature.

If after the stern judgement of your rector I will be allowed to give a second talk, then tomorrow I would like to continue with this theme, saying something about our knowledge of God and of certain difficulties which lie on the path to such knowledge.

II: Knowledge of God

To begin with, I would like to say something about our knowledge of God and of our knowledge of creation and to underline the fact that every time that God reveals Himself to us, this revelation of God corresponds at the same time to a revelation concerning creation. Every time that we discover something about God, we simultaneously discover something very significant about ourselves, namely that we are capable of knowing God, not only as we did before, but in a different and new way. So any revelation of God opens to us a new depth in what we as creatures represent. It is very important to remember this, and it coincides with what I have already said, that Man is infinitely deeper and more significant than we often think, and that only if we see Man in relationship to God, can we measure the scope and depth of that which Man is.

Secondly, the revelation which God gives us of Himself is always twofold. On the one hand he give us the ability to know Him in a new way, with new freedom. On the other hand, this revelation always places before us new depths in

God, and a new sense of God's inscrutability. That is also very important to remember. The example I would like to give you is the Incarnation of the Word of God, and that knowledge of God which we received through it.

God as revealed in the Incarnation

In popular piety, especially in the West, a tremendous amount of attention is given to mankind and the human, incarnate side of God as Man. It is absolutely natural that the feeling exists that – speaking in a very simplified way – in becoming incarnate God thus became comprehensible. That is not more simplistic than what many of our believers think and feel: that God having become Man, He is totally here, the infant of Bethlehem, 'for in him dwelleth all the fullness of the Godhead bodily' (Col. 2:9). There is a God, and I can see Him, I can embrace Him. He is here, He is comprehensible. This does indeed seem so to people, and one must put them on their guard concerning it. Yes, it is true: in His Incarnation God became flesh. It is true that the incomprehensible God lived among us and 'took upon Himself the form of a servant' (Phil. 2:7) – but not only that. In the Incarnation something more incomprehensible is revealed than an imagined transcendental God, whom we can invent.

It may be possible to invent a heavenly God, a God whom we could characterise as having all the best human characteristics and qualities, infinitely multiplied. In his day Voltaire wrote that if there was no God, Man would have to invent Him.[7] And indeed if our God displayed only infinitely multiplied human characteristics, He would be all-powerful, He would be wise, He would be kind and so on. But God as He is revealed in the Incarnation is impossible to invent, because no one would begin to invest God with qualities of which one would be ashamed: a God who is vulnerable, a God who is defeated, a God who is humiliated, a God who is condemned by a human court, who is slapped across the cheeks, a God who displays some incomprehensible weakness and unfathomable helplessness. Such a God no-one could invent, and no-one would. If one is going to invent a God, He must be a support, an ideal, who would be one that in time of need people would turn to with certainty that He would help, that He would stand like a wall between them and sorrow or danger or need. But such a God who becomes a man, such a God who takes on Himself the total defencelessness, the total weakness, the total vulnerability, the total apparent defeat of a man, could only be 'invented' (if one can express oneself in this way) by God Himself, could be presented only by God. In this sense, Christianity is more invulnerable in its faith in God than any other religion. The Christian God demands of us the very opposite of what we would like to receive from Him, and for which we naturally strive. Take the Beatitudes:[8] Blessed are those who in one way or another are unhappy – that is not what a normal person seeks for. I once gave a lecture on the Beatitudes and a very conscientious man said to me, 'Your Grace, if that is the blessedness which Christians seek, please be blessed in your own way, but I want nothing of it.' A normal person does not wish for such blessedness, and a normal man does not wish for such a God. And it is only because God showed Himself to be like that, that we are able to know Him to be such. Man would not wish to invent such a God.

Thus, in every one of God's revelations, as in this one, something is revealed about God that is incomprehensible, unfathomable. In other words, God allows us to know something that we can catch hold of, that we can grasp, that we can understand about God. And at the same time, because we have grasped something, an abyss of in-comprehension opens before us, which passes all under-standing, that is so marvellous, so wonderful as to be overwhelming, before which we can only stand in silence and in amazement, with a trembling heart.

Contemplation and silence

There are various names for this silence, depending on from which point of view we approach it. One could call this silence faith, that condition of the human soul which stands before a mystery totally convinced that in this Divine darkness shines an unattainable Light – and remains silent.

That contemplative condition which is described by Isaac the Syrian[9] can also be called silence. He says that when the soul is in a state of ecstasy, when it is beside itself, then it has no power over its thoughts or its feelings. It simply remains silent, observes and perceives, but cannot itself make a single movement. It observes and takes in as the earth absorbs rain, or as the earth receives the shining of the sun and its light. It is warmed through and through, it is lit throughout, and becomes fully alive from this life-giving moisture and from this life-giving light – but remains silent. This silence is that mystical, mental and ascetic silence which encompasses many aspects of man's spiritual life and activity. Silence, that deepest calm of the soul of which I am now speaking, also lies at the root of true prayer. That hesychastic state, the silence of the Hesychasts,[10] who prayed in the Jesus prayer,[11] here joins the silence of the intellect in faith, with the silence of the whole being of man in the following words: 'Let all mortal flesh keep silence'.[12] When we speak about flesh we speak not only of the body's composition, but of everything within us that is fleshly, that is earthly, that is not heavenly.

In this way, any knowledge of God opens up to us something that we can grasp with the mind and with the heart and which has living consequences in our actions, which moves us forward to a new life. For one cannot comprehend Christ in His boundless humility, His self-giving, His love and so on, and not follow Him! It means that our will, and our very flesh are actively, creatively, drawn into this comprehension of God. The mystery expands our soul, and deepens it, and makes it capable of prayerful contemplation and leads it to a knowledge of that which is incomprehensible.

But, as I said earlier, any knowledge of God is at the same time a greater understanding of Man himself. Call to mind the troparion of the Transfiguration, in which it is said that Christ revealed His glory to his disciples *as far as they were able to bear it*.[13] That is, as much as they *could* understand they understood. They saw as much as they could see, they carried away as much as they could: they had seen a vision of God's glory. The same can be said of Moses, when he went up to Mount Sinai: he was given the knowledge of as much as he could see and comprehend: '[The Lord] said: "Thou canst not see my face for man cannot see me and live ... And it shall come to pass, while my glory passeth by, that I will ... cover thee with my hand until I have passed by: then I will take away mine hand, and thou shalt see my back"' (Exod. 33:19–23).

Here we are given a measure of what Man is capable of: not only a measure of limitation, but also a revelation of Man's possibilities. Every time we meet with this question it seems to us that the limits have been underlined: 'Thou canst not see my face ...' The Apostle Paul says that the time will come when we will see face to face, when we will know as also we are known, and so on (cf. 1 Cor. 13:12), but that is in an age to come. And we very rarely notice or emphasise that although it is too soon for us to stand face to face, in the meantime we can see *something* – and how much there is that we can see, how much there is that we can get to know!

There certain things which are incomprehensible by their very nature, but which we can grasp to a certain extent and by certain means. Even in the world of the senses we cannot grasp light. We do not 'see' light – we are surrounded by light. Light shows us what surrounds us, but we do not see or grasp light itself. If we find ourselves in darkness we see nothing; then a torch starts to burn, or the electricity is turned on, or a window is opened – and we are surrounded by riches of colour, of movement and of form. The same can be said to a certain extent of our knowledge of God.

You have probably seen pictures of the many-coloured windows which are to be found in Western churches: huge windows composed of mosaics of small pieces of glass of different colours, joined together into a colourful harmony, a vision of colourful beauty. We are used to looking at them and marvelling, to revelling in their beauty and to being satisfied by this. But let us think about them a little. First of all it is self-evident (but not all things that are self-evident can be left unsaid): if there is no light behind the window, then that splendid window is no longer there. If it is night outside the window, all we see is a dark space on the wall, which is sometimes even darker than the wall itself. If you take an electric lamp and shine it on that window, you will nonetheless see nothing, not a single colour. You can see that it is made up of small pieces of glass, joined together by something, but you will not get to know either colour or form or beauty; however much light you will shine from where you are standing in the direction of that darkness, you will not be able to see anything.

So it also happens with God, when we try to throw in God's direction all the light of our mind, all our capability for creative imagination. We can make up something, but we only see very dim, dull, meaningless and empty outlines.

But it is enough for the light to rise behind this window in order for us to begin to catch something living and beautiful, something which has significance for us – because beauty is always significant. Let us now look carefully at this window. It may represent some event from the Old or the New Testament: the Transfiguration, God's entry into Jerusalem, Mount Sinai, it matters not which. It already tells us something about God. It is a whole philosophy represented in lines and in drawings but it becomes what Prince Evgenii Troubetsko[14] in his book about icons called *Philosophy in Colour*, only because the light of the sun is capable of bringing to life every small bit of glass. It is relevant to mention icons here, because an icon gives us much more than lines and colours. An icon is a scene from the world to come, of the Kingdom of God coming with all its glory into the world. An icon from within itself opens up to us the mystery of both heaven and earth, and of earth's reception of God and of God's proximity to us.

When we look closely at the window, apart from the subject and the story it tells us, we begin to grasp the richness of colours, and the beauty of the heavenly world appearing in our earthly world, because the light of heaven pours out all over this world's substance. And then it comes about. The light manifests to us not only itself in the refraction of these small pieces of glass: it manifests to us the true beauty, the potential, that is all the possibilities of beauty and the heavenly illumination, of our earthly substance.

This is a double revelation: of God and of us, of heaven and of earth, of time and of eternity. And here we see how closely they are intertwined, how inseparable they are from each other, because everything is contained in the creativity of God's Word, which has called everything out of non-being – not as lifeless matter, but as humanity capable of eternal life, capable of living in God, capable of containing everything that cannot be contained. These words are not mine but of Maximus the Confessor.[15] He says that if only we could grasp the mystery of Resurrection, we would reach into infinity.

In this way revelation puts before us a whole sequence of reality. We see a window and we receive a first impression of it. Then we get to know that behind this window there is light, and that the whole meaning of this window and all its beauty are not in the window but in the light behind the window. On the one hand something concrete and real is opened up; and on the other hand a mystery is revealed, because if, having seen the light in its refraction of the seven colours of the rainbow, you say: 'Now I understand, now I know, what light is, now I can look at it and see it', and throw the window wide open – there will be nothing in front of you. There is the inscrutable light, which is once again invisible, because as light you are incapable of seeing it.

This leads me to the following: the difference between an inseparable union which exists between reality itself and our understanding of reality – that is the truth as we express it. We are tempted, especially in Russian and especially in the wake of Pavel Florensky's definition,[16] to say that the truth is reality, that is the truth is that which is. To a certain extent this is the case, because if some assertion does not correspond at all to what is, it is a lie and not the truth. But the danger of such an assertion, which is so accurate and vivid, and so easy to remember, lies in the fact that one can come to identify as one actual reality and our knowledge and expression of it. In this respect whatever we say about God, however deeply we understand Him, be it by means of God's revelation, what God says of Himself, even by God's revelation in Jesus Christ, we still only know in part and see in part, 'as through a glass darkly' (1 Cor. 13:12). I have just spoken about a stained-glass window – coloured, living glass, which reveals God to us and does not separate us, but in fact these two – revelation and separation – are the same. Just as you cannot know the light without this glass, so you cannot express in words this knowledge other than by limiting it.

These thoughts, of course, are not my own. I am drawing a parallel between the word (be it theological) and the image (be it glass or an icon) on the basis of a troparion from the Great Canon of Andrew of Crete, where he speaks of King David: 'once [he] composed a hymn, setting forth, as in an icon ...' (Canticle 7, troparion 5).[17] This is where the connection lies between these two concepts. When we speak of God, we are, in fact, painting an icon in words. This verbal icon has all the characteristics of an icon: it both expresses something and brings it to our consciousness, and it becomes as it were a window opened for us on to eternity. At the same time it has all the limitations of an icon. An icon is not God, however well it portrays Him, just as verbal truth is not that of which it speaks.

This may seem complicated, but I want to underline precisely this difference between reality and its expression. St Gregory Palamas[18] says that everything that we say about God in accordance with His own revelation may appear the complete truth as far as the world is concerned, but is not the complete truth for God. We must always remember this because many of the hopeless, bitter arguments, full of hatred, between believers start here: when a man thinks that the words he uses to express truth, do not only express truth, but are in fact the truth itself, and that those who protest against what he says are blaspheming, are speaking against God, and are trampling the Face of Him of whom they speak. This leads to schisms, to divisions and to the spilling of blood on the basis of that which *should* unite us in the spirit of wonder concerning how much we can know about God, and the deepest humility in the face of the fact that He remains unknowable.

If we were to pray more, if we were capable of praying even a little more, we would not have this difficulty. When we pray we come to God basing ourselves on what we have already come to know of Him. But if we want to meet the Living God, then in that moment when we come to stand before God, we must stand before a God who is at one and the same time known and inscrutable – or, more correctly, a God whom we have come to know but have not yet grasped. In other words while we are seeking in our imagination, in our heart, in our experience, for that God we have known up till now, we will pass by that God who at that very moment is opening up to us, and we will not recognise Him. We will even possibly dodge past Him because that God may appear not to resemble the God towards whom we were moving, whom we expected, whom we long for in our heart. This is very important.

The same thing happens in our theology. There is a certain boundary which marks the limit of what we can know of God on earth. We need not fear this boundary. It is far beyond any limit which we have reached. However much we were to know God, however much we were to marvel at Him, however much our spirit might be grasped by what we do know of Him, we must always remember that we know so little and could know so much more. Therefore we can strive further and further, but knowing that when everything that is within our powers of comprehension has been achieved, God will still remain unknowable, and will remain the object of silent, wondering and loving contemplation.

Creative doubt

If that is the case, then it has enormous importance for us not only in our theologising, which on the one hand calls for creative boldness and on the other hand for obedient humility – that is, for the ability to listen in silence to what Man cannot create for himself – but also in our practical life in one particular aspect: that of doubt.

I want to say a few words about this, because doubt is one of the most tragic elements in the life of believers. It shatters the soul and sometimes erodes faith in the very place where there was absolutely no need for faith to be shattered or eroded. The word 'Doubt' is etymologically in Russian 'the conjunction of two opinions' – in the weak sense of the word 'opinion' and not in the strong, contemporary sense when a well-grounded opinion is expressed. The merging of two opinions is the coming together of two seeming realities. This, of course, creates a tension in the soul, which sometimes comes near to breaking it apart.

Two opinions, poles apart in our consciousness of God (either for God, or against Him) or of creation (for one view or another) are in no way incompatible. Indeed it often happens that they *are* incompatible, that one cannot continue to hold both one and the other opinion at the same time, but there is something which merges them, or which so overshadows and alters one of them that they come together in perfect harmony.

What it is important to remember is that often people become shattered by doubt because they transfer the doubt from themselves to the object of their doubt, to God, say, and forget that the coming together and the struggle of these two opinions is only taking place within oneself and in one's own consciousness. 'I knew little. I got to know something new. How can I bring the one together with the other? I do not know.' This only tells me that I have not matured to a fuller, more integrated understanding of things. It certainly does not mean that I have to choose between one and the other, choosing, moreover, not between things which seem right to me, but between God and no God.

Here we might be helped by a parallel example, and, I hope, my past will be of service to me. As some of you know, I first studied Natural Sciences, and then was a doctor. I had to do quite a lot of scientific work. And one of the first things that I learned when I was working at Physics, Chemistry and Biology at university level was that every time that you are certain of something, you must hasten to question it before someone proves to you that what you thought is foolish. That is how it is: as soon as you look at your wonderful idea, at your latest discovery, it will turn out that you are standing and looking at a barrier across the road. People are passing you, crowds are passing – and you are just standing and looking and do not see that there is a road and not a barrier in front of you.

The scholarly approach I am talking about appears as a systematic state of doubt, doubt born not of uncertainty but from a ripe and bold approach. A man does not doubt that there exists an objective reality towards which he is going, but knows that all the approaches to this reality must be superseded. He is certain that it is necessary to pass by each approaching barrier in order to reach his goal, rather than trembling before each barrier: 'Suppose there is no further sign, no pathway but only a desert, and I get nowhere and perish in it?' Through painstaking, arduous work people gather facts, one after another. When enough facts have been collected, in order to retain them and use them in some way that can be generally understood, people try to systematise them, to form a model of the world as it appears given these facts, as we know it now. This allows all these facts to be held together, rather like a sum total of knowledge. One has in one's hand a model, a *maquette*, an outline scheme of everything that one at present knows and understands. But at the same time, each one of us understands and knows that the facts of the current year will be surpassed by the facts of the following year.

I was a pupil of one of the Curies, who discovered radioactivity and was the first to study the structure of matter. My professor of Physics specialised in the structure of matter (this was thirty-five years ago).[19] He explained to us clearly that the atom could never be split, because at the very moment when the first atom was split, the universe would also split, because too much of a certain kind of energy would have been let out into the world. But, after he had said clearly that one cannot split the atom, for all the succeeding years he studied the question as to how in fact it could be split. A man has curiosity: if he is fated to be blown up in this task, he still wants to split an atom. And now atoms are split just as children crack nuts.

If this man had dug his heels in saying, 'But I know that one cannot split an atom', people would now look at him simply as an old man who had gone off his head. This is the root of the matter, that in science everybody says: 'I know that this is impossible – and now let us see how it can be done.' This doubt concerning one's own opinion is a genuine doubt. It is very bold, even sometimes heroic, because scientific research may lead one a long way. I know, for instance, a doctor who is a specialist in forensic medicine. He studies, for instance, the question as to what is the minimum that is necessary in order to strangle a man, and he carried out experiments on himself with the help of an assistant. He created a whole system of ropes and hangers, and would hang himself up, and attach weights up to the moment when he lost consciousness – and then, of course, his assistant had to take him down. That is a very bold approach, because one could die in this process. The assistant might not notice or might simply think, 'Well, let him.'

Another thing: this form of doubt is not only bold but systematic. It must apply to everything, and not just to what we do not 'like'. A discovery does not coincide with my view as of yesterday – then let us see what we can do to prove that it is not so.

Further: doubt must be optimistic and based on faith, because you are breaking up your view of the universe in order to build something better. In the worst case, it is the story of the rich man in the Gospel who said, 'I will break down my present barns and will build new ones' (see Luke 12:16–21); and at best it is the building of a view of the world in which a man can live more fully, more spaciously, with a more profound understanding of things, with a deeper understanding of Man, and with infinitely greater creative powers.

Why do believers so often divide on the subject of doubt, whereas scientists do not? Because a scientist is quietly confident that if he goes beyond today's view of the world, tomorrow's will be more true, more authentic, and will

CERTAIN CATEGORIES OF OUR EXISTENCE IN CREATION

correspond more closely to the existing objective reality. He does not transfer his own doubt onto reality, whereas a believer for some reason does this. And I will tell you why: because we develop very unevenly. If you will think of yourself and of the more mature or elderly people, who surround you, you will see that intellectually we have developed a long way. Any child now is more learned than a learned man of the sixteenth century. We develop far less as far as personality is concerned. I am not now thinking of the cult of personality, but of personality in the best sense of the word: that man should see himself as an unrepeatable being and not as just one of many in a flock of sheep.

But where we develop very little is in the sphere of our faith. Mostly doubts consist for a man in the argument between the boy he was when he was eight or nine and believed as a child, and the grown man into which he has intellectually developed. The experience of a religious eight-year-old boy is under fire from the mature mind of a grown man, and we are surprised that the eight-year-old child within, somewhere in our heart, does not find the intellectual means of beating that clever man that the owner's brain has become. This is not surprising, but it is very reassuring, because if that is how things stand, then doubt is very simple: it is a state of flux on our part. We have blown up like tadpoles: the head is big, but the body is like a thread.

The whole question, then, lies in how to mature in the sphere of faith and religious experience so that the mature believer can engage in a dialogue with the mature person within us. We should not fear this dialogue because that child who has not yet matured, who is still an infant in faith, may grow fully if he listens to his interlocutor – his mind – and combines the objections of that mind with his inner experience.

Yes, we shall see that we are children as far as faith is concerned and need to grow up. Such people as Basil the Great,[20] or Gregory Palamas were not afraid of the ideas and learning of their times, because they had combined them together. If only we were to mature spiritually, we would be able to start this dialogue with ourselves, but putting the stress there where it should in reality be: precisely on the fact that I have not yet found in myself that balance whereby the mind and the heart are merged together and can as one not only think about God, but think about Man, about the cosmos and about learning. A person who is half developed on one side or another is fit for neither the earth nor for the sky. He limps in both legs, as the saying goes. I would like to end with a heartfelt appeal: do not be afraid of your doubts! Do not be afraid of the doubts of others! Do not think that they cast doubt on God, or the sky, or the earth, or man, or knowledge. They are only telling you your baby clothes have grown tight, that the view of the world which you held yesterday is beginning to squeeze on the right side and on the left, that the image that you formed for yourself of God and of the world, has become too small for the experience of God and the world which has developed in you. Rejoice, and build a view of the world which is wider, deeper, wiser, and more spiritual. And then you will grow up, into a person who is everywhere in the right place, who can be a first-class scholar or a public figure in the world, and at the same time a citizen of heaven, God's man on earth.

Answers to Questions

Our students have to study a great deal, and often go to church to pray. Having great opportunities to become good theologians and good leaders of prayer and pastors, how should one combine one with the other so as not to become big-headed?

It seems to me that during one's studies one has to learn, one has to collect with much effort, concentration and with total conviction everything which might be useful in life later. It is early to begin forming a final view of the world, because in order to build up one's view one first has to have the facts. It is impossible to have an opinion based on a very primitive, elementary knowledge of the Christian faith. One has first to read, to think, and not to generalise into systems that which you have learned from others. For instance, in our attitude to the Holy Fathers one has to preserve the individuality of each one of them, with his particular problems, and their varying opinions in order to remember (and this is very important: we have to live with a sense of history) that the Orthodox theology which we have acquired involves a consciousness of the Church only in outline, even though it contains tremendous richness. And while we have not yet learnt what others already learnt before us, we have to hasten to find out. Otherwise it will seem to us that we are extraordinarily original, but unfortunately that appears so only to us. One of the French writers said that nobody thinks of himself as so original a thinker as he who has not yet read other people's ideas. The richness of the ideas of others which are current in the world, is very great, and without noticing it one can pick up half a dozen, not even knowing where you got them, and base oneself on them; but that is insufficient.

I had the same problem, because when I had finished secondary school, we lived in general in considerable poverty; I wanted to go to work in a factory, but my family insisted that I went on studying. And it seemed to me: why should I be studying, when firstly I only wanted to pray, and secondly we needed money to live on. I thought that there was betrayal, as it were, on two fronts. And after seven years of study at the university I understood that my family had been right. It became clear to me that the state of frigidity in which I lived (well, I had been put in a refrigerator for seven years, it seemed that I was doing nothing useful, I did not find food for my family, I managed to find a bit of food for myself, and did nothing for God) was only external. In fact these seven years gave me the opportunity to become a doctor, which is a very useful thing, and I had also been taught a great deal concerning mental discipline, at least concerning my approach to doubt. My working years taught me a great deal about the depth of human relationships.

That is why I think that one should not fear such a position. Only, firstly, one should seek knowledge, objective knowledge, of what exists – and not what 'should suffice for my parishioners' – because your parishioners perhaps do not need the theology of Gregory Palamas; and, as far as spiritual life is concerned, if they are Orthodox Christians they live according to the theology of Gregory Palamas. But there is no dogma in Orthodoxy which does not have a direct, clear relevance to the clergy. I cannot call myself a spiritual father. However 'when there are no fish, even a crab takes on the role of a fish'.[21] People come to me every single day and I see people for fourteen hours every day, who come to speak about their souls, about prayer, about doubts, about one thing or another; and I constantly see how their problems, their questions, or simply the patterns of their inner lives are the very things which are expressed in Orthodox dogma about the Holy Trinity, about the procession of the Holy Ghost, about energies, about the essence, about the substances, about the Hypostasis, about all those things which one has to teach, like a form of

Chinese grammar.[22] But these people did not invent theology: theology arose in them from the necessity of expressing in words their genuine religious experience – theirs and that of whole communities of people.

Therefore never think that there is something which one can call abstract theology. There are people who are in a state of abstraction, who are incapable of standing on the earth, and who, of course, cannot reach the sky, but float somewhere like clouds between heaven and earth – but there is no such thing as abstract theology. I have already said that I could easily show you how the teaching about the Holy Trinity forms the basis and roots of sociology and of human relationships, and how in it a whole lot of psychiatric problems of our time are resolved. I know this from experience of working in psychiatric clinics and among people. And if the dogma concerning the Holy Trinity can have such an application, then even more so can dogma concerning the Incarnation or the teaching about the Mysteries[23] and so on. Therefore learn and try to understand, try to grasp not only the general knowledge which is to be found among all spiritual writers – because that is more easily done – but to grasp that which is exclusive and unrepeatable in each one. That is the first thing.

Secondly – learn to pray! There is a difference between the words of prayers and prayer. Learn specifically to pray; and not to be good technicians. You know there are people who read wonderfully, sing beautifully, sometimes even serve touchingly, and at the same time are tottering in their souls, or who simply can convey to someone else that which they themselves do not understand (because God has helped them, has given them a voice or a good style). No, it is necessary to pray! And here the question of time arises.

We are all in the grip of time, but it is our own fault, for time has nothing to do with it. The fact that time flows by and that we are hurrying somewhere are two quite separate things. To be in a hurry – that is an inner state. To act quickly, accurately, and to the point – that is something quite different. Take the following example: it happens that when on holiday in the country one is walking across a field, quickly, cheerfully and briskly – and not hurrying to get anywhere, because there is nothing to hurry for. And sometimes one sees a man carrying two suitcases and three bags and is in a tremendous hurry, but is moving at a snail's pace. Haste lies in the fact that a person wants to be half a kilometre ahead of himself: not where he finds himself but always a little further. And while a person lives like that he will not pray, because someone who is not here cannot pray, and the person who is here does pray. That is all there is to it. It seems to me very important.

I want to speak of this in greater detail. I discovered a certain quality of time in an incident where I was very lucky. At the time of the German occupation of Paris I was an officer in the French Resistance and I was arrested. (Of course everything that I am going to say now I was then unable to think through theologically, but the experience was there for a purpose.) It happened like this. I went into the Metro and I was promptly seized. At that moment I discovered that my past had vanished – for two reasons. Firstly, if I was to be spirited away, there would be no past. I would be imprisoned, and what had happened before would not define me any longer. Secondly, everything that had indeed happened would lead me to the executioner's block, and therefore it must be wiped out. That past must be totally cut off, and at the same time I must invent a past which would be helpful. The future, if you think about it, lies within us, as far as we can foresee and plan it. For instance, when you walk in total darkness there is no future; you go along and do not expect anything, although you are prepared for whatever may happen. That future towards which we are always striving is only real either because it is vividly before our eyes, for instance like a departing bus, or because we are going towards it: I am going home, I am going to the cinema. But if you cut that off, if you find that you have been arrested, you have absolutely no idea what is going to happen. That soldier might hit me in the face, he might shoot me, he might put me into some German cell, he might do something quite different – and every moment will be like this and there will be no moment when I shall know what is about to happen next. In such cases there proves in fact to be no future.

We live as if there is no present, as if we are rolling along from the past into the future. And the present is that fleeting moment in which one is rolling over, and it proves that the only reality – the only place where I entirely am – is the here and now. And I understood at that moment what one of the ascetic Fathers of the fifth century had in mind when he said, 'If you want to pray, retreat into your own skin.' We do not live under our skin: we live here, there, and everywhere. Think of yourself when you are sitting at table. Your eyes wander about: you are in the cucumbers, you are in the fish, you are in the vodka,[24] you are in the one or the other. Your personality has spread across the whole table. And if you think of life in general, we do not live under our skin. We have spread ourselves in all directions through our desires, our wishes, our friendships, our enmities, our hopes, our aims – whatever you will. I do not want to say that that is all bad. I only want to say that in fact under our skin only our inner organs remain, but we exist outside ourselves, like some sort of squeezed-out liquid. So get back under your skin.

If you are arrested in the Metro, as I was, suddenly you are all under your skin. And you realise how used you are to this skin, and how much you like it and so you do not want that anything unpleasant should happen to it – that is the first thing. Secondly you realise that it is so cosy within this skin that you do not want to get out of it. And furthermore, the past minute has been dangerous and the coming minute is even worse. Oh, if only one can keep going for this minute! And it proves to be possible to creep in under one's skin, that it is comfortable within it, that the present is the only reality, and that one desperately wants to stay in this present. And tell me: what happens to time? Yes, it flows on without you! You think that if you move, time moves with you? Certainly not. Time moves on its own.

In order to pray one has to learn to live like that, in the way I have just described. Here is another example. When you are riding in a car or in a train, the machine moves, and you are sitting, reading a book, looking out of the window, thinking your own thoughts. So why not live like that? Why can't one, for instance, walk fast while at the same time doing something with one's hands – and at the same time be in a completely stable state of calm within? It is possible! This is shown by the experience, not just of the saints, but of the most ordinary people. But in order for this to happen one has to learn to stop time, because (unfortunately!) not all of us are arrested, and so there is nobody about who can teach us. But one can learn for oneself – after all one can do things for oneself. I will give you two exercises and you must try them. If you are able to do this, they will teach you all the rest.

The first is very simple. When there is nothing to do, when there is time, sit down for five minutes and say to yourself: 'I am now sitting and not doing anything, and will be doing nothing for five minutes, I only exist …' And you will see that this is an extraordinary feeling, because we very rarely discover that we exist. We usually feel that we are a part of some collective whole and a small part in relation to what surrounds us.

Then, try this. When I first became a priest, an old lady from an old people's home came to see me and said, 'Your Reverence, I have been studying the Jesus Prayer[25] for fourteen years. I repeat it all the time and I have never felt that God exists. What should I do?' 'Well', I said, 'Turn to someone who knows how to pray.' She replied, 'You know, I have asked all the learned people, and they told me that you have only just been ordained and do not know anything yet, so you will speak from the heart.' I thought, 'What a sensible old woman!' And I said, 'I shall speak to you from the heart: how can God put a word in, when you are speaking all the time?' 'So what should I do?' she asked. I replied, 'This is what you should do. Go into your room, close the door, put an armchair in a comfortable position. Then place the light so that you can see the icon with its icon lamp, and sit for fifteen minutes in front of the Face of God. Only do not have any pious thoughts and do not pray.' My old lady said, 'But it is wicked to behave in this way!' I replied, 'Try it, since you ask me who am ignorant.' And she went away.

After a time she came again, and said, 'Do you know it really worked!' I asked what had worked. She told me: 'This is what happened. I locked myself in. There was a ray of light in the room, and I lit the icon lamp. I put the armchair in a position from which I could see the whole room, I took up my knitting, and sat down and breathed, and looked round – I had not noticed for a long time that my room was both warm and cosy. The icon lamp burned. At first various worries would not calm down, my thoughts flew about; then

I began to knit, and my thoughts began to become calm. And suddenly I heard the quiet clicking of my knitting needles. Through this clicking I suddenly noticed how quiet it was around me – and then I felt that this quiet is not at all because there is no sound, but that it is something' – as she said – 'substantial. It is not emptiness, but has substance. I continued to knit, and suddenly it became clear to me, that at the heart of this silence there is Someone: God.'

Well try it – not for fifteen minutes, because for that one has to be a wise old woman – but at least for five minutes. And if you will learn in the course of these five minutes to remain in the present, not in the future, not in the past, to remain nowhere but *here*, you will know what it means to exist. One old man, a French peasant, was asked the question: what do you do for hours in church, sitting, not even moving the rosary beads? To which he replied: 'Why should I do anything? I am looking at Him, He is looking at me – and we are happy together ...' What more do we want?

When you have learnt, when there is nothing to do, to do nothing (which, probably, none of us is really capable of doing), learn to make time stop when it is rushing past. And when it seems to you that the world cannot carry on without you ('If I do not do something, everything will begin to collapse, the universe will waver'), remember that Christianity has existed for almost two thousand years without you, not to mention the universe, which existed for ages before that – and has managed very well. Learn to stop time at such a moment, when it normally does not stand still. In order to do this at a moment when you are busy, say: 'Now, stop. I am freeing myself from my occupation.' For example, you have just been reading with pleasure. Stop for five minutes. You are throwing your head back, you are sitting down, you are silent. Do not dare to think of anything useful. You are before God. That is more difficult. When you are studying it is not so difficult to do, because it is not a major sadness to distract yourself from learning. And so, when you are reading some interesting novel, say to yourself: 'I will stop in the middle of the next page, on the sixth line, where there is not even a comma in the middle of a phrase. I will stop, in order to stop time.' That is harder.

When you have learnt to do this, learn to stop not only your reading but events themselves. For example withdraw from a conversation. Three or four people are speaking, and you are too. Lean back inside yourself, retreat into your own skin, like a snail into its shell, and stay at the heart of your being, in the place which in ascetic literature is called the heart: not in a state of emotion, but of *hesychia*, in silence, in the absence of talk. If you learn to do this, you will see that you can read, sing, work, talk, without losing a single moment of being in a prayerful state. And this is not a wish beyond the clouds, because if you want this even a little bit, then God wants it as much. He will come towards you from Heaven, while you have only taken one step on earth. I think that if you will work at yourself like that, you will be praying, and you will be able to learn and to pray in the most creative way and never lose anything.

I cannot say that I can do this, but I would die simply from boredom and exhaustion if I were unable to do it just a little, because in the course of a year in London alone more than three and a half thousand people come to my hour-long talks. So one has to somehow find some support, one has to somehow switch off. That does not mean to fall asleep or to doze off spiritually: you must get under your skin and stay there.

How can one combine the fulfilling of monastic vows with theological and pastoral work?

When I took my monastic vows a little more than twenty-five years ago, my confessor said to me, 'You are seeking spiritual achievement and self-assertion in monasticism. Remember that monasticism consists only of the victory of God's Love in you, that is, in God's victory over you.' I think that is the heart of the matter. If monasticism is defined by the fact that you, as a fully professed monk, must perform a thousand obeisances and recite the Jesus Prayer five thousand times, in addition to all the statutory services – of course there will not be time to study theology and there will not be time for pastoral work. They cancel each other out in terms of time, and they cancel each other out physically.

If monasticism consists in 'not being', so that only God is in you and acts through you, so that there is nothing left of you except obedience, except transparency, except an inner God-inspired silence and God-inspired weakness, then one can at any rate do pastoral work, because pastoral work is love.

It is harder in a way to work at theology, because people who are not gifted intellectually and lack cognitive powers can find that the effort of concentrating their attention, which is required for mastering and understanding the material, does not leave any room for inner toil. That is a mistake, but that mistake can be rectified – not by a lecturer but by a confessor. I can tell a single person what he should do, but I cannot lecture on it: it is too private, too personal a question, one that pertains to an individual.

But I think that monasticism consists in detachment. Do you know what is meant by the words in the Gospel 'to untie an ox or a donkey' (Luke 13:15)? That freedom from being tied up is the state of a man who is completely free to follow the behest of the Spirit, the behest of God. This takes a monastic form in a monastery, but it can also take on a secret form of monasticism, which many have experienced in the last fifty years. Their activity is not marked in a specifically religious way, and a person can be religious regardless of his activity or his clothing. That, I think, is all that I can say in such a short time.

Is it possible to find some criterion or standard, by which one could define the truth of religion?
I cannot give you either an exhaustive answer or even a reasonably deep one to this question, because I have never thought in these terms, and I have never been called upon to think this theme through. But I will point out two things: firstly an image of that God of whom a given religion speaks; and secondly what this God accomplishes for people. The second I define in this way. The Church is a society of love. If those around us were to see in us people transformed by love, they would not ask which is the right God, and is there a God, and which religion is best. As the Apostle Paul said a long time ago, 'For the Name of God is blasphemed among the Gentiles through you' (Rom. 2:14). The answer does not lie in good works but in love, because there are many kind people who are dry as sticks, in spite of doing everything that should be done – nobody will be drawn to God by this. But the God of love, the God who teaches us that the other is more important than oneself, that my neighbour is the person who needs me and not the one who happens to live near me – that is one of the criteria. In this sense, of course, we make many people question the Christian faith.

The image of that God of whom we are speaking: I want to return to the quotation from Voltaire, that if there was no

God, Man would invent Him. Every invented God is a human being multiplied to infinity. It is everything that man delights in, blown up to huge proportions. In this sense, various cultures provide us with various gods, more or less attractive to other cultures. But any god who appears only to be an idealised man should be questioned. What is characteristic of Christianity, which convinces me more and more, is that Man would have never invented such a God as ours.

For example, people say that Christ appears as a sort of image of the Egyptian god Osiris, who also died and was resurrected. The point is not that he died and was resurrected – that would have been easy. The point is that Osiris never became a man, never experienced the profanation of fallen mankind. The God that is revealed to us in Christ – powerless, vulnerable, defenceless, cursed, defeated – such a God will never be invented by Man, because that is the very opposite of what he needs in a God and that he seeks in God. Such a God cannot be imagined.

I cannot go into details now, but I want to underline two things: this God is in a certain sense absolutely incomprehensible, and arouses the deepest perplexity: 'How can this be?' And that is exactly how we could understand God, who became Man and endured everything, and would be in sympathy to the end with everybody who is capable of knowing God, who is capable of being saved. But what is characteristic of Christ is that He remains in sympathy – once and for ever, through the inalienability of His Incarnation – not with the person who is saved but with the fallen one, not with him who is already beginning to improve, but with him who is sitting deep in the ditch; and this solidarity of His goes much further than we imagine. He links His fate specifically with the sinner, with the rejected one, with the disenfranchised, with fallen Man: and not only outwardly – and here I think is where the criterion of the love of God is sharpest – but inwardly.

Think about it. In the garden of Gethsemane, Christ goes through everything which surrounds approaching death, but according to Maximus the Confessor, even in His body He is not, in fact, subject to death, because death is the result of separation from God; whereas the absolute authenticity of the combination in Him of Divine and human nature makes Him an immortal Man.[26] We bear witness to this when we speak of the fact that the Body of Christ was imperishable in the tomb, and he descends to hell in God's glory. He accepts an impossible death: 'O Life, how canst Thou die?'[27] This death would only be possible as a result of some totally incomprehensible rift with God, what one of our Western Orthodox theologians called 'metaphysical unconsciousness'.

Christ on the cross cried out, 'My God, my God, why hast thou forsaken me?' (Mark 15:34). This is not a mere repetition of the prophetic psalm. It is a real experience of the loss of God, which alone makes the death of the Immortal one possible. And when we think about it, we see that Christ experienced more deeply than any unbeliever the experience of godlessness, the deprivation of God, and here there is not a single person who can stand outside the mystery of the Man who is Christ. If you think about these two or three points, you will see that in this respect in Christianity there is something absolutely unique, which can be found nowhere else. We have an unknowable God with all the wealth that Man can only imagine and which he cannot attain, but there is also an historic God, who makes history comprehensible and incorporates it in Himself, right up to the very limits of Man's fall and the utmost tragedy.

This is what convinces me, if I need to be convinced,

because I came to faith a different way, simply, not philosophically, because I ran into God and there was nowhere for me to go from Him. I simply, well, bumped into Him.

Is salvation possible for someone who does not believe in Christ and can grace be active outside the Church?
Grace is spread so widely that we simply cannot comprehend it. The Apostle says to us that 'no man can say that Jesus is the Lord, but by the Holy Spirit' (1 Cor. 12:3). This means that before you called Jesus Lord, the Holy Spirit whispered something into your heart. We have this conception that only within the Church does the Holy Spirit speak, teach, reveal things. (Honestly speaking, if one looks at us this is not obvious! One has to be honest: stand in front of a mirror, look into it, and ask yourself, 'Am I indeed a temple of the Holy Spirit? Is this something that everyone can see on my face and in my eyes?') But God acts throughout the world, saving, possibly the dispossessed – if the voice of God reaches someone foreign to Him and not to his own. So it is simply much richer than we often imagine. We think that there is a kingdom of Grace, and then a desert like the north pole. No! Christ bestows grace on us in such different ways. Can we, for instance, say that in the Old Testament the prophets and the patriarchs lacked grace? We cannot. But at the same time we can say with the Evangelist that the Holy Spirit was not on the earth because Christ had not yet risen to the Father (John 14:26). Both things are simultaneously true, because the presence of the Holy Spirit and the influence of grace vary in different circumstances, but there is no 'radical' absence of grace.

So that means that salvation is possible without Christ?
I would say yes. Take the words of the Apostle Paul that the

Gentiles are guided by God's law which is written in their hearts, that Jews are guided by God's Law given by Moses, and that Christians are guided by Christ's law (see Rom. 2:14 ff.).

But they have to approach Christ?
They might not approach him, because that depends on history. You cannot question the eternal salvation of a person only on the basis that he was born in Central Africa in an epoch when there was not a single missionary there. In that case salvation would really be determined by geography and history. England is an island. No Eastern Orthodox person had been seen there before the time, say, of Ivan the Terrible. Does it means then that the English are doomed to perdition, condemned for eternity, because they were born there? That would be too simple! It is a different matter if Truth stands in front of you and you walk past it, but even in such a case there are the words of Christ, 'All manner of sin and blasphemy shall be forgiven unto men … And whosoever speaketh a word against the Son of man, it shall be forgiven him' (see Matt. 12:31–32). It means that one can walk past something and not be finally condemned.

I will give you a personal example. I read the Gospels for the first time when I was fifteen years old, because of indignation with what I had heard about Christianity, in order to ascertain whether it was true and if it was true, to have done with God once and for all, with Christianity and with everything else. This is what happened; the person who spoke about Christ in my presence had aroused in me such repugnance, such loathing and indignation, that it ended by my reading the Gospels – and this turned me around. But this might not have happened. I might, for instance, have heard all this, come to feel loathing and anger (as I did), come home and found that we had no Gospel book in the house and that none of the people we knew had them either, and said to myself, 'Well, that is that!' And I would have felt very determined about it, because at that time I was very determined in myself. So it is all very complicated.

I know that I am now raising very difficult questions. The question of finding Christ and of salvation through Christ I see as follows: one cannot be saved except through Christ – that is one thing. But if you could not have heard about Christ, then you cannot be judged for that. Otherwise it would be a case of predestination, worse than in Calvinism, worse than in the Reformed Church: it would simply be a case of an arbitrary fate from God – you have been born there and so you are condemned. There is no moral connotation here, there is no morality. There is simply chance, or God's evil will, but nothing else. In what way can you be guilty of having been born here or somewhere else?

Does this mean that you can think of people in other religions as catechumens?
It falls to me to see very many people, both Orthodox and non-Orthodox, both believers and non-believers. And at one time I had to work for three years, which is quite a long time, with people from the Far East. And it is amazing how much knowledge of God there can be in a man when he gets to a certain point: the one thing that is lacking is the name of Jesus, in order to provide the key and explanation to everything. When a person who, through life's experience, with the help of even his pagan faith, comes to such knowledge and finds himself in front of God's face, is it possible to imagine that he does not recognise him as the one he has been searching for all his life, the answer to all his perplexities?

I remember the words of St Isaac of Syria: 'Do not call God just. If He were just, you would already be in Hell.'[28] There is a great deal of hope in that. If He was simply just, like a good judge, what hope would there be? All hope is based on God's 'injustice', which is expressed in the parable of the labourers in the vineyard: 'Am I not allowed to do what I choose with what belongs to me? Why do you begrudge my generosity?' (Matt. 20:15). Whether you are capable of receiving is another matter. It may happen that a person loves you, but you are not capable of returning that love.

St Isaac of Syria has another marvellous passage, where he points out that when a person dies, the body is separated from the soul, and the soul finds itself face to face with God, and sees that life's only content is love; and everything that is in him, all the love which is somewhere in Man, all the yearning for love which is in him, all the striving for wholeness, for true being, becomes for him like the pangs of childbirth: all this is striving to come out and cannot be born. And here St Isaac introduces an interesting thought: that the soul cannot hear the final judgement on itself before it is reunited with the body, because the body is its friend, with which it communed, doing good and doing evil, and it is only together that they can bear this fruit.

All this is not such blind hopelessness as it often seems to us to be: 'When I die it is all over.' Then what are we praying for when we say: 'Give repose with the righteous' in Panikhidas and elsewhere?[29] We cannot pray for God, who has judged rightly, to act wrongly because we want him to: that would not be Christianity. There is something else here. Indeed at this time something else is happening. Every drop of love, which has come through our prayer, might change something in Love's Kingdom, because this love belongs to the person whom you love. And when this love costs you a lot, then you really think: yes, it seems this could help.

I am thinking now of somebody I knew, who was considerably older than me. He was taken to a German concentration camp and spent four years in Buchenwald. When he returned I asked him, meeting him in the street, 'How are you, Fedor Timeofeevich?' And he answered, 'I have lost peace.' 'Fedor Timeofeevich, have you lost faith?' 'No, I have lost peace, because day and night I think of those miserable people, who were so mad that they tortured and tormented us in such a way. They do not know that one day they will stand before the judgement of God, and I know they will. When I was in the camp, I was their victim and I felt: I can pray for them, because God cannot fail to hear my prayers. And now, when they are no longer torturing me, I have the feeling that my prayer was not heard. It was too lightweight.'

This is where we are most closely integrated with God, where through sacrifice, through suffering, we receive Christ's power to say: 'Father, forgive them, for they know not what they do' (Luke 23:34) – 'Forgive!' Another sufferer said to his disciple before he died, that only a martyr will be able on the Day of Judgement to stand before the Judge as a defender of his tormentors and say, 'Following Your example and Your word I forgave. You have nothing more to exact from them.'

Here destinies are spun together. Here everything is spun together, and one feels that the Body of Christ is not only the object of worship, but also a tragedy. The man who torments you has not entered into the Body of Christ, but without him the Body of Christ will not shine fully.

Tell us, your Grace, about your past.
You know that it is always awkward and even absurd to talk

about oneself. I never spoke of it until two years ago, when there was formed in London a public discussion between non-believers and believers. I was asked to be one of those who would speak for the faith. The talk was roughly two hours long, and the people taking part in the discussion had the right to intervene: anyone who happened to be in the hall could ask any one of us a question. There was a rather long discussion about the truths of faith, and about the trust-worthiness of one idea or another, until the moment when a man got up and said, 'I am asking Bishop Anthony a question: what is the basis of his belief?' – and he sat down. At this point I felt that I had no right to defend the privacy of my soul, especially because this question might not be prompted just by curiosity, not only a challenge, but a cry from one soul to another. And then for the first time I told him what I am now about to tell you.

One could say that I had no contact either with the Church or with the Gospels till I was fifteen years old. I was born into an Orthodox family, was christened an Orthodox, but knew nothing of the Church. This was due to the Revolution, the constant moving from place to place, and material circumstances amounting to poverty. There was also the fact that I was in a French boarding-school where no religious teaching was done. I should add, as well, that nothing drew me to God. I discovered a wonderful method to prevent myself ever being in church. I was taken there once a year, on Good Friday, and I discovered at once that if I inhaled the incense and then held my breath, I fainted, and was immediately taken outside. I used this method for several years, and then they got tired of taking me. As far as God Himself was concerned, I had no time for Him. In fact my feelings tended to be hostile, because at times, at certain moments, He complicated life. There was a time when émigré children were offered places in Catholic schools on the condition that we became Catholic, and this put me off not only from Catholicism but from God Himself.

This went on until I became fifteen. I was then a member of a Russian national organisation, where we studied the Russian language, literature and history because there was a hope that we would return to Russia and would then dedicate all our talents to our native land; but in general we were not involved in questions of faith. Then one of our leaders suddenly got the idea of inviting a priest during the Great Fast.[30] And when we heard of this we all began to find excuses, one referring to his oxen, another to his fields, and some simply tried to get away as far as possible from the all-seeing eye. I was caught between the others and I was told that even if I felt so hostile to the whole business, I still must understand that one must show loyalty towards the organisation, and if nobody went to the talk we would be disgraced. 'You do not need to listen,' my teacher said to me, 'just go in and sit down.' I thought to myself: I can do that – and I went and sat down. But it was difficult not to listen, because there were five of us young folk and the priest spoke too loudly, interfering with one's thoughts, and I had to listen to him. He was a very eminent theologian, but he had no experience of working with young people. And what he said to us made me so deeply angry, and brought on such indignation, that when he finished, I did not even contemplate staying with my friends and decided immediately to try to find out if Christ was indeed what he said he was, and whether Christianity was indeed that disgusting, loathsome, horrible thing, which he had described to us. I went home with a deep feeling of hatred towards everything. At home I asked my mother whether we had a copy of the Gospels, and she gave one to me. I went to my corner and, not expecting anything good to come from the Gospels, I decided to choose the shortest – so I began to read the Gospel according to Mark. I cannot explain to you what happened at this point. Anyone who knows will understand, and anyone who does not know will not understand anyway. It happened that between the first and the third chapter of the Gospel according to Mark, it became absolutely and concretely clear to me, that at the other side of the table at which I sat reading stood the living Christ. That is all.

Years later, in England, we had an argument in our youth group, to which I had invited the Chairman of the Union of Non-believers. He said to me, 'If you are a believer, it means that you are mad.' Maybe you, too, think that such an approach as mine does not explain anything: it does not. It is simply a fact of my life, and what happened then has stayed with me to this day: an absolutely clear awareness that Christ is here, more real than this platform or anything else.

What came afterwards was not the acquiring of faith, but something more like a great banquet. I read the Gospels and they simply opened up life to me. I was then amazed by three things. I was amazed that the God of the Gospels was not the God of some small – or big – bunch of people, not only the God of the Orthodox, or of the Catholics, or of the Protestants, not only the God of the kind, not only the God of believers, but also the God of the wicked, of non-believers, and of those who hate you: that He encompasses everybody, that He has his approach to each person, but nobody is foreign to Him, even if some alienate themselves from Him. This opened up the world to me as something whole, profound and significant. And when I entered university about a year and a half later, during all my studies I took in learning as a branch of theology, words about God and about that which He had created. And to this day I think like that, after many years of experience in study and in the spiritual life.

The second thing I was amazed by was that out of all the gods of whom I had heard, our God stands for human dignity. Everywhere in the Gospels God treats Man with the deepest respect. I do not say with mercy or pity – one can be merciful and have pity for those one despises. But his approach is never 'wholesale' – for Him everyone is unique. Later, I began to read the lives of the saints, and there I came on a story of how one priest, indignant about the sins of those surrounding him, began to pray to God for retribution, and God said to him, 'Do not pray like that! If there was only one sinner on the earth, I would be ready for a thousand years to experience that which I had already experienced in Gethsemane and on Golgotha.' And it is this God, who is God indeed, who gives infinite value to Man. When St Paul says: 'Ye are bought with a price' (1 Cor. 6:20), it simply means that God puts the question to Himself: 'What is the value of, what does a single sinner mean to me?' And He replies: 'The entire life, the entire death, all the blood of My Only Son.'

And the third thing is freedom. I obviously had not thought this through when I was fifteen or sixteen years old, but it is this: we are not called to show false modesty, to turn ourselves inside out and become evasive, so as to somehow ingratiate ourselves with God. We have to become ourselves in the most absolute way, to an infinite degree, but we can be ourselves only if: 'I live; yet not I, but Christ liveth in me' (Gal. 2:20), if I live not only with that amount of God's breath, which He breathed into me at the beginning, but with everything that has been communicated to me from the Source of life – only if I become the son of God in Christ.

Then, of course, Christ's image amazed me by its combination of gentleness, love and enormous power which gives Man the possibility of giving himself over for the whole of his life to love and service: 'No one takes my life away from me; I am laying it down of my own free will' (John 10:18). This prefigures the crucifixion. If you remember what I said about the God-forsaken nature of Christ's death you will understand, how deeply felt and significant this is for me.

That is what I can say. Probably all of you have experienced equally significant things, but since you asked me the question, I have answered you.

In the Church, we are called to be servants and handmaids of the Lord. I think that this expression contains an antinomy. We are still sons and daughters by our calling, and I would say: thank God! – but if all that one can achieve is what you or I, or we together can show at present, if the whole fullness of being a son could be expressed in each of us as we are now, it would be very sad, and the eternal Kingdom would be infinitely boring. But with God, being a son is a calling. That is, it already exists here as a mutual relationship with God. We are his children by birth, He is to us our own Father: that is the truth. On the other hand, we have to mature to the measure of this state of being sons, and become such as Christ, such as the Mother of God: that and no less should be our measure. And herein lies the antinomy. In fact everything on the earth has two faces: we are already in eternity, and we are still within time. We are still slaves and servants because psychologically we fear God's punishment, hope for reward, and have not learned to love only so that everything should be easily achieved through love – but at the same time we are already God's own children.

How should one understand Christian love – the basis of all good works?

I think exactly as I have just said, for the words 'good works' ring false. This has been briefly expressed by a Catholic saint of the eighteenth century: the more I hate doing something, the more virtue there is in my action. But the fact is that, seen like this, good works only tell us that there is little love in you and that you are very far from heaven. In some sense good works are excluded by love from the point of view of him who loves: they only appear to be good works to someone looking on. Let us say a mother spends the whole night sitting by the bed of her sick child – she does it because of love. It does not occur to her that she is doing a good deed. She loves the child – how can she act otherwise? Put a carer in her place. If she does not fall asleep and does everything that is needed, she will be doing good – why? Because she does not have enough love for it to absorb everything and take away the fact of doing good. And in this sense such acts develop out of love that we call the fruits of the Spirit, on the one hand, and good works on the other. But love for him who acts, or rather for him who lives by love, causes the idea of good works to vanish.

If the holy prophet David said: 'I am a worm, and no man; a reproach of men, and despised of the people' (Psalm 22:6) – then what can anyone else say? How is one to understand this?

When a man is worthless, he does not see himself as worthless. Most often an evil man sees in himself a great deal – not so much of good works as of attractive qualities and traits. We start to lose sight of our splendid qualities, which only we see, when we are fascinated by something greater that we ourselves, and are astonished by great beauty. Then we begin to comprehend: maybe we are not so splendid after all?

One of the mistakes made by preachers and teachers of a falsely ascetic state lies in instilling into a person humility, having first trodden him thoroughly in the mire. One does not achieve humility in this way, because however much one has been trodden into the mire, even if you are indeed a worm, you will try to break free from the heels that trample you, and will only begin to be angry. And this is a fact. It is simply a fact not only from my worm-like life, but out of your worm-like life too. None of us gains humility through being trodden on. Humility appears when we are truly astonished by the disproportion between ourselves and that which we can only contemplate in silence and amazement. The saints acquire humility through seeing God, and certainly not through endlessly gazing at themselves.

The Irish writer Beckett has a play[31] about a family that lived in dustbins, and how they communicated with each other from these dustbins, and what they found in them. You know, we often live like that. We are told, 'Be humble.' We think: how can I achieve humility? Let me find more grime in myself. And we begin to dig into our inner dustbin. Humility does not increase from this. We only find more and more grime. Then we either get used to it – which, unfortunately, very often happens – or we fall into despair – which also often happens.

The answer does not lie in this. John of Kronstadt said that God does not reveal any man's failures to him until he finds in that man enough faith and hope so that he will not become dispirited. Therefore the problem of a spiritual life certainly does not lie in us digging down to the depths of all our cesspools – there would be no end to them if we began to dig – it lies in finding some way to what we can attain so as to feel how beautiful God is and how all could be well, if only we were not lying like a dark and dirty stain on His creation. And so, when man sees the greatness, the infinity and the captivating beauty of God, he becomes quieter and more humble.

I remember a young woman, who before getting married came to see me and said, 'You know, from the time that I knew that I was loved I experienced trembling and humility in my soul because love is such a holy thing that I know that I cannot be worthy either of Peter or of John or of this miracle of love.' This is where humility starts: there where we come to comprehend God's beauty and the miracle of love. Then we cease to be petty, we grow up to a great height but feel that compared to the greatness of God we are nothing. And what joy there is in this impoverishment of the spirit: to be loved not according to our deserts. Remember the prayer, 'If thou wert to save me in accordance with my deeds, this would not be grace or a gift but rather a duty.' This would not make happiness. Happiness lies simply in being loved and in being something just because you are loved.

Take the line in the marriage service: 'Christ chose the Church as a pure bride for Himself.'[32] The Church is us, and can we be called a pure bride? We cannot. If He had looked at us first, could he have loved us? He would never have loved us. But the truth lies in the fact that He loved us first, and in that love we began to radiate beauty. 'The servant of God, *N.*, is crowned to the handmaid of God, *N.*...':[33] he becomes a prince, a married king, because she loves him and vice versa. That is what it consists of: an anticipated and transforming love. And when you are blessed with love, there only remains the need to fall down in veneration – there is nothing else you can do. To answer with love – you will always feel that you are in debt, that you lack the strength to love this miracle: of being loved. That is where humility, that is where saintliness is found.

And this expresses itself in – 'yes, I am a worm' and so on. 'I am the last in line among people, the most unworthy.' This is said more sincerely because everyone feels himself to be lower than everything and everyone else.

When St Seraphim was in the Spirit, his face shone as if lit by the Holy Spirit, as did that of many saints. What is this effect of the Holy Spirit?

Remember what is written of the work of the Spirit: 'But the fruit of the Spirit is love, joy, peace, long-suffering … against such there is no law' (Gal. 5:22–23). This shows to us in the right order what is the effect of the Holy Spirit's coming to us, that there settle within us quiet, order, joy and lucidity in the heart, the quelling of passions, the mind's irradiation, a fervour for God, sobriety and a mortification of the flesh. We know all this through experience, because each one of us at some moment experiences this. Only we forget; and we forget because we are inattentive: we are at one and the same time making much of ourselves and inattentive to ourselves.

In the case of Seraphim of Sarov, I would say the invisible became visible. Let us move from Seraphim of Sarov to Mount Tabor: the Transfiguration of the Lord. For the Lord did not change. The Lord was the same from the very beginning; He was the incarnate Son of God, nothing happened to him at that moment, but something happened to his disciples. He shone out in front of them and they saw His glory in so far as they were able. And then they ceased to see, because this vision of glory plunged them into horror and they fell down flat, and Peter began to say some mad words: let us put up three tabernacles – it is good for us here. He did not know how to express what was going on in his soul.

We encounter the same thing with St Seraphim when he says: 'You see, your Grace, the wretched Seraphim did not even cross himself, but only said in his mind: "Show him in what glory people can be when Thou comest" – and He showed them.' I cannot explain anything, I can only say, that that inner state, which is described in the Holy Bible as the gifts of the Spirit (in Isaiah), and as the fruits of the Spirit in two places by the Apostle Paul, we also experience – in small measure, but at certain moments we know that an incomprehensible quiet is descending upon us, when all the powers of our soul and body enter the deepest calm of silence, and we hear and see and live and reign freely – that is already a phenomenon, that is something which became visible through the salvation of man's soul.

Chapter 5

❦

The Vocation of Man

Address given at the Russian Orthodox Cathedral of the Dormition and All Saints, London, on 6 June 1991.

We are ever more conscious of the necessity of preserving nature and preventing the destruction of animal and plant species, which has recently reached a frightening scale. In connection with this the word 'crisis' is used. 'Crisis' is a Greek word, which means, literally, judgement. A critical moment is one when all that has passed is put in question. It is very important to see a crisis as a judgement. This could be God's judgement on us. It could be Nature's judgement on us, a moment when Nature with indignation and outrage refuses to co-operate with us. It also could be that moment when we should judge ourselves – and in many cases condemn ourselves. The question as to what have we done to our earth in the last half century is placed before our conscience. The question is not one of what is profitable to us – that the earth should be fruitful and that everything in it should be at its best – but is one of our moral responsibility before the world, created by God for love and with love, a world which He called to be in communion with Him.

It goes without saying that each part of creation relates to

God in an individual way, but there is no part of creation which has no relationship to God. Otherwise our understanding of the miraculous would be impossible. When Christ orders the waves to be still, and the wind to cease to blow, it does not mean that He has some sort of magic power over nature, but that the living word of God is apprehended in some way by all of His creation.

Apart from the concept of judgement which is contained in the word 'crisis', there is another understanding of it which I heard recently. The same word in Chinese means 'a revealed opportunity', and that is very important. Judgement speaks of the past; but when you have come to a judgement of your own value and of the situation in which you find yourself, when you have pronounced judgement on yourself, the next step is to go forward, and not only keep looking back. That is why indeed at the moment of judgement a person probes deeply into his conscience, looking at what he has done – both personally, and collectively as a member of the human race – and thinks further as to how he should proceed. And at the moment when we begin to think of the future, we speak of what is possible. We have not yet got to the point from where there is no going back nor any way forward. When there is neither any path back into the past nor a way forward, it will be the end of the world. We have not yet got to that point. But we are all responsible for something in Nature, in which we live; we all poison the earth, poison the air, we all play a part in the destruction of that which God has created. And therefore we should think about the relationship between God, the world created by Him, and Man.

The first thing that is clear from the Scriptures is that everything that exists was created by God. That means that by the power of His Word he called into life everything which previously did not exist. Besides, He called it all to life in order to bestow blessing on everything and to bring everything into a state of blessedness and perfection. If one can express oneself in this way, at the moment that He was creating Man and the other creatures, He was creating them out of love, He was creating them in order to share with them all the riches which belonged to Him – and more than that: not only the riches that belonged to Him, but even Himself. We know from the Epistle of the Apostle Peter, that our human vocation (we will think later about how it reflects on the rest of creation) is not only to know God, not only to bow down before Him, not only to serve Him, not only to tremble before Him, not only to love Him, but finally to become 'partakers of the divine nature' (2 Peter 1:4): that is, precisely to unite with God in such a way that God's nature should be grafted into us, so that we should become like Christ in this sense.

St Irenaeus of Lyons[1] uses a wonderful, and maybe even terrifying, but at any rate a sublime expression. He says that at the end of time, when the whole of creation reaches its full measure, the whole of mankind, in unity with the only begotten Son of God, by the power of the Holy Spirit, will become *the only begotten son of God*. That is finally our vocation. That does not mean that we are called to that, while the rest of creation is not. I want to draw your attention to some moments in the story of creation as it is told in the Bible.

We read how God utters the Word, and that is the beginning of what had never happened before. Things start to happen and things are created for the very first time. First there appears light. There is a saying (not a Biblical one, but Eastern) that light was born from the word. This is a wonderful picture: God pronounces the creative word, and suddenly light shines forth, which appears already to mark the beginning of reality. Later we see that other forms of life are formed by the order of God, step by step growing to perfection, and we arrive at the moment when Man is created. It would seem that Man appears as the peak of creation (and this is indeed seen both in the Scriptures and even in the simplest worldly experience). But the story of the creation of Man is very interesting. We are not told that God, having created the most highly developed animals, moves on to the next step in order to create an even more complete living creature. We are told that when all creatures have been created, God takes up some wet earth and makes Man out of this mud. I do not want to say that this is a literal description of what happened, but that by this we are shown that Man is made from the same basic material as the whole of creation. It follows that from the same substance other creatures are also created, but it is here underlined that Man is not different from other creatures, that he is, as it were, at the root of the existence of all creation, that he is created from the same elementary, basic material from which all the rest of creation has come. That somehow makes us kin, not only – as a non-believer would say – 'the highest form of the animal kingdom', but kin to the lowest forms of life on earth. We are formed from the same material. And this is very important, because, being kin to the whole of creation, we have a direct link with all of it. And when St Maximus the Confessor contemplates Man's vocation he writes that man is created of elements of the material world and of elements of the spiritual world, that he belongs both to the spiritual world and to the material world, and he underlines that because of this, containing within himself both matter and spirit, man can bring all that is created to spirituality and bring them to God. That is man's basic vocation.[2]

This is a very important moment, because it is followed by another moment – that of the Incarnation of the Word of God. God becomes man, Our Lord Jesus Christ. He is born of a Virgin. He receives His full humanity from the Mother of God. He has His entire divinity from the beginning from God the Father. As John the Evangelist says, 'The Word became flesh' (John 1:14), 'for in him dwelleth all the fullness of the Godhead bodily' (Col. 2:9). He is fully God, He is fully Man. He is a perfect man exactly because His manhood is combined with His Godhead both indivisibly and inseparably. But at the same time both natures remain themselves: the Godhead does not become matter and matter does not become divine. Speaking of this, Maximus the Confessor gives the following example.[3] You take a sword which is cold, grey and dull, and put it into a fire, when you take it out after some time the sword is burning with the fire and gleaming. The fire has penetrated the sword so much that it has united with the steel, and now one can cut with fire and burn with steel. Both substances have joined and penetrated each other while at the same time remaining themselves. The steel has not become fire, and the fire has not become steel. At the same time they are inseparable and indivisible.

When we speak of the Incarnation of the Son of God, we are saying that He became a perfect man. He is perfect because he achieved the fullness of everything that Man can be, and He became one with God. At the same time He is perfect in that He is in the full sense man; we clearly see that He became a descendant of Adam, and that the flesh which belongs to Him is our flesh. And this flesh which is taken from the earth makes Him kin both with us and with the whole of the created world. He is linked by His flesh to everything that has substance. In this sense one can say (and once again Maximus the Confessor writes about this) that Christ's incarnation is a cosmic event, that is, that this phenomenon links Him with the whole cosmos, with all that is created; because at that moment when energy or being arises it recognises itself in Christ and its unity with Divinity. And when we think of matter and of that earth on which we live, of the world which surrounds us, of the universe of which we are a tiny fragment, we have to imagine and to understand that by our fleshliness we are related to all that which is material in the universe. And that Christ, being Man in the full and absolute sense of that word, is linked by his fleshliness to all creation: the very smallest atom or the largest galaxy recognises itself in Him and in His glory. It is very important for us to remember this and it seems to me that apart from Orthodoxy not one branch of religion in the West has taken in the cosmic nature of the Incarnation and the glorious opening for the whole of the universe through it. We think and speak of the Incarnation too often as something which happened only for Man, for mankind. We say that God became Man in order to save us from our sins, to conquer death, to overcome the division between God and Man. Of course this is so, but beyond it there is something else, which I have tried to explain here.

If one thinks of things in this way, then we can with much more realism, depth, fear and reverence take in the Mysteries, the Sacraments, of the Church, because in the Sacraments of the Church something absolutely amazing occurs. Over a piece of bread, over a little bit of wine, over the water used for Baptism, over the oil which is brought as a gift to God and is blessed, something is done which brings it at that moment into communion with the miracle of Christ's Incarnation. The waters of Baptism are sanctified by the corporality of Christ and by the grace of the Holy

Spirit, which descends on them and brings about this miracle.[4] The bread and the wine are brought into communion with both the corporality and the divinity of Christ through the descent of the Holy Spirit. Already eternity is entering into time: eternity, the future, are already to be found before us and among us.

The same can be said of anything that is blessed. There is a wonderful prayer which we never hear, because we have no occasion for it: the prayer for the consecration of a church bell. In it we ask God to bless this bell in such a way that when it sounds, it will bring to people's souls something which will wake them up. We ask that because of this sound, eternal life will start to vibrate within them.[5]

There is a poem by Koltzov which elaborates this thought:

> The evening bell, chiming in the endless plain
> Rings in the shifting heart and a strong soul.
> Ring long, ring a dirge of forgiveness and farewell.
> Ring in a sleeping heart, hopeless and tearless.
> Maybe the heart will awaken and shake off its torpor,
> And come to life for an instant, only an instant ...[6]

And so, when we bless a bell this is exactly what we have in mind. We ask this bell to make not only a musical sound (which, with enough skill, can be created easily enough), but we ask that the blessing of God will rest on this bell. This is so that its sound (which is like any other sound – it will not sound different from any other bell created with no specific purpose, without a prayer to renew and enliven souls) should ring in such a way as to reach a person's soul and that this soul should wake up. So, you see, we are not talking only about blessing matter: water, oil, bread, wine and so on. We are saying that everything should be brought

to God as a gift from us, to be accepted by God; and that
God should pour His divine transfiguring power into His
creation. I think this is central to our understanding both
of Christ and of the cosmic – that is, the universal, all-
embracing – significance of Christ's Incarnation.

This also relates to the spoken word. After all it is not
only a bell that sounds and renews souls, but words can
sound and renew souls – or kill them. If the word is dead, it
kills. If it is living it can penetrate to the depths of human
beings and awaken the possibility of eternal life. You
probably remember the place in St John's Gospel, when
what Christ had said threw into confusion the people around
Him, and they began to move away from Him. The Saviour
says to His disciples: 'Do you not also want to leave me?'
And Peter replies for the others: 'Where should we go? You
speak the words of eternal life.'[7] What Peter says does not
mean that Christ knows eternal life so well, and describes it
in such a way, that his disciples burn with the desire to enter
it. If we read the Gospels, we will see that Christ nowhere
specifically speaks about eternal life, in the sense that He
does not describe it, and does not put before us pictures of
eternity, either of hell or of heaven. No, the very words of
Christ were such that, when He spoke to people, His words
reached their depths, where dwells the possibility of eternal
life and, like a spark falling on dead wood, eternal life
blazed up in people. I think that it is very important to
imagine this for oneself.

This does not apply only to Christ, whose words, of
course, were more penetrating than those of anybody else,
but also to those great teachers and preachers who by their
words have transformed the lives of other people.

Both sound and light are material. Everything that exists
and everything that is material (whether it is so great that we

cannot even imagine its scope, or so small that we cannot capture it with any instrument) – everything is contained in Christ, is included in Christ. It is precisely because Man is made of earth – that is, he belongs in his flesh to matter – that it is Man's calling to enter into God's depths, to become so closely linked to Him that we become one with God. By this means we transform our corporality, and through this transfigure the whole surrounding world. These are not mere words: they are reality. This is our concrete calling, that which is given to us as a task.

But why are we so unsuccessful? It seems to me that it is worth taking a look at the Scriptures and asking ourselves: 'What then has happened?' When Man was created he was given the opportunity of enjoying all the fruits of paradise, but he did not depend for his being on those fruits. As Christ said to the devil, when he was tempted by him in the desert: 'Man shall not live by bread alone, but by every word that proceeds from the mouth of God' (Matt. 4:4). Man lived, of course, not through God's words, but by the creative Word of God and by his communion with God.

At the moment of his falling away from God, this is what happened. First there appeared a division between man and man. When Eve was created out of Adam, they looked at each other and Adam said: 'This is now bone of my bone, and flesh of my flesh' (Gen. 2:23). That is, he saw himself in her, no longer locked up within himself, but in front of him. He saw in her not a reflection, but his own reality – as did Eve also. And they were as one. Sin not only divided them but it broke the unity of Man's relationship with the whole of the world around him. And now, when Man broke away from God, he lost the ability of living solely according to God's word. God gives him an opportunity and sets him a task: the opportunity to survive by the fact that he will receive a certain part of his life from the fruits of the earth – and the task of cultivating that earth. Without that he will die. He can no longer live only through God. Man is, as it were, rooted both in God, whom he has not finally lost, and in the earth, into which he has rooted himself – which he should not have done because his mission was to lead this earth to God, to be, as it were, its guide. We read in the Bible that man was made to have dominion over the earth (Gen. 1:26), and we constantly take this to mean that we should have power over it and should rule it. But it does not necessarily mean this. In the Gospels, there are the words of Christ: 'You know that those who are supposed to rule over the Gentiles lord it over them … but it shall not be so among you; but whoever would be great among you must be your servant, and whoever would be first among you must be slave of all … And whosoever of you will be the chiefest, shall be servant of all' (see Mark 10:42–44). That was Man's vocation: to be the servant – not in some humiliating form, but to serve the whole of creation and its ascent to God, and its gradual rooting of itself in God and in eternal life.

Then comes another moment. If you will read carefully the story of the generations from the Fall of Adam to the time of the Flood, you will notice that the number of years for which people live diminishes all the time. It is said that after the Fall, death gradually began to take over, death began gradually to rule over mankind more and more, because mankind moved further and further from unity with God and became more and more absorbed in the created world, which cannot by itself bestow eternal life, which cannot even extend life on earth. However, there are two exceptions to this. One is Methuselah, who lived longer than all his ancestors and descendants, of whom it is said that he was the friend of God, and because of this he lived a long life. The other was Enoch, who, because he was the friend of God, died young, according to the story in the Bible, only about three hundred and sixty-five years old.[8] For us, of course, that is not young, but compared to others he was young. For all that, the long life of the one and the early death of the other were both determined by the fact that they were both, more than anyone else, united with God. God needed that the one should live, and God needed that the other should come to Him.

And then comes the flood, and in the text there is another place that one can ponder. People were getting further and further away from God, to the moment when God, glancing at them, said: 'These people have become flesh.'[9] There was no spirituality left in them, and the flood came, and death overcame them. And after the flood God says for the first time: 'Now all living things are given to you for food. They will serve you as food and they will fear you and dread you' (see Gen. 9:2–3). This is very frightening. It is frightening to imagine that Man, who was called to lead every being along the road to transfiguration, to the fullness of life, came to the point that he could no longer ascend to God, and was compelled to obtain his food by the killing of those which he should have led to perfection. This is where the tragic circle closes. We find ourselves inside this circle. All of us are still incapable of living only for eternal life and according to the word of God, although the saints have in a large measure returned to God's original conception of Man. The saints show us that we can through prayer and spiritual endeavour gradually free ourselves from the need to feed on the flesh of animals, and, becoming more and more assimilated to God, require less and less of it.

This is the world we live in. This is what we are called to

be, this is what has been bestowed on us. This is our Orthodox understanding of what the world is like and how God is connected to this world. He is not merely a Creator who simply creates and then remains a stranger to His creation. Even an artist does not remain a stranger to what he has made. Everyone can recognise the hand of the artist, his imprint on his work. Here we are speaking of something else. God does not simply create and then leave his creation to live. He remains connected to it and calls it to Himself, so that it should grow in full measure according to the possibilities given: from innocence to saintliness, from purity to transfiguration. That is the conception we have in the Orthodox Church of the created world, of the relationship of God with Man and with all that is created without exception – and of Man's role in this. Then the question of our role and what we are now doing on the earth becomes understandable, from the point of view of the Orthodox Church. The problem is not: 'What we are doing with the earth will destroy us', but 'What we are doing with the world is destroying our human vocation'. We are destroying ourselves, and we are blocking the way for other creatures to reach a transfigured life.

Faith in Our Lives

Chapter 6

❦ ❦

Christianity Today

In June 1990, the current Patriarch, Alexis II, was elected. It was a moment when it seemed that the Russian Orthodox Church would be playing an ever increasing role in the development of Russia, which at that time was still the Soviet Union. The following interview, conducted by D. A. Chernyakhovsky on 11 June 1990, addresses aspects of the part played by the Church in the life of society. It was first published in the Russian journal *The Star* (1991, No. 1).

Do you consider that the influence of Christianity in Russia has grown? If so, then why? If we can speak of a revival of Christianity, then what exactly is revived? – the doctrines, ritual and ethical teaching of the Church, or Christianity itself as part of Russian identity?

It is difficult for me to judge to what extent Christianity influences Russia's destiny at present. I get the impression that interest in and response to spiritual values has grown; that people are much more responsive to the legitimacy of these values than at any previous period, and that they understand that it is possible to be a modern, educated person and at the same time someone who does not deny the spiritual domain. It is not necessary to be a materialist in order to be a person of our time. On the other hand, people have not yet discovered – talking of materialism – that Christianity is the only absolute form of materialism: in the sense that a materialist regards matter as building material, whereas for us, through Christ's Incarnation – 'Christ in whom dwelleth all the fullness of the Godhead bodily' (Col. 2:9) – matter is endowed with absolute importance, meaning sanctity. And in this way we could build a bridge linking the Christian Orthodox world view to that of unbelievers, showing them that in materialism Man's image is too small and that matter itself is debased. For matter has an enormous potential, which they do not even suspect exists: it is called to deification[1] and being imbued with the sacred – as in the sacraments – because of the actual presence of God in it.

I think that the reason why Russia is opening up to spiritual treasures, and in particular to Christianity, is that for the last seventy years people have been starved of them. One cannot live a life which is purely carnal and materialist (and at the same time often extremely hard) resting on purely rational propositions. It is very restricting because one has to conform to a specific ideology and cannot cross any thresholds. And also (and this is linked with your other question, when you asked what exactly it is to be reborn), Russian Orthodoxy, Russian Christianity, was from the very beginning characterised by worship, that is the ability to bow down before God, to venerate Him from one's innermost being. Theology and doctrine were the province of a particular group of people, but as a whole Russian Orthodoxy is essentially prayer and the Church services, in which various elements come together. On the one hand there is immense beauty. As Plato said, beauty is the persuasive side of Truth. When you cannot say of something, 'How splendid!', it means that it has not reached you: this objective fact is still outside you. And therefore the beauty and the majesty of Orthodox worship is not just a matter of presentation, but is the expression of the spirit of the people, for whom all that has been inwardly, spiritually absorbed is made incarnate in the beauty of the Liturgy. On the other hand there is also the danger of ritualism. This is a serious risk because it is very easy to consider ritual as self-sufficient, and to respond to the ritualistic side of the service while overlooking the depth of its content.

All the same, it seems to me that the rebirth of Christianity in Russia is connected most of all to the fact that in Russia, God, Christ – the whole reality of Christianity – was perceived as a personal spiritual experience which people also shared with each other. That is, it was at one and the same time both general and profoundly personal. And in that I think lies its great strength, because if Christianity was only a social experience, it could not have taken into itself all the layers of society, but only the privileged, the intellectual or the aesthetic classes; whereas here we find deep personal experience shared by all kinds of people.

But there is another problem here too. Leskov[2] had already said in the nineteenth century that Russia had been baptised, but had never been enlightened. That is, there had been no religious, spiritual education and therefore it was an amorphous experience, ill-defined for the people at large. It was not systematised in such a way that it could, on the one hand, be formally expressed and, on the other hand, be defended, nor enrich a man except in his heart. I am not speaking here, obviously of professional theologians. Maximus the Confessor[3] said that a theologian is a man whose heart is a flame and whose mind is ice: in other words, one who can think coldly and soberly, but against a background of leaping flames. And this is now a huge problem which faces us.

When you use the word 'doctrine' – if you take that to mean what is taught about God, about Christ, about the Church, about the sacraments, about Man, about matter – which expresses itself with the power of a deep inner experience, then yes, that is doctrine. On the other hand, if it is simply the speculation of some theologians, which sometimes resembles higher mathematics which is inaccessible to everyone, or abstract art – of which the abstract painter Lanskoy[4] said that it is a language which only one man can speak and three or four people understand – then, of course, that is not for us. But we have to find ever more methods of expressing the whole inner experience, both personal and collective, in ways that do not diminish it, and which retain its spirituality. And that is not simply a matter of education in doctrine.

It seems to me that Christianity is everywhere weak, including in Russia, in the matter of ethics. I say 'everywhere and always' because the Apostle Paul wrote in his Epistle to the Romans: 'For the name of God is blasphemed among the Gentiles through you' (Rom. 2:24). If we do not live up to the standard which we preach, we are evidently and openly denying before people the truth which we are professing. I remember the first General Secretary of the World Council of Churches, who said one can be a heretic in one's life while professing the truth in words, because if your life is at variance with this truth, you have betrayed your faith. And that problem seems to me very acute at present. Some of the basics of faith have to be preached, some of the verities of faith have to be explained and assimilated; but, on the other hand, as some ancient writers have said, the understanding of the Gospel comes from fulfilling that which is said in it. If we only read it and marvel at its beauty, then we cannot attain to its truth; and that is a major problem for contemporary life. This should be the sermon of every priest, and of every bishop: live according to your faith.

As the Apostle James said: 'Shew me thy faith without thy works, and I will shew thee my faith by my works' (2:18). If that does not come about, if the coming together of spiritual experience and the attainable but unsullied and truthful mental expression (both of this experience and of this understanding in its beauty) does not come about in life as it is lived, then finally nobody will be able to believe in Christianity.

Does your Grace not want to say anything about Christianity as part of the Russian identity?
I simply left it out. I think that the identification of Christianity with Russian-ness gives an exaggerated impression of the Russian identity: Christianity is in fact on a much higher plane. Russian identity was to a very large extent inspired and formed by Christianity, but Russian Christianity does not represent the fullness of Christianity for the world. We cannot say that we must inculcate it into all the countries of the world. And I think that to speak of the coming together of Russian-ness and Orthodoxy is to lower that which is Godly, eternal and universal. Nestor[5] said that every nation must contribute its voice, like a musical note, to the general harmony of the whole world in the phenomenon and the glorification of God – and the Russian people can put in their unique contribution. But that is not all. We have to learn from other peoples what they have discovered, precisely because they are not like us. Therefore to say that Christianity was, is and can become to an

extraordinary extent the inspiration, the content, and the form of the Russian soul and of Russian life is one thing; but to identify Christianity or Orthodoxy as one of the expressions of Russian culture or the Russian soul or Russian identity would be a great pity.

The truths of Christianity are unalterable, but in varying historical situations certain doctrinal aspects become more important. What is the specific message of Christianity for Russia today?

I am in total agreement with the way you framed the question. If we think about the development of theology in the Christian Church, we see that it was gradual. The first generation knew Jesus Christ personally. First they probably knew him as a youth. After all Cana in Galilee and Nazareth are only a few kilometres apart; it is impossible to imagine that the child or the adolescent Jesus Christ who lived in Nazareth would not be known by Nathaniel, who lived in Cana.[6] Therefore at first he was known simply as a local resident, and probably people were amazed by the uniqueness of his human personality; and then gradually newer and greater depths opened up before people until the moment when they understood who He was: the Living God, who had become a living man.

This was the first experience, the absolute centre of which was the living Jesus Christ, known and renowned among them. When Christ died and was resurrected, they went about talking of Him whom they had personally known. The calling of the Apostles was addressed to those who had known Christ from the very beginning. They could all bear witness to that. And then questions began to develop and to be asked: 'Who then is He?' 'Yes, He is God, but He said of Himself that He was the Son of God.' He talked of

God as of His Father; and people began to think about what this could mean. The descent of the Holy Spirit[7] was not a theological concept but a purely empirical, living experience. The Apostles, because they people in whom the Holy Spirit dwelt, could speak of Him as one can only speak of a power which moves you concretely and through experience. Therefore the theology of the Trinity began to develop, and to become more and more clear-cut. There were arguments, which was in a sense a very good thing. The Apostle Paul said: 'There must be also heresies among you, that they which are approved may be made manifest among you' (1 Cor. 11:19). And Orthodox theological teaching gradually, through seeking both in light and in shade, through battles between schools of thought and personalities, crystallised into something which holds in balance that which one can express in words or by liturgical actions, and that which in no way can be expressed, because in the final moment when one meets God face to face, one can only be silent. The English and German words *God* and *Gott* come from an old root which means 'he before whom one falls on one's knees' – and that is the final step.

It now becomes increasingly essential that, if the history recounted in the Old and New Testaments is true, if indeed God became Man, we learn to speak of Man in a completely new language. Man is no longer the most remarkable ape, which has learnt to do what other apes cannot do: Man is a being who from the start bears within himself the image of God, who in depth and scope can become the receptacle of Godhead – a receptacle not like, say, a cup which contains something, but, as Maximus the Confessor once said of the Incarnation, which in Christ combines Godhead and manhood as fire and iron can be combined.[8] If you put a sword into a brazier, you put it in colourless, grey, dead, and you take it out incandescent. And the fire has remained a fire and the iron has remained iron, but now one can cut with fire and burn with iron. Man is so deep, so great and mysterious, that he can be totally united with God, without ceasing to be man. And this cannot be said by any materialist.

And another thing. When we speak of Incarnation, as I previously said, Incarnation means that Godhead has united with matter. It says that the matter which makes up the whole universe is capable of being united with God in an indescribably marvellous way, as the Apostle Paul expresses it: 'God may be all in all' (1 Cor. 15:28). And it seems to me that now we must speak much more than before of Man's greatness, of the fact that we can *believe in* Man – believe with the same depth and assurance as we say we believe in God.

There is another thing which inspires me very much: God is not mad. If He creates anything, it is not that it should be destroyed, and not that that world which He created should be defaced. It means that every time that a man enters the world, it shows that God has faith in him: God believes in us – both individually and collectively – in the whole of humanity and in each one of us. And that is a wonderful thought: that God believes in us, and God hopes for everything from us. And we must speak much more about this. We speak of God as out of proportion with Man, as if Man is tiny and God is huge. We see this in the icons, and that is our only method of expressing the greatness of God. How often does one see Christ sitting is majesty, and at His feet some two saints looking like little mice. That does not speak of man's greatness, but only of God's greatness. And we have no icon which would show us the greatness of Man – except icons of Christ. 'Behold the Man': *this* is a man – not you, and not her, and not us, but Him – the Man, the only one. If you want to be a human being in the full sense of the word, that is what you have to be. And that seems to me the problem for our time, because people have lost faith in Man. Man has shown too many of his dark sides, and only a Christian, I think, can believe in Man. I remember a priest in the West once wrote that when God looks at us, He does not see either our good deeds or our successes (which may not exist), but in the depth of every one of us He sees His image shining, which could grow and fill everything through Transfiguration. This, it seems to me, is what we should be saying, in one way or another: 'I believe in Man, God believes in Man.'

Probably, Metropolitan, this is no less important for other countries, or do you think it is specifically important for Russia today?
It is important for all countries now, because we have lost the sense of Man's greatness everywhere. I speak of this in the West, and I think that we have to talk about this much more. Man has become a political beast, or some higher animal: the world is turning into an ant-heap. But a real ant-heap is constructed in a very talented way; whereas we build our ant-heap in a far less talented way. And I think that Christians must work together with all other peoples, with good or bad intentions, without distinction, in the building of a human city, but adding to this human city dimensions of depth, breadth and sanctity, so that it could at some time become the City of God, the first citizen of which would be the Man Jesus Christ. This applies to the whole of humanity at present, in all circumstances, whether Christian or pseudo-Christian.

What then is specifically important for Russia?
I think that for Russia it is now very important to revive faith

in Man not as a slave or employer, not as, say, a learned genius or participator in the ant-heap, but as a unique personality.

There is no human being that the universe could dispense with: every human being is like a little tile in a colossal, splendid mosaic. You know what happens if one little tile falls out: gradually the mosaic begins to crack and all the tiles fall out. And therefore every human being is unique, unrepeatable, and not only in his knowledge of God. There is a wonderful passage in the Book of Revelation, where it is said that at the end of time everyone will get a name which only he will know and God will know.[9] That will be the name which will express him completely, which will express the fact that his relationship with God is unrepeatable, that only he knows God in the way he knows Him. And we have gradually to imbue people's consciousness with the absolute value of individuality – of the individual not as a fragment of humanity, but as a specific personality who can creatively interact with other personalities, losing nothing in the process and at the same time giving everything. You know that the sun shines, but it does not grow poorer by giving out this light – but through this light, others begin to see everything differently.

Can an indisputable devotion to the truth of Christianity be combined with an acceptance of the pluralistic world-view which has arisen in the present day, which accords legitimacy to foreign truths?

I think that Christianity must recognise the fact that the pluralism which now exists and is often antagonistic to Christianity, is the result of the fact that Christianity did not produce the world-view which would have revealed to people new life and happiness. We are responsible for the fact that people began to look for other world-views, because what we said about Christianity could not satisfy them. That is the first thing. And in the given circumstances we have to be conscious of the fact that we are responsible for all the heresies, for all the deviations, for all the imperfections; and we are responsible for the fact that people turn to the East, and to the most outlandish sects, and to political and social world-views because they do not find fulfilment in that Christianity which we preach and which we have shown them.

On the other hand, there is no doubt (that is, obviously, *I* have no doubt, but that does not necessarily apply to others) that if we look at the whole of Christian society in all its diverse forms, there is not one Christian body, which – precisely because it grew apart from others through some intuition that one thing or another was colossally important – could bring the Christian world in its entirety nearer to that completeness which has been partly lost. This applies to Orthodoxy as well: we have that which we can give, but we also have things to learn, both in the field of morality and in our actions, and in the understanding of that which we ourselves preach. So I consider that pluralism is not an affront to Christianity: it is a multitude of voices, who question not Christianity but Christians. Berdyaev[10] once wrote a pamphlet, *The Worth of Christianity and the Unworthiness of Christians* – well that is exactly my position. If Christianity was the Christianity of the Gospels – fulfilled, real – then everybody would say: 'Yes! That is the fullness of life. That is worth living for.' But can we say that about Orthodoxy in Russia, about Russian Orthodoxy abroad, or of any other branches of the Church?

That is why I think that the existence of pluralism is a challenge to us, and that we have to look into ourselves every time we meet with the views, opinions or reactions of people who know Christianity but reject it. We have to ask ourselves: Why could I not reveal this? Why could I not provide that which they seek, but which they only partly find? That is what seems important to me.

And besides, a dialogue will always be a dialogue. At certain periods of history the triumph of the Christian worldview was achieved with fire and the sword. That is not a triumph: that is the ultimate downfall. Take, for example, the idea of the Inquisition (I am not blaming anybody – Catholics or anyone else – for this, but simply taking the Inquisition as an example): the idea that it is necessary to break a man and force him to think in one way or another. That is a sin, that is simply a crime, because God wishes to have for Himself people who have chosen Him, and not slaves. 'Henceforth I call you not servants; for the servant knoweth not what his lord doeth; but I have called you friends; for all things … I have made known unto you' (John 15:15): that is what Christ says. And one cannot expect that anyone, without seeking, would find the final form of truth which corresponds to God's truth. And, without fail, seeking sometimes becomes confused. Things are questioned which finally can be justified, but which must be analysed along the way, seeing that we have to put them into words.

And I will say one more thing. Pascal[11] prayed to God and said, even shouted, that he could not find Him, and God said to him: 'You would not seek Me if you had not already found Me.' And I would apply this to all the religions of the world. One cannot invent God. I am not speaking of the ugly forms, which can afterwards be applied to this primary experience; but when a person says: 'I know by experience that God's power exists' it means that he has touched at least the hem of God's garment. And therefore we have to regard with great seriousness that which people know of God through experience, even if they express it in completely unacceptable forms of piety or worldly notions, and we have to be very careful. There is a passage where the Apostle Paul says that the gods of the Gentiles are devils because they denied Christ.[12] The word 'Satan' in Hebrew means 'enemy', that is not 'devil' according to our understanding. They are enemies – yes, and those that hold such world-views, especially if they hold them fanatically and passionately, are mistaken; but one must take care how one reveals the great truth to them.

There is a story in the life of the Starets[13] Silouan[14] which tells how he once asked an Orthodox missionary in the East, 'How is your mission going?' 'Not well at all. The Chinese are so obtuse, so unresponsive – they do not take anything in.' Silouan said, 'And how do you deal with them?' 'Well, I go to the heathen temple, and say to them: "Look at your idols, throw them down: that is stone, that is wood, that is idolatry!"' 'And what happens then?' 'They throw me out of the heathen temple and keep to their own ideas …' And then Silouan said to him: 'You know what. You could go there and see how they pray, and how much reverence and piety they have, and call together a few of their priests and say, "Let us sit down on the steps and have a talk; tell me about your faith …" And every time that they say something that is close to Christianity, you could say to them: "How splendid this is! But you are missing something. If you like, I will tell you". And that will add that grain of salt, which can change the cloying sweetness of what you have heard into something "tasty", and living. Well, if you were to do this, gradually they would assimilate a great deal of the Christian faith; but when you say to them that everything that they believe is false, they cannot agree with you, because they know from experience that much of it is true.'

I lived for a long time among people of different faiths, and for a long time I had that radical attitude: only Orthodoxy – and that's it. But gradually, especially during the war, I observed how people of other faiths behaved: a Christian may sit behind a bush while the shooting is going on while the atheist comes out of hiding and brings back the wounded. And then you ask yourself which of them is like the Good Samaritan and Christ the Saviour.

I am always amazed by the parable of the Last Judgement. We are always told at the Last Judgement there are the goats on one side and the sheep on the other – but what questions does Christ ask? He does not ask people whether they believe in God – He does not ask anything about their attitude to Him. He asks them: 'Did you clothe the naked? Did you feed the starving? Did you visit the sick? Were you ashamed to admit that the prisoner was your friend?' He only puts one question to them: 'Were you a man – or were you not a man? If you are not a man, there is no road that you can take to the Kingdom of God, because only a man can become like God. But if you were a man – here is the road you must take.'

It seems to me that that is how we must regard everybody who believes in something. Even the materialist believes in Man in his own way. He has from our point of view a very imperfect, incomplete conception of Man, but he believes in something. And so, you must listen to what he believes. He very often believes in some moral truth, in integrity – which we frequently replace by piety. You know that it is much easier to say to a man who is hungry, 'Go in peace. I will pray for you', than it is to share with him the little that we have to eat.

What can you say about tolerance within the Russian Orthodox Church towards representatives of other faiths or other ethnic groups, towards unbelievers?

The word 'tolerance' can be understood in various ways. One way is to say, 'We know these people deeply and well enough not to pass judgement. We regard with respect the fact that they keep to their convictions, and live by them in a real way; but we retain our own conviction that Orthodoxy is the most perfect expression of the Gospel, even if we regard others thoughtfully and with complete respect.' Another form of tolerance is expressed by saying, 'Well, yes, there are so many different opinions – and maybe mine is worth nothing ...' You know that form of compromise. This, I think, never helps anyone, because as the Apostle Paul says: 'For if the trumpet give an uncertain sound, who shall prepare himself to the battle?' (1 Cor. 14:8). And to say, 'Of course, your opinions may be nonsensical, but you are a good man, and maybe mine are not so perfect either', helps neither of you. A dialogue can only take place between people who are convinced in what they say, but who are prepared to listen to others in case someone opens up for them something which they themselves had not found and did not know. Therefore I think that we must regard with deep respect people of other faiths and other outlooks, seeking in what they say to us or what is obvious to us from their lives, an enrichment for ourselves and a way of understanding them; and then, as the Starets Silouan said to that missionary, to share with them the riches which we have – which maybe neither you, nor he, nor she embodies, but which still remain real.

There are people who do not know how to embody something, and cannot do it, but who can say with conviction that it is the truth. I would like to give you an example. Once our parish priest in Paris was arrested by the Germans. Another priest replaced him, who had attended church but had very rarely officiated, because he mostly arrived dead drunk. I was then the parish warden and I used to put him in the corner and stand in from of him, so that if he should fall he would fall on me and I could hold him up. Many people condemned him. I even remember an interesting conversation when he spoke about himself, saying that he was a bad priest, but somebody else said: 'You know, you are not a bad priest: you are a bad man, but you are a good priest.' And I completely agreed with this because I once went to Confession with him when the incumbent priest was absent. I remember how he listened to my confession. He listened from the depth of his own penitence, and he wept over me – not with drunken tears – he was completely sober – but at the fact that here was a young man of about twenty years old who was struggling and who might also fall to pieces. I remember when I finished my confession, he said to me, 'You know what my life is like, you know that I have no right to speak about how people should live and what sort of people they should be; but although I am unworthy even to speak of this, I will say to you what Christ would have said in my place, because you are young and you may not fall into the state into which I have fallen.' And then he spoke to me, quoting the Gospel. And that was a man who to an outside observer was merely a drunkard: how disgraceful – a priest who drinks! But he could speak God's truth from the depths of his own suffering.

Later I found out more about him. He had been with a unit of the White Army leaving the Crimea. He was in one ship, and in another ship were his wife and two children, and that ship sank. They perished in front of his very eyes, and he could do nothing about it. And he began to drink. To this somebody may say: 'Job did not start to drink.' Well, if you can say that, if you dare to say that Job did not start to drink, then first grow to Job's stature: he would not have condemned him. And so it seems to me, that neither moral perfection, nor worldly perfection, but the inner truth of a man plays an important part. And therefore a man of another faith, a non-Orthodox, a heathen in our eyes, an unbeliever – if he lives according to his faith with all his heart and mind and believes in what he says, he utters the word of truth and we can learn something. You can condemn me for this, but I will say yet again that I have seen too many worthy people with whom I could in no way agree, but whom I marvelled at all the same: marvellous people.

Chapter 7

❧ ❦

The Church Must Be as
Powerless as God …

The following interview was given to M. B. Meilakh in London and printed in the paper 'The Man of Letters' (21 September 1990), published by a Leningrad writers' organisation.

Your Grace, maybe from a distance it is easier to see what is happening in the Russian Church in our homeland?
You know, maybe from a distance one can see certain things more clearly, but some things cannot be seen at all. Because the situation in Russia is so complicated, and there are so many varying currents in it, one can catch certain things and miss a great many others. It seems to me that the Russian Church has survived thanks to the love of the Russian people for Church worship and the beauty of the Liturgy, of which Nil Sorsky spoke.[1] I am not speaking specifically about the Jesus Prayer, but of the personal contact between a living soul and the Living God which takes place during a divine service, but does not necessarily depend on under-standing it but simply on standing before the Living God and on the fact that the Living God is amongst us.

What is certainly missing in the Russian Church is the knowledge which an ordinary believer has concerning matters of faith. Already in the nineteenth century Leskov[2] wrote that Russia had been baptised but was never enlightened. And indeed a Russian's knowledge of God is within himself, within his soul. As Leskov says, 'He has Christ in his bosom.' On the other hand, he has yet to acquire a great deal of knowledge: not any specific knowledge, but simply a deep understanding of the meaning, for instance, of the Creed, and the Lord's Prayer. And as a result it seems to me that we have in Russia a great many people who could not defend their faith should it be under attack or stand up for it in a dispute, but who could die for it, because they know it with their whole being, and with their inner selves know that what they believe is the Truth, the Way and the Life.[3]

Therefore the Church is now faced with the question as to how to educate its believers, how to teach their faith to them. First of all there is the Gospel. The Gospels were for many decades inaccessible. We have somehow to disseminate the book of the Gospels throughout the population so that more people can read it and live according to what is the living strength, the fire, the life-giving spirit of our faith: the words and the example of the Saviour Jesus Christ Himself.

On the other hand, it is also essential that people should understand the divine service in which they are taking part, not because it is necessary to have some sort of intellectual understanding, but because the divine service is so constructed as to transmit the essence and content of our faith, and the more one understands it the further one can penetrate into the content of Orthodoxy.

So now we have two tasks, which we shall probably have ever-increasing opportunities to tackle. One is to educate the laity: in groups, at open meetings, and in catechetical courses. The second task, which is now becoming more and more important, is to instruct the young clergy. New courses – not seminaries – are being started to prepare the clergy, and that is very important. However, one must of course say that it is not only theological knowledge which makes a man capable of becoming a priest.

To be a priest is an art. There are things which a theological school does not teach, because it is totally absorbed in theological education. I have met many young priests who were insufficiently prepared in many spheres, who had not yet entered into the life of the parish. They had not been taught, for instance, how to make their confessions and teach others to do so, how to hear confessions, and what sources to draw upon when preaching. Spiritual writers and the holy Fathers have written on various themes, but a sermon is spoken from the heart – it is spoken first of all to oneself. If it does not touch you to the heartstrings, it will not touch anybody to the heartstrings. If it does not flow from your mind and experience, it will not transmit itself to others. A further problem is how to learn to pray oneself, not only with words, not only as prescribed, but from the depths, and how to lead others into the mystery of this prayer.

And, finally, there is one more thing. Many people – bishops, clergy and laity – have come to me after services and spoken to me along the following lines. They were brought up in a totalitarian, authoritarian State, and they got used to the fact that they did what they were told to do, let alone the fact that many people wait similarly to be told what to think. But now they had a new problem: they had to learn how to make decisions and choices and they did not know how to do this. One well-educated and sophisticated man asked me, 'Tell me how to do this.' I replied, 'If I were to tell you how to do it, you would again be acting under direction. You must learn to think for yourself, to act according to your conscience, to take risks (and I am not speaking now of worldly risks) and learn that you might make mistakes: you must learn to think deeply in order to understand how well you are doing and in what you are mistaken.'

This is, of course, the most important part, but there is another, closely related question. It is easy to understand what took place during the long years of the Church's persecution. It is not known if this period has ended; but at any rate now, in the course of Perestroika, the Church has acquired a somewhat different status. But does that not hold in itself new dangers? Are not these more organic freedoms fraught with the possibility of unfavourable developments in connection with co-operation with the State?

Political conformity – this has for long been the cause of ill-health for the Russian Church. Even before the Revolution the Church and the State existed in a sort of unified harmony, which was, incidentally, not always pleasing to the Church. After the Revolution the Church fell silent. During the time of repression and extreme persecution nobody expressed political views. And to start to think politically, and to speak of politics from within the Church will require a long and – more specifically – a deep period of learning. The Church cannot belong to one party or another, and at the same time it is not without or above party politics. It must be the voice of conscience, permeated with the light of God. In an ideal state the Church must be in a position to speak for every party, for every point of view, to say, 'This is worthy of Man and God, and this is not worthy of Man and God.'

Of course this can be done from two positions: either from a position of strength or from a position of total helplessness. It seems to me – and I am firmly convinced of this – that the Church must never speak from a position of strength. It should not be one of the powers that be, acting for the State. It should be, let us say, as helpless as God, as helpless as Him who does not force His will on us, who only calls us and reveals the beauty and truth of things, but who does not force them upon us and, like our conscience, prompts us with the truth but leaves us free either to listen to the truth and the beauty or to deny them. It seems to me that the Church must be just like that. If the Church represents some organisation which has power, which can coerce and control events, there always remains the risk that it will want to exert power, and as soon as a Church begins to exert power it loses its deepest essence – God's love, and the ability to understand those whom it must save, rather than break or reconstruct them.

And finally, Your Grace, this is a very general question, but we know both from your books and your sermons that you have considered very deeply the question of what happens in life and what happens in the world. Tell us how you rate the position of a Christian in the world today, in view of all that takes place in it.

This is a difficult question, because what I want to say will probably offend a lot of people. I think that today the whole Christian world, including the world of Orthodoxy, has become cut off from the simplicity, the all-inclusiveness and the triumphant beauty of the Gospels. Christ with his group of disciples founded a Church which was so deep, so all-embracing, so complete, that it contained within itself the whole universe. Over the centuries we have made the Church one of mankind's societies. We are smaller than the world in which we live, and when we speak of the conversion of this world to Christianity, we are saying in fact that we should convert as many people as possible into being members of a limited society. This, I consider, is our sin.

We should understand that the Christian Church, the believers, should be believers not only on account of their view of the world but also in their lives, through their inner experience, and that our part consists in bringing light into this world where it is so dark and at times so frightening. The prophet Isaiah says: 'Comfort ye, comfort ye my people' (Isa. 40:1). Those were God's words to him and, of course, also to us: 'Comfort ye'. That means: understand in what sorrow the whole world exists, both materially and in its confusion, and spiritually, through its lack of God's grace. It means that we should bring comfort to this world: God's tenderness, God's love, and God's concern, which should enfold every person. There is no point in speaking to a man about spiritual things when he is starving – feed him. There is no point in saying that a man errs in his view of the world when we fail to provide him with the living experience of the Living God. And that is our position in the world today – it is the position of people awaiting trial. The world, in turning away from God and from the Church is saying to us: 'You Christians cannot give us anything that we need. You do not give us God: you give us a view of the world. It is very doubtful whether at its heart there is any living experience of God. You do not give us instructions how to live – yours are as arbitrary as those which we get from other people.' We need to become Christians – Christians in the manner of Christ and his disciples, and only then will the Church acquire not power – that is the ability to coerce people – but authority – that is the ability to speak such words that once any soul hears them it will shudder and will open itself to the eternal depths.

Perhaps my view of our condition is a pessimistic one,

but after all we are not Christians. We profess to believe in Christ, but we have turned everything into symbols. I am always struck to the soul by our service on Great Friday.[4] Instead of the Cross on which a living young Man is dying, we have a beautiful service. We can be touched by it, but it stands between us and the brutal, horrifying tragedy. We have replaced the Cross with an icon of the Cross, the Crucifixion with an image, the story of the horror of what was happening with a poetical and musical version of the event. This of course reaches us, but at the same time it is so easy to take pleasure in this horror, or even to experience it deeply and be shaken by it but then to calm down; whereas to witness the killing of a living man is something quite different. *That* remains like a wound in the soul, *that* one does not forget: once having seen that, one can never return to one's previous condition. And this is what frightens me – in some sense the beauty and the depth of our service should be opened up; we should tear a hole through it and take every believer through that hole to the terror and majesty of what is taking place.

Yes, this is a very profound thought. After all our contemporary world is so established, so well ordered, that in principle it can exist without God, and without spirituality. It rolls on in an established manner, and in it one can safely sleep one's whole life through and then die.

But what strikes me as even more frightening is that one can call oneself a Christian and live one's whole life studying the depths of theology – and never meet God. One can take part in the beauty of Church services, be a member of the choir or of the congregation, and never break through to the reality of being. That is frightening. An unbeliever has still the possibility of coming to believe, but for a pseudo-

believer that possibility is very far removed because he has
everything: he can explain every detail of the service, and of
the Creed, and of dogma, and then it suddenly becomes
obvious that he has not met God. He is at peace with himself. In Leskov there is a passage in which he speaks of such
a person: 'Think of it! He has read his way to Christ!' And
his interlocutor replies, 'Well then, there is no hope of
changing him.' Such a person imagines that through Church
services, through the Gospels, and through everything that
we have one could indeed 'read one's way to Christ' and not
be left behind – I became a believer through the Gospels and
through a meeting with the living Christ. Everything else
came later, and everything else remains transparent to me: I
do not shut myself off from what I once experienced, nor do
I react to it with sharp pain. Yet how can one, for example,
in Holy Week sing lightly of certain things which are so
tragic? How can one, for example, when celebrating the
Divine Mysteries [the Eucharist], listen to the music of 'We
hymn Thee ...'[5] and not allow oneself to be carried by this
music into the frightening depths of the Divine, where the
blessed bread and wine become the Body and Blood of
Christ? To me – for I am an unmusical man – it is totally
inexplicable how one can sing at such moments: it seems to
me that everyone should be numbed into a state of contemplative terror. And when they hear the words: 'And make
this bread ...'[6] – I do not even want to repeat the words of
the Holy Offering. But that, of course, is my own reaction. I
do not wish to say that it is the right one because I know
people who are a thousand times more spiritually conscious
and gifted than I am who are not troubled by this, who are,
on the contrary, carried into the depths; but I also know
many others who are brought to a halt at this point. One has
to have enormous experience of prayer within services in

order that the service should cease to exist as a thing apart, should become simply imperceptible, as water is imperceptible to the fish that swims in it. I remember an old deacon in Paris, Father Evfimy, who used to read and chant with me in the choir. And he read and chanted so quickly, that I could not catch the words. And after the service – I was then twelve years old and was both cheeky and self-assured – I said: 'Father Evfimy, you stole the whole service from me today and, what is worse, you could not have experienced it yourself, reading and chanting in such a way!' And then he burst into tears and said to me, 'Forgive me, I did not think of you, but I was born into a very needy family in a very poor village. When I was seven years old, I was sent away to a monastery, and now I have been hearing and chanting these words for sixty years. And you know,' he said, 'at the moment I see a word, before even pronouncing it – it seems to me that some hand has touched the heart-strings, and all my soul begins to sing.' And I understood then that his soul had become a musical instrument, and that at the lightest touch it sang with all its being like the Aeolian harp which sings at the touch of the slightest breeze, that it reacted to these words without their having to pass through the mind, the heart, or even consciousness. These words had become a song, a religious experience. But in order to reach that point one has to become like the Elder, Father Evfimy, whom people laughed at because he had lost his voice and drank a lot, and did not stand out in any way, but before God his whole soul sang – may God grant this to everybody!

Well, if what I have said should prove useful to anybody – that would be splendid!

Chapter 8

❧ ❧

Without Notes

Please tell us about your childhood.

I have very few memories of my childhood. For some reason I do not retain memories. That is partly because so many layers have built up one on top of the other, as they do on icons – it is sometimes impossible to make out the first layer under the fifth – and partly because of something I learnt very early on – or was taught it – that in fact one's life is in itself of no interest: the interest lies in what you live for. And therefore I never tried to remember either events or their sequence, as they have no relevance to anything. Whether I am right in thinking this or not is another matter, but that is how I was schooled to think at a very young age. And that is why I have many gaps in my memory.

I was born in Lausanne, in Switzerland. My grandfather on my mother's side, Scriabin, was the Russian Consul in the East, which at that time was in the Ottoman Empire, first in Turkey, in Anatolia, and then in what is now Greece. My father met this family because he too was a diplomat and was a secretary to my future grandfather in Erzerum. He met my mother there, and subsequently they married. My grandfather had retired by the time I was born – 1914 – and was living in Lausanne. My father at that time was nominally

appointed Consul in Colombo. It was an official appoint-
ment but in fact nobody went there because nothing was
happening in Colombo and people were put to more useful
tasks – however that is what he officially was. And so, to rest
from his exertions in Colombo, he and my mother went to
Switzerland, to her father and my grandmother.

My grandmother, my mother's mother, was born in Italy,
in Trieste, which at that time was part of the Austro-
Hungarian Empire. All I knew about her father was that his
name was Ilya, because her patronymic was Ilyinichna; they
were Italian. My grandmother's mother later joined the
Orthodox Church and took the name Xenia; when my
grandmother married, her mother was already a widow and
went with them to Russia.

My grandmother was one of three sisters. The oldest
(who subsequently was married to an Austrian) was clever,
lively and energetic and remained so to her late old age, and
she was self-sacrificing to the end. She was a diabetic and
finally she developed gangrene. They wanted to operate on
her (when she was nearly eighty) and she said no. She was
going to die anyway and an operation would cost money,
and she could leave this money to her sister – so she died.
That was so courageous and beautiful on her part. The
younger sister was married to a Croat and was very
unhappy.

My grandfather Scriabin was the Russian Consul in
Trieste and met this family, and decided to marry my grandmother, to the great displeasure of her family because it was
considered proper, of course, to marry off the eldest daughter first, whereas my grandmother was the middle daughter.
And so she married at seventeen. She must have been exceptionally naïve and pure in heart, because even when she was
ninety-five she was still exceptionally naïve and pure in

heart. For instance, she could never imagine that anyone could lie to her; you could tell her the most incredible stories and she would look at you with such warm, childlike, trusting eyes and say 'Was that *really* so?'

Did you try to do this? In what circumstances? When it was necessary to do so?

Of course I did. Not out of necessity, but simply to tell her something unimaginable in order to amuse her, just as one tells a joke. Neither she nor I could ever laugh straight out; when we were told something funny, we always sat and thought about it first. When my mother told us something funny, she used to sit us down side by side on a sofa and say, 'I am now going to tell you something funny. When I give a sign you must laugh and then you can think about it ...'

My grandfather decided to teach my grandmother Russian. He gave her a grammar book and the complete works of Turgenev and said, 'Now read and learn ...' And my grandmother did indeed speak the language of Turgenev to the end of her life. She never spoke Russian very well, but her choice of words was in the style of Turgenev.

So you are also Italian?

Hardly so, I think. I am so anti-Italian in my reactions, I find the Italians do not suit my character in the slightest. That is a country in which I would really hate to live. When I was Exarch,[1] I would travel always to Italy with this feeling: my God I have *got* to go to Italy! I always felt that life in Italy was operatic and unreal. I do not like the Italian language, I do not like the Italians' constant state of excitement and drama, so that, of all the countries that I know, Italy is probably the last in which I would choose to settle.

After their marriage my grandparents went to Russia.

Later my grandfather served in the East, and my mother was at the Smolny Institute[2] and would visit her parents in her holidays (six days by train from St Petersburg to the Persian frontier, and then by horse carriage to Erzerum), and there she met my father, who was a 'dragoman', which – as used in Russian – means a translator at the Embassy. Then, in 1912–13, my grandfather retired and, as I said, they left for Switzerland – my mother by that time being already married to my father. And then came the war, and my grandmother's eldest son died in the war; and then Sasha, the composer, died,[3] by which time we, my parents and I, with my grandmother, found ourselves in Persia (where my father had been posted). My grandmother being passive, indeed very passive, was always being taken in tow.

And it seems that your mother was very intense?
She was not intense: she was energetic and courageous. For instance, she went with my father on all his mountaineering expeditions, she rode well, played tennis, hunted boars and tigers – she was capable of all that. On the other hand she was totally unprepared for life in emigration, but as she spoke French, Russian, German and English this of course proved her salvation, because when we arrived in the West in 1921 life was hard and there was unemployment. But with her knowledge of languages it was possible to find work; then she learned to type and she learned shorthand and continued to work for the rest of her life.

I am not sure how my father's ancestors got to Russia; I know that they came from the north of Scotland to Russia in the reign of Peter the Great, and settled there. My grandfather on my father's side continued to correspond with a cousin living in the north-western Highlands; she was already an old woman by then, living on her own in complete solitude, far from everything, and it seems she was a brave old woman. The only story I know about her came from a letter in which she told my grandfather that one night she heard someone climbing up the wall; she looked out and saw that a thief was climbing to the first floor up the drain-pipe, so she took an axe, waited till he grasped the window-sill, chopped his hands off, closed the window and went to bed. And she described all this in such a natural way as if that is just the kind of unpleasantness that happens when one lives alone. Most of all I was astonished by the fact that she could close the window and go to bed – the rest was up to him.

They lived in Moscow. My grandfather was a doctor and my father was taught at home with his two brothers and a sister. Besides, my grandfather insisted that they should speak Russian for half the day since it was the local language; and for the second half of the day they had to speak Latin one day and Greek the next, as well as one other foreign language which they had to learn in order to qualify for the school-leaving certificate – and that was all at home. Then he studied Mathematics at University and took his degree, and went on to the school for diplomats run by the Ministry of Foreign Affairs, where they studied Eastern languages and all that was necessary for diplomatic service.

My father began to travel to the East early. When he was seventeen or eighteen he went to the East in the summer during the holidays, riding alone across the whole of Russia and Turkey – this was considered a useful thing to do. I know nothing about his brothers. They both died: one was shot, the other, I think, died of appendicitis. And his sister was married in Moscow to one of the early Bolsheviks; but I do not know what happened to her and I cannot remember her surname.

My paternal grandmother was my godmother. She did not attend my christening but was written down as such. In general I think it was not taken very seriously, for no one in my family ever went to church, until later when I began going and taking them with me. My father started going before I did, but that was much later, after the Revolution, at the end of the twenties and in the early thirties.

In Lausanne in 1961 I met the priest who had baptised me. It was a very amusing meeting, because I arrived there as a young bishop (young in consecration), met him and said, 'Father Constantine, I am so glad to see you again!' He looked at me and said, 'Forgive me, you must be mistaken for I do not think that we have ever met.' I replied, 'Father Constantine! You should be ashamed of yourself. We have known each other for years – and you do not recognise me?' 'No, forgive me, I do not recognise you …' 'But you baptised me!' He became very agitated, called some of his parishioners who were there and said, 'Look, it seems that I baptised a Bishop!' And the following Sunday I was at his church, and there was a book in the middle of the church in which baptisms were recorded. He showed me the entry, saying 'What does this mean, I baptised you as Andrew – why are you now Anthony?' He wanted to know why I had changed my name. We had conversed in French, and he conducted the service in Greek, but in my honour he read the Gospel in Russian. I did not recognise that it *was* Russian. It was a good thing that someone prompted me: 'Did you notice how he tried to oblige you, and how splendidly he reads in Russian?' I thanked him with great caution, choosing my words with care.

After I was born, we lived for about two months in Lausanne and then returned to Russia. At first we lived in Moscow, in what is now the Scriabin Museum, and in 1915–16 my father was once more appointed to a position in the East and we went to Persia. And it was there that I spent the second half of my early childhood, till I was about seven.

I have no clear memories of Persia, only snatches. For example, I can now see before my eyes a whole lot of places, but I could not say where they were. I can see big town gates, which might have been in Tehran or maybe in Tabriz, or maybe not; for some reason I think they were in either Tehran or Tabriz. At that time we travelled a great deal, and lived in about ten different places.

Then I have a memory of how (when, I think, I was about five or six) we settled not far from Tehran in a house, which was surrounded by a big garden. We went to look at it. It was a rather large house and the garden was overgrown and dry and I remember how I dragged my feet through the dry grass, because I liked the rustling it made.

I remember that I had my own sheep – a ram – and my own dog. The dog was mauled to death by the street dogs and the sheep was also mauled by somebody's dog, so it was all very tragic. The sheep had an odd habit of coming every morning into the drawing-room, and pulling all the flowers out of the vases with his teeth and then, rather than eating them, laying them out on the table next to the vases, after which he lay down in the armchair, from which he was usually driven out – that is, he was always driven out, but with varying degrees of indignation. You know everything gradually becomes a habit; the first time it happened it aroused great indignation, and then the sheep having to be driven out became a regular feature of life.

There was a donkey which, like all donkeys, was obstinate. And in order to ride on him one had first of all to hunt for him, because we had a big park and the donkey, of course, preferred grazing in the park to performing his donkey duties. And we used to go out in a large group and crawl between the trees surrounding the animal. One person would scare him from one side and he would rush to the other side and people grabbed hold of him, and finally after about an hour or an hour and a half of such animated hunting, he was caught and saddled. But that was not the end of it because he learned that if, before the saddle was put on him, he threw himself on the ground and rolled about on his back, it was much more difficult to put the saddle on. Local Persians overcame this by using, rather than a Russian Cossack saddle, a Persian wooden one, and on the first occasion that he threw himself on his back in one of those he immediately leapt up with a shriek, because it proved so painful. But this was still not the end of it because he had a principle that if anything was wanted of him he would do the opposite, so that if you wanted him to go in a certain direction you had to cheat him by pretending that you did not want him to go that way. The best method was to sit very far back in the Persian saddle, grasp the donkey by the tail and drag him backwards, and then he would quickly go forwards. That is what I remember.

I have another memory about the first railway. In the whole of Persia there was only one railway, about fifteen kilometres long, either between Tehran or Tabriz and a place called Kermanshah, which was considered (I do not remember why) a place for pilgrimage. Everything went well when one travelled from Kermanshah to town, because the line went downhill. But when the train had to drag itself uphill, it would reach a small humped bridge, and then all the men would get out and Europeans and men of rank would walk next to the train, and the less important men would push it. And when they had managed to push it over the humped bridge they would get back into the train and reach their destination very successfully, which was, all in all, very entertaining and a big event. Think of it – fifteen kilometres of railway line!

Then when I was about seven years old, I made my first major discovery in European culture; for the first time in my life I saw a car. I remember my grandmother took me up to the car, stood me up by it and said, 'When you were little I taught you that one must not stand behind a horse, because it might kick; now remember not to stand in front of a car, because it might start moving.' At that time cars were only held back by brakes, so that one could not know whether they would move or not.

Did you have any tutors?
In Persia I first had a Russian nanny. Then there was a time more or less from 1918–1920 when I had nobody except my grandmother and mother; but there were various Persians who taught me how to ride the donkey and various similar skills. As far as cultural matters are concerned I cannot say anything, because in fact I do not remember anything. It was a blissful time – I did not go to school, I was taught nothing, I was being 'brought up', as my grandmother would say. My grandmother was wonderful. She read aloud to me, so that I had 'read' a great deal for my age: three or four volumes of Brem's *Life of the Animals*, and all the books for children. My grandmother could read for hours and hours, and I could listen for hours and hours. I lay flat on my front and would draw pictures, or simply sat and listened. She knew how to read aloud; she read very beautifully and clearly and she could pause at the very moment when it was time to allow one to react. Occasionally she would stop reading and we would go for a walk, and she would start talking of what she had been reading to me. These were moral judgements, so

that what I had heard would not simply be a matter of recreation but a moral investment, and I think that that was very valuable.

In 1920 we began leaving Persia: there had been a change of government and the Embassy had been handed over. My father stayed behind while my mother, grandmother and I set off for an unknown destination in the West. We had a diplomatic passport for England but we never reached it; or rather we only reached it many years later, in 1949. We travelled across northern Persia in the depth of winter, partly on horseback and partly in a carriage, escorted by a convoy of brigands, because that was the safest thing to do. In Persia at that time one could travel escorted by a convoy of brigands or by a convoy of Persian soldiers. A convoy of Persian soldiers was the most unreliable, because they would rob you without fail and you had no possibility of redress. 'What do you mean? We did not dream of robbing them! We were defending them! Somebody attacked them but we do not know who – probably people in disguise!' If brigands appeared, the convoy would immediately disappear: why should soldiers fight and risk their lives in order to be robbed as a result?! It was much safer being with the brigands; they either protected one, or simply robbed one.

So it was that we travelled through the whole of northern Persia escorted by a convoy of brigands, crossed through Kurdistan, embarked on a barge, and passed the Earthly Paradise, where up to the Second World War they still showed people the Garden of Eden and the Tree of the Knowledge of Good and Evil, which is where the Tigris and the Euphrates meet. It is a wonderful sight: the Euphrates is wide and blue, and the Tigris is fast-flowing and its water is red, and it flows into the Euphrates and for several hundred metres it is possible to see the red water of the Tigris in the midst of the blue water of the Euphrates. In the forest there is a large meadow and in the middle of it, surrounded by a fence, is a little dried up tree. It was covered all over with little bits of rag: in the East at that time (I do not know if that is still so) when you passed a holy place you tore off a piece of your garment and hung it on a tree or a bush, and if that was not possible you laid down a stone, and piles of them were formed. There stood that little tree and it almost perished because in the Second World War American soldiers dug it up, piled it into a jeep, and were preparing to take it to America: the Tree of Good and Evil is of course of much greater interest than bringing over some Gothic cathedral – after all it is much more ancient. But the local population surrounded them and did not allow the jeep to move until the American command had been warned of this and forced them to re-plant the Tree of Good and Evil. So it is probably still standing there.

In those days I smoked for the first and last time. I was extremely hungry during the journey, and even more bored, and I was continually grizzling, asking for something to eat to help pass the time. Since there was nothing to eat my mother tried to distract me by offering me a cigarette. During the whole week I tried to smoke: I puffed on one cigarette and then puffed on a second, and then on a third, but I understood that cigarettes were cheats, that they provided neither nourishment nor diversion, and on this my career as a smoker came to an end. I did not take it up later either, but not for virtuous reasons. I was told that I would start smoking like everyone else did – but I did not want to be like everyone else. Later they said that I would start to smoke when I found myself in an operating theatre, because no one survives the experience unless they do, and I decided that I would die, but would not start to smoke. Then I was told that when I joined the army I would start to smoke, but I did not.

So we reached Basra and, as at that time there were mines in the ocean, the shortest route to the West was to go from Basra to India, and we went East to India. We lived there for a month and the only thing that I remember about it was the red colour of the buildings in Bombay; the tall towers in which the Parsees lay their dead, so that they can be eaten by birds of prey, and whole flocks of eagles and other birds of prey circling around these towers; this is all that I remember, except for the barely endurable heat.

Then we were sent to England, and I was full of hope, which unfortunately was not fulfilled. We were put on a boat, having been warned that it was so dilapidated that should there be a storm it would *inevitably* sink. And I, having read *Robinson Crusoe* and many other interesting books, obviously longed for a storm. Besides which the captain was full of imagination, if not of good sense, and decided that all members of the family should not perish together, and so he assigned my mother to one lifeboat, my grandmother to another, and me to a third, so that at least one of us should survive, if we began to drown. My mother was extremely negative about the thought of a shipwreck, and I could not understand how she could be so unromantic.

We sailed for thirty-three days from Bombay to Gibraltar, and in Gibraltar we stuck, the ship having decided never to move again. We were disembarked and though we retrieved the greater part of our luggage, one large wooden box sailed away, or rather was taken to England, and we only got it back many years later; the English somehow traced us and made us pay pounds sterling for its storage. This was a huge event, because this was one of those chests into which everything which one *could* not leave was thrown at the last minute. First we had reasonably packed all that was *necessary*, then what could be added, and left that which we could not *possibly* take, and at the last minute – for the heart is not made of stone – into this chest were, of course, put all the most precious things, which I as a boy was a thousand times more interested in than in warm underwear or sensible shoes. But that came later.

So we journeyed through Spain, and my only memory of Spain is of Cordoba and the Mosque. I cannot see it before me in my mind's eye but I remember the overwhelming impression made by its incredible beauty and silence. Then we came to the north of Spain, which is wild, dry and stony, and which so well explains the character of the Spanish.

Then we got to Paris, and there I made two further discoveries. One was that for the first time in my life I came into contact with electricity – and learned of its existence. We drove in somewhere and it was dark, and I stopped and said, 'We need to light a lamp.' My mother said, 'No, one can switch on the electricity.' I did not understand what she meant and suddenly I heard a click – and it was light. This was a momentous event. Later generations will not understand this because they are born to it, but at that time it was such an incomprehensible experience: suddenly it can become light, and then suddenly the light can be extinguished; and there is no need to light an oil lamp, the light does not produce soot, one does not need to clean its glass … an entire world had vanished.

The second discovery was that there were people whom one should not run over in the street. In Persia a rider would gallop along the street or a carriage would drive along, and every pedestrian would fight for his life by flattening himself against the wall. If you did not flatten yourself quickly enough, you would be struck by a whip, and if you still did not get out of the way you would be thrown down and told that it was your own fault that you were lying under the horse's feet! And here we were on our first day being driven from the station in a taxi along the Champs Elysées, that is along a very wide street – at that time there were almost no cars and everything was very open, and there were also no shops along the street and it was very beautiful – and suddenly I saw that a man was standing in the middle of the road and was not moving out of the way but was just standing there, as if rooted to the ground, and the carriages and the cars were simply passing. I grabbed my mother by the arm and said: 'Mama! We must save him!' After all we were also in a car and we could stop and say: Hurry, hurry, jump in, we will save you! And my mother said, 'No, that is a policeman.' 'Well, what of it, if he is a policeman?' And Mother said, 'One cannot run down a policeman.' And I thought: what a marvel! If one were to become a policeman, one's whole life would be free from all mishaps and accidents! Later I somewhat changed my point of view, but at that moment I really regarded it as an example of diplomatic immunity: there you stand and no one can run you over! Can you understand what that means? Well, that was the second momentous event in my European life.

That was all that I found out in Paris at that time. We then travelled to Austria in order to find some work for my mother. My grandmother's elder sister, who was married to an Austrian, was still living there. We then went on to northern Yugoslavia, near Zagreb and Maribor. There we lived for a time on a farm. I was seven years old and I managed to earn a little money doing odd jobs for people. Then we returned to Austria, because there was nothing for us to do in Yugoslavia, and we remained in Vienna for a year and a half.

There I experienced my first contacts with culture. I was taught to read and write and I responded very unwillingly. I could not understand why it was necessary for me to learn these things when I could be peacefully sitting and listening to my grandmother reading aloud so fluently and well – what need was there for anything else? One of my relations tried to make me understand, saying, 'You see I studied well and now have a good job, with a good salary, and can support my family.' My only comment was to ask if he could not do it for the two of us.

Be that as it may, I went to school in Vienna and studied for a year and a half and performed disgracefully: school did not bring out anything either honourable or glorious in me. One day, I was taken to the zoo and on the following day we were set to write an essay on the subject: 'What do you want to do as a career?' Of course, the little Austrian children wrote down all sorts of worthy aims: one wanted to be an engineer; another, a doctor; a third, something else; whereas I had been so inspired by what I had seen the previous day that I wrote an essay, even illustrated with what I thought was a wonderful picture, on the subject: 'I would like to be a monkey'. The following day I came to school hoping that my creative powers would have been appreciated. The teacher walked into the classroom and said: 'Well, I had one piece of work unlike any other handed in to me. Stand up!' I stood up and I got a dressing down that 'it was quite clear that I was a Russian barbarian, a savage, and could not think of anything better than returning to nature,' and so on and so on.

That was the principal event in my school life there. Two years ago I was in Vienna once more recording two tapes for broadcasting, and the man who was recording my talks asked me whether I had been to Vienna before. 'Yes.' 'And what were you doing then?' 'I was at school.' 'Where?' 'At such and such a school …' It turned out that we had been class-mates fifty years before, but of course we did not recognise each other, and our acquaintance went no further.

What languages could you speak as a child?
From my childhood I was made to speak Russian and French. I spoke in Russian to my father, in French to my grandmother, and in both to my mother. The only thing I was forbidden to do was to mix the two languages. This rule was adhered to very strictly and I simply got used to it. I also spoke fluently in Persian. Of course I forgot it three or four years after we had left Persia, but it is interesting that later, when I was at boarding-school, in my dreams I spoke in Persian, whereas when I was awake I could neither say nor understand a single word. It is curious how it had remained in my subconscious, whereas consciously it had completely vanished. Then I spoke German. I had been taught as a small child how to pronounce German correctly, and this has helped me a great deal and still does. On good days I have less of an accent in German than in French. When you do not speak a language for a year you forget it. But I recently received the most wonderful compliment concerning my German from the Cardinal of Cologne, who was blind; and when I met him we exchanged a few words and he said to me, 'Can I ask you an impertinent question?' I replied, 'Yes.' 'How did you, a German, come to be Orthodox?' I was very pleased, because being blind he would be very sensitive to sound. But that must have been a very good day, because when I am tired I cannot always speak as well but once in a while I can. I can read in Spanish; Italian is no problem; Dutch is easy because it is very like German of the twelfth and thirteenth centuries. When I am mentally

exhausted, I read German poetry of that period as a form of relaxation.

And when you were small, did you have any special duties, or were you just allowed to grow up naturally?
Oh no! First of all nothing unreasonable was expected of me. I was never made to feel that something was being asked of me because my parents were bigger and stronger and so could break me in as a child. But, on the other hand, if anything had been said it was *never* gone back on. I do not remember this but my mother later told me that she once asked me to do something and I refused; I was told that I would do as I was told and for two hours I rolled about on the floor, chewed the carpet, and screamed with indignation, despair and rage, while my mother sat in an armchair in the same room and read a book, waiting for me to stop screaming. Nanny came in several times and said, 'Madam, the child will over-strain himself!' And my mother said: 'Nanny, go away!'... When I had stopped screaming, she said, 'Well, have you finished? Now do what you were told to do ...'
That was a firm principle. Another principle defining my upbringing was that I would develop my own convictions in time, but that I must grow up to be an absolutely truthful and honest man, and so I was never put in a position which would cause me to lie or to conceal anything because I was being victimised. I might be punished, but that was always for a good reason. I did not have a secret life, as happens when children are brought up so strictly or unfairly that they simply start to lie and to do as they please.

We lived a family life, and I had certain duties – for example, from my earliest childhood I tidied my own room, made my bed, cleaned up after myself. The only thing that I was not taught was how to clean shoes, and it was only later, during the war, that I discovered a moral reason for not doing so, when I read in the Curé d'Ars[4] a sentence which said that polish for shoes is the equivalent of cosmetics for women, and I was absolutely delighted that I now had an excuse. You know how every child has certain things which he finds terribly boring. I always found it terribly boring to dust, and to clean shoes. Now I have learned how to do both. All other household tasks we did together, literally together: it was not a case of being told 'Go and do so-and-so while I read', but 'Let's wash the dishes', 'Let's do this or that job', and I more or less learned to do everything.

Was this while you were still in Persia?
No, as far as I can remember life there was completely free; there was a large garden attached to the Embassy and the donkey – and nothing was asked of me, except, that is, for tidiness. I would never be allowed to go for a walk if I had not tidied my books or toys, or had left my room in an untidy state – that was out of the question. To this day I continue to live like this. For example I tidy the vestments and the sanctuary after every service. Even if, as on Great Friday, there is only an hour and a half between the service of the Procession of the Shroud and that of the Burial of Christ,[5] I fold everything up. This is based on the principle that at the moment when something is over it should be so completely over that it appears that nothing has happened, and, on the other hand, everything can start anew: this is a great help in my life! I was taught to prepare everything for the following day the evening before. My father used to say, 'Life is easy for me because I have a servant, Boris, who in the evening will fold everything, will clean my shoes, and will get everything ready – and when Boris Edvardovich gets up in the morning he has nothing to do.'

And were you spoilt as a small child?

I was treated with affection, but I was not spoilt – in the sense that nothing was allowed to get in the way of order, discipline, or upbringing. I was also taught from my earliest childhood to value little things; and, when the emigration came, then to value particularly some thing, or some little object – that was a marvel, a joy, that was something one could value for *years*. For example, some little tin soldier or some book – I lived with them for months, sometimes for years, and I am very grateful for this, because I am able to take pleasure in the minutest object that presents itself and never to undervalue it. I was given presents, but never showered with them, even when this would have been possible, so that I should not become overwhelmed and could take pleasure in a single object. At Christmas I once had a present which I can remember to this very day: a small tricolour Russian flag made of silk; and I carried this flag around so long that I still seem to feel the silk under my arm and see the three colours as I stroked it. It was explained to me that this was our Russian flag; made up of Russian snows, the Russian seas and Russian blood; and that's how it has stayed with me: the whiteness of the snows, the blueness of the waters, and Russian blood.

When my parents and I reached France, life became rather hard. My mother worked, knowing languages, but we lived scattered, each in a different part of town. I was sent to live in a *very* tough school on the outskirts of Paris in a run-down district, which was a no-go area at night, from dusk onwards, even for the police, because people got killed there. The boys at the school were local boys, and this made things extremely difficult for me at first: I simply did not know how to fight and could not take being beaten. I was beaten mercilessly – in general it was considered normal for a newcomer to be beaten up throughout his first year, until he learned how to defend himself. As a result it was possible to get beaten up in front of a teacher to the point of having to be sent to hospital. I remember I once broke out of the crowd and rushed toward the teacher, crying out for pro- tection – he simply pushed me aside with his foot and said, 'Do not whinge!' At night, for instance, it was forbidden to go to the lavatory because it disturbed the master's sleep. It was therefore necessary to creep out of bed, crawl under the other beds to the door, manage to open the door noiselessly and so on … and for this one was beaten by the master himself.

They beat me and they beat me, but in the end they did not beat me to death! At first I learned how to bear beatings; then I learned how to fight back and defend myself – and when I fought, I fought to the death. But never in my life have I experienced so much fear and so much pain, both physical and mental, as at that time. Because I was a sly creature, I promised myself not to breathe a word about all this at home, for there was nowhere else to go, and why should I burden my mother with yet another worry? So I first told her about it when I was about forty-five, when it was all in the past, finished and done with. But that year was a really difficult one – I was eight or nine and I did not yet know how to live.

About forty-five years later I was once riding the Metro on the line to that part of Paris. I was reading and at one point raised my eyes and saw the name of one of the last stations before the one for the school – and I fainted. So it appears that the effect of that whole experience had lodged somewhere very deep down inside me, because I am not given to hysteria and I have considerable powers of endurance in life – but this had pierced me to the very core.

This shows how deeply an experience can penetrate one's flesh and blood.

What I learned at that time, apart from physical endurance, was something which I later took a very long time to get out of my system: firstly, that *any* person, of either sex and of any age or size, is an enemy and a danger; secondly, that one can survive only if one becomes absolutely insensitive and stony-hearted; thirdly, that one can survive only if one knows how to live like a wild animal in the jungle. I did not become aggressive, but this deadly other aspect – the feeling that one has to become absolutely insensitive and stony-hearted in order to survive – took me years to overcome, positively years.

We were let out of school at midday on Saturdays, and we had to go back at four o'clock in the afternoon on Sundays, because it was dangerous to walk through that district any later. But on our free days there were other difficulties, because my mother lived in a tiny room, where she was allowed to entertain me during the day but where I was not allowed to stay the night. It was an hotel and at six in the evening my mother would solemnly lead me out by the hand, so that the owner of the hotel could see her doing it; then she would return and engage the hotelier in conversation, while I crawled on all fours between his desk and my mother's legs, turned into a corridor and made my way back to her room. In the morning I would crawl out the same way, and then my mother would solemnly lead me in, which was my official return after a night spent 'in some other place'. This was very unpleasant – to feel that one has no place of one's own, anywhere. It is not surprising therefore, that on my free days I would sometimes wander through the streets in the hope that I would be run over by a car and that all this would come to an end.

There were however some very happy moments. For example, the day that I spent at home was very happy: there was a great deal of love, a lot of friendship, and my grandmother read aloud to me. During the school holidays, which were long, we would go away somewhere into the country, and I would get work on a farm. I remember my first disappointment. I had worked a whole week and had earned fifty centimes. I was happily holding them in my fist as I walked back to our village, walking like small boys do, waving my arms about, when suddenly these fifty centimes flew out of my hand. I searched for them in the field, in the grass – and I couldn't find them anywhere, and so my first earnings were lost.

Toys? If I think back to my toys, I remember the donkey, which had a special place, because he was an independent animal; the Russian flag, two little soldiers and a little machine; I remember that in Paris they sold such little wind-up side-cars, motorcycles with seats attached – it was one like that. I also remember the first book that I bought for myself – *Ivanhoe* by Walter Scott. I 'chose' it because it was the one book in the shop: it was a tiny shop and this was the only book for children. My grandmother had decided that we could afford to buy ourselves a book, and I set off. The shopkeeper said to me, 'No, we haven't got anything, except for some book translated from the English, called *Ivanoe*' (which is the French pronunciation of *Ivanhoe*) and advised me not to buy it. When I came home and told my grandmother, she said 'Run and buy it immediately, it is a very good book.' Before that, in Vienna, my grandmother and I had probably read the whole of Dickens. Later I was disappointed by Dickens: he is so sentimental. At the time I did not notice, but the sentimentality is so pervasive that a great deal gets lost. Walter Scott is an uneven writer: he is a wonderful writer when he is in a good vein, and a dull one when something does not come off. But this book I liked straight away. *Ivanhoe* is the kind of book which a boy cannot dislike.

Were there things that you were afraid of – dark rooms or wild animals?
No, I was not particularly frightened of wild animals, there simply had not been any occasion to feel fear. We had wild boars in Persia, who lived in the steppes and used to come into the garden; and there were other wild animals but they roamed at night, and anyway I was not allowed out of the house at night, so there was nothing especially frightening around. I was afraid of dark rooms, and I did not conceal this. Nobody laughed at my fears, or at any childish phobias I might have. My father, on those occasions when we were together, used to cultivate manly qualities in me simply by telling me stories about manly behaviour and heroic characters, so that I myself aspired to those qualities – not to any particular act of heroism, but simply to the knowledge that such a thing as *courage* exists, and is highly regarded and splendid. Therefore as a boy I cultivated a high degree of discipline in myself.

When I was about eleven or twelve and I had begun to understand more, I schooled myself in physical endurance. My father, for example, would consider it shameful if one were to pick up a hot saucepan and then drop it. 'Hold it!' he would say, 'And if you have burned your fingers we will see to them later.' The same applied to tiredness, to pain and to feeling cold. I was very disciplined in this respect, because it seemed to me that this was important! It was part and parcel of manliness. When I was about fifteen or sixteen, I began to sleep by an open window without a blanket, and when I felt cold, I used to get up and do some gymnastics and then lie down again – it seems, some good has come of it!

I spent a further three years at the same school. Why? Because, firstly, it was the cheapest, and besides it was the only one near or in Paris near which I was able to live. Then I was moved to another one, which was heaven on earth after what I had experienced at my first school.

Did you accept school discipline?

I was too lazy to be a mischievous boy: it was not worth the effort. I was not interested in school, I was only interested in Russian organisations, but I discovered that if you study badly you remain sitting in the same class for two years and as I wanted to leave school as soon as possible I always studied hard enough to make sure that I moved up: that was my main motivation. There were some subjects that I liked and worked at, though using the plural here is somewhat of an exaggeration, because it was just Latin that I loved. I was always interested in and drawn to languages, and I loved Latin because at the same time I was attracted to architecture, and Latin has much in common with architecture: it is a language which is constructed according to fixed rules, just as a building is – in its grammar, its syntax, its word order, and in the relationship between words. And this is what fascinated me about Latin. I liked German and German poetry, which I enjoy to this day. I had read a great deal about architecture when I was ten, and then I had had enough and was drawn to other things – to the military, and to knowledge of my homeland, that is to everything that related to Russia – its history, its geography, and, again, its language – and in living for one's native land. I was studying in a French school, which had absolutely no ideological framework: people came, studied and left, or lived there as boarders, but there was nothing behind it.

Were your friends from school or from the organisation you belonged to?
No. I had friends in the organisation, that is there were boys whom I liked more and some I liked less, but I never went to anybody's house and never invited anybody to mine.

Was that on principle?
I simply had no desire to – I liked to sit in my room at home alone. I had hung on the wall a quotation from Vauvenargues:[6] 'He who will visit me will do me an honour: he who does not visit me will give me pleasure.' And the one time when I invited a boy to come and see me, he read the quotation and left.

I have never been very sociable. I liked to read, I liked to live with my thoughts, and I liked Russian organisations. I regarded them as places where we were forged into something and it made no difference to me *who* was with me provided he shared my ideas. And I did not care whether I liked him or not, *provided* he was ready to stand up for these principles.

When I was no longer a boarder at school I had more time, and I joined my first Russian organisation – a Scout group, which differed from the others because apart from the usual summer camp activities, such as living in tents, sitting round campfires, cooking out of doors, forest excursions and so forth, we were inculcated with Russian culture and the consciousness of being Russian. From about the age of ten or eleven we were taught military drill, and all we were taught was so that sometime we might return to Russia and give Russia everything that we had managed to learn in the West, and that we should indeed be both physically and mentally prepared for this. We were taught this over a period of several years: summer camps lasted about a month and a half, and they were strict and demanding camps. Usually three hours every day were spent on military drill, gym, sport, and there were lessons on Russian subjects. We slept on the bare earth, and ate very little, because at that time it was very difficult to find any money, but we were very happy. We returned home looking very thin; and however much we had bathed in the river or in the sea we got back indescribably dirty, because of course we swam much more than we washed. And thus from year to year a large group of young people grew together. On the last occasion, when I was no longer a boy, but an adult in charge of one such summer camp, there were more than a thousand young people and boys and girls involved in various camps in the south of France.

In 1927 I joined another organisation, simply because the group in which I had taken part had scattered and fallen apart. This was called 'Heroes', and was run by the Russian Student Christian Movement, where I put down roots and remained; in fact I have never left it. It was very similar to the previous organisations, but there were two differences: the cultural level was much higher and much more was expected of us both in reading and in our knowledge of Russia; and the other feature was religion. The organisation included a priest and there was a church at each camp. In this organisation I made a series of discoveries. As far as culture was concerned, it seemed that all I had to say about culture was to my shame, but that could not be helped. I was given a first task in our circle – I think I was about fourteen years old – to give a paper on the subject of 'Fathers and Sons'. My cultural knowledge at that time had not taken in the fact that Turgenev had written a book with this title. So I sat and thought and sweated over what I could say on this subject. I remember I came to the meeting of the circle and crept into a corner hoping that I and my essay would be forgotten. Of course I was called out, settled on a stool, and was asked: 'Well?' I sat there humming and hawing and said: 'I have thought about the subject given to me for a whole week ...' Then I fell silent. In the total silence that ensued, I added, '... but I could not think of anything.' Thus ended the first lecture I ever gave in my life.

As far as the Church was concerned, I was very against it, because of what I had seen among my friends, both Catholic and Protestant. God did not exist for me, and the Church was simply a negative phenomenon. The basis for my experience in this sphere was maybe the following. When we found ourselves in 1923 as émigrés, the Catholic Church offered grants to pay for Russian boys and girls to attend schools. My mother took me to an interview. Someone talked to me and to my mother and everything was arranged and we thought the matter was 'in the bag'. We were getting ready to go, when the man who had talked to us asked us to stay for a minute and said, 'Of *course*, it is assumed that the boy will become a Catholic', and I remember how I stood up and said to my mother: 'Mama, let's go. I am not for sale.' After that I had finished with the Church because I felt that if this was the Church, then there was no reason to go or to take any interest in it; there was simply nothing for me there. I must say that I was not the only one who felt like that; in the summer in camp, there was Vespers on Saturdays and a Liturgy on Sundays, and we *systematically* did not get up to go to the Liturgy, and turned back the flaps of our tent so that those in charge could see that we were lying in bed and *not going anywhere*. So the foundation for religion in my life was an extremely doubtful one, though several attempts were made for my development in this regard: once a year on Good Friday I was taken to church, and on the first occasion I made a remarkable discovery, which served me well for the whole of that period of my life. I discovered that if I took three steps into the church, took a deep breath and inhaled the incense, I immediately fainted. And therefore I never took more than three steps into a church. I fainted, and I was taken home – and that was the end of my yearly religious torture.

It was in this organisation that I discovered something which at first perplexed me very much. In 1927 there was a priest at the children's camp, who seemed to us very aged – he was probably about thirty years old, but he had a large beard and long hair, sharp features, and one characteristic which none of us could explain: and that was that he loved everybody. He did not love us in response to love or affection being shown to him, he did not love us as a reward for being 'good' or obedient or anything of that kind. It was simply that his heart overflowed with love. Everybody could share in it, and not just a fraction or a drop, and it was never withdrawn. The one thing that did happen was that this love for a certain boy or girl was for him either a source of joy or of great sorrow. These were two aspects of the same love; it never lessened, and it never wavered. Indeed if one were to read what the Apostle Paul wrote of love: 'Charity ... believeth all things, hopeth all things ... never faileth', all this could be found in him, although I did not understand this at that time. I knew that my mother loved me, that my father loved me, that my grandmother loved me, but that was the extent of the circle in my life as far as tender feelings went. But why a person who was a stranger to me could love me, and could love others who were also strangers to him, was an idea that was foreign to me. It was only many years later that I understood where all this sprang from. But at the time it was a question mark in my consciousness; a question which could not be answered.

I remained in that organisation and life proceeded normally. I developed my Russianness very consciously, very passionately and with great conviction. At home we always spoke Russian, Russian was the element we lived in, and I spent all my free time in our organisation. We did not like the French particularly (my mother would say that France would be fine if there were no French people in it!); we called them 'natives' – without malice, but we simply walked past them: they were part of the fabric of life, like trees or cats or whatever. We met French people and French families at work or at school, but not otherwise. A certain amount of Western culture was absorbed but we did not feel any attachment to it.

Another memory of our relationships with the French comes from the time when we had moved to the Ile St Louis and Mother got a job as a literary secretary at a publisher's, and her boss said to her on one occasion when she could not come in to work, 'You know, Madame, that only death, your death, could justify the fact that you did not come in to work …'

When I was fourteen, for the first time we got accommodation (in Bois Colombes) where we could all three live together: my grandmother, mother and I; my father lived elsewhere. Before that, as I have said, we lived here, there and everywhere. For the first time in my life since my early childhood when we left Persia, I suddenly experienced some sort of feeling of happiness – and to this day when I have dreams of blissful happiness, they take place in that flat. For about two or three months it was simply a state of cloudless bliss. But then a most unexpected thing happened to me: I came to fear happiness. I suddenly felt that happiness was more frightening than the hard times that had gone before, because then life was a constant struggle, endless self-defence and survival, and it had a purpose: one had to survive *here and now*, one had to secure the possibility of surviving a little while longer, one had to know where one would spend the night, one had to know how to get something to eat – in that order. When it suddenly appeared that this constant struggle was no longer required, it seemed that life had suddenly become totally empty, because could I really build my life round the fact that my grandmother, my mother and I loved each other? It was pointless, there was no depth to it, there was no sense of eternity or of the future. Life was shackled to time and space. Maybe it had some substance that one could measure, but there was nothing else – only emptiness. If life was indeed so pointless, as it suddenly appeared to me – a pointless happiness – then I was not prepared to live. I gave myself a pledge, that if within the course of a year I did not find a point to life, I would kill myself, because I was not prepared to live for a happiness that was meaningless.

My father lived apart from us. He had taken up a distinctive position when we found ourselves as émigrés. He decided that his class, his social group, bore a heavy responsibility for all that had happened in Russia, and that he had no right to profit from the privileges which his upbringing, education and social position had given him. He therefore avoided looking for any work in which he could use his knowledge of Eastern languages, his university education, and Western languages, and he became an unskilled labourer. Very soon his strength gave way, and then he worked in an office and died when he was fifty-three (2 May

1937). But he had inculcated certain convictions in me. He was a very steadfast man of great courage and faced life fearlessly. Once when I came back from a summer holiday he met me and said: 'I was worried about you this summer.' I replied, half joking, 'What were you afraid of – that I would break a leg or injure myself in some way?' And he replied, 'No. That would not have mattered. I was afraid that you would lose your honour. Remember: it should be absolutely of no consequence to you whether you are alive or dead, as it would be of no consequence to others. The only thing that is important is what you live for and what you are prepared to die for.'

He once said to me something about death which remained with me and subsequently had a very strong impact when he himself died. He said, 'One should wait for death as a young man waits for the arrival of his bride.' He lived by himself, in extreme penury; he prayed, he observed a vow of silence, he read books on asceticism and lived totally, unremittingly alone. He had a tiny room at the top of a tall building, and pinned to the door was a note: 'Do not bother to knock. I am at home but I will not open the door.'

I once went to see him and knocked, saying 'Father! It's me!' ... but no, he did not open the door, because he only saw people on Sundays. All the rest of the week he went home from work, locked himself in, fasted, prayed, and read.

And so, when I had decided to kill myself, I had in my mind two phrases of my father's, some things which I had noticed in him, and the strange experience of that priest (a love the quality and type of which was impossible to grasp) – and that is all, there was nothing else. It happened one year – I think it was 1930 – that during Lent we boys were taken by our camp leaders to a volleyball court. Once

FAITH IN OUR LIVES

gathered there, it turned out that a priest had been invited to give us, wild boys that we were, a spiritual homily. Well, of course we all tried to shirk it as best we could. Those who had time to run away, ran away; those who had the guts to stand against it did so, but I was prevailed upon by the camp leader. He did not persuade me that I should go because it would be good for my soul (if he had brought my soul or God into it, I would not have believed him). But he said, 'Listen, we have invited Father Sergei Bulgakov, and you can imagine what he will say about us if nobody comes to his talk.' I thought, 'Yes, loyalty to my group demands this of me.' He then added a marvellous sentence: 'I am not asking you to listen! You can sit and think your own thoughts, as long as you are there.' I decided that this would do, and set off to the talk. Everything went off very well, though unfortunately Father Sergei Bulgakov spoke too loudly and prevented me from thinking my own thoughts. I began to listen to what he was saying, but this brought me to such a state of fury that I could not tear myself away from what he was saying. I remember that he spoke of Christ, about the Gospels, and Christianity. He was a remarkable theologian, and he was a remarkable speaker in front of adults, but he had had no experience with children and he spoke to us as though he was talking to little animals, concentrating on what was sweetest in the Gospels, which was exactly what we would shy away from: meekness, humility, quietness, all the qualities of servitude, which we are rebuked for, from Nietzsche onwards. He brought me to such a state that afterwards I decided not to return to the volleyball court for a game, in spite of the fact that this was my life's passion, but to go home and see if we had a New Testament somewhere in the house, so that I could check this and be done with it. It never even occurred to me that this would not be the end of it, because it was absolutely obvious that he knew what he was doing, and that meant that it was so.

So I asked my mother for a New Testament, which she did have, and I tucked myself away in my corner, looked at the book and found that there were four Gospels, and as there were four of them one of the four must be shorter than the others. As I did not expect any good to come from any of the four, I decided to read the shortest one. And there I fell into a trap – as I was to discover many times in the future how cunning God is when he casts his nets in order to catch a fish – because had I read a different Gospel I would have had difficulties. Each Gospel has a certain cultural foundation: Mark, however, wrote exactly for young savages like me – for Roman youngsters. I did not know this – but God knew it and maybe Mark knew it when he wrote more briefly than the others.

So I sat down to read. And at this point you will have to trust my word because this cannot be proved. Something happened to me which occasionally happens in the street, when you are walking along and suddenly you turn round because you think that someone behind you is looking at you. I was sitting and reading, and between the beginning of the first and the beginning of the third chapter of the Gospel according to St Mark, which I was reading slowly, because the language was unfamiliar to me, I suddenly felt that there, at the other side of the table, stood Christ. This feeling was so intense that I had to stop reading and look. I looked for a long time and I did not see anything, did not hear anything, nor did I feel anything. But even when I looked straight ahead of me at the place where there was nobody to be seen, I still had the same vivid sense that Christ was without any doubt standing there. I remember that at that point I leant back and thought: if the living Christ is standing here – it means that it is the risen Christ. It means that I know personally and for certain, within the limits of my own, personal experience, that Christ has risen and that means that everything that is said about Him is true.

This follows the same logical path that the early Christians experienced when they discovered Christ and came to believe in Him, not through stories about what happened at the beginning, but through meeting the living Christ, from which it followed that the crucified Christ was the very man that was spoken of, and that everything that had gone before also had a meaning.

I read on – but now it was all completely different. My first discovery in this field I can remember very clearly to this day; I would probably have expressed it differently when I was a boy of about fifteen, but the first thing was this: that if this is the truth, it means that the whole of the Gospel is true, it means that life has a meaning, it means that one can live for nothing other than sharing with others this marvel which I had discovered; that there are certainly thousands of people who do not know it and that they must be told of it quickly. Secondly that if this was the truth, then all my ideas about people were false; that God had created everyone, that He loved everyone even unto death; and therefore that even if they think they are my enemies, I know that they are not. I went out the following morning and walked as though in a world transfigured, looking at everyone I passed and thinking: God created you out of love! He loves you! You are my brother, you are my sister; you could destroy me, because you do not understand this, but I know it, and that is enough for me. That was the most striking discovery for me. Later, when I continued to read, I was astonished by God's respect and care for Man. If people are prepared to trample over each other, God never does it. In the story of the prodigal son, for instance, the prodigal son admits that he has sinned before God and before his father, and that he is not worthy to be his son. He is even prepared to say 'Take me on as a hireling.' But in the Gospel his father does not let him say this last phrase. He lets him say the words, 'I am unworthy to be called your son' and he interrupts him at this point, taking him back into the family: 'Bring shoes! Bring a ring! Bring clothes! Because you might be an unworthy son, but in no way can you be a worthy servant or slave: one cannot stop being a son.'

What also astonished me at the time, and which I would probably have expressed quite differently then, is that God – and this is the very nature of love – is able to love us so much, that He is prepared to share everything with us to the last: not only creation through His Incarnation, not only the limiting of life through sin, not only physical suffering and death, but that which is the most terrible – mortality as a state of being, hell as a state of being: the deprivation and loss of God, from which Man dies. That cry of Christ's on the cross: 'My God! My God! Why hast Thou forsaken me?' – this experience not only of being abandoned by God but also of being deprived of God, which kills a man, this readiness of God to share our loss of God, as if descending with us into hell, because Christ's descent into hell was precisely a descent into the Old Testament abyss, that is to the place where God is not. This amazed me because it meant that there was no limit to God's readiness to share Man's fate, in order to find Man. When very soon after this I entered the Church, I found that my personal experience was the experience of a whole generation of people, who before the Revolution[7] had known the God of great cathedrals and of solemn services, who had then lost everything – their motherland, their loved ones, and often their self-esteem, their sense of their place in life, that gave them the right to life – who were deeply wounded and therefore so vulnerable. They suddenly discovered that through His love for Man God wanted to become just as they were: defenceless, totally vulnerable, weak, powerless, and despised by those people who believe only in the triumph of might. I then became aware of an aspect of life which means a great deal to me: that our God, the Christian God, can not only be loved, but can be respected: that one can bow down to Him, not only because He is God, but out of a feeling – and I can find no other words for it – of deep respect.

That was the end of a whole stage in my life. I began to experience my newly acquired faith in different ways. I was so overcome with joy and gratitude for what had happened to me that I let no one alone. I was a schoolboy and travelling to school by train, and in the train addressed adults with the words, 'Have you read the Gospels? Do you know what they contain?' Not to mention my friends in school, who had to endure a great deal from me.

I began to pray. Nobody taught me how to do it, so I experimented: I simply knelt down and prayed as best I could. I then came across a teaching guide to the Book of Hours, and I began to learn how to read Old Slavonic and read out the services – this took about eight hours a day, but I did not do this for long because life did not allow for it. By that time I had already entered university and it was impossible to combine this with a full university course. But then I began to learn the services by heart and as I walked to the university and to the hospital for my clinical practice I managed to recite the Morning service on the way there, and to read the Hours on the way back. I did not *set out* to read them: it was simply that it was a great pleasure for me, and therefore I read them. Then Father Michael Belsky gave me the key to our church in rue Montagne Sainte Genevieve, so that I could go in there either on the way to work or when returning home, but that was difficult. In the evening I prayed for a long time – simply because I am very slow, and my method of praying was also very slow. In effect I read the evening prayers three times: reading over each sentence, then falling silent, reading it a second time with a full veneration – bowing to the ground – and then again for a final understanding – and this applied to the whole set of evening prayers. All this took two and a half hours, which was not always easy or convenient, but it was very nourishing and satisfying, because it then comes to the point when you respond with your whole body: 'Lord, have mercy!' First it is said with a clear understanding, and then with a full veneration, and then again to imprint it on the mind, and this process is repeated throughout. Through this I acquired a sense that this was life. While I was praying I was alive; without it there was something lacking, something missing. I read the lives of the saints in the *Chitiya Minei*,[8] simply page by page until I had read all the Lives of the Desert Fathers. In those early years I was extremely fascinated by the lives of the saints and the sayings of the Desert Fathers, which to this day mean much more to me than those of many theologians.

When I had finished secondary school, I wondered what I should do. I thought of becoming a desert father; but it turned out that there were very few deserts left, and that with my passport I would not be allowed to go to any desert, and besides I had a mother and grandmother, who had to be supported in some way, and this would be inconvenient from a desert! Then I wanted to become a priest, and later decided to enter a monastery on Valaam,[9] and in the end all this came together into one idea. I do not know how this idea came about, probably from a combination of various ideas: that I could take monastic vows secretly, become a doctor, move to somewhere in France where there were Russians who were too poor and too few in number to have a church and a priest, and so become their priest. This could be achieved by being a doctor on the one hand, and thus earning a living and maybe even being able to help the poor; and on the other hand, that being a doctor I could remain a Christian all my life, which would be easy in terms of caring for others and showing compassion. This started with my joining the Faculty of Natural Sciences (at the Sorbonne) and then going on to study Medicine. It was a very difficult time, when I had to choose between buying a book or buying food, and in that year I got to the point of virtual exhaustion: I could walk about fifty paces along the street (I was about nineteen at the time) and then would sit down at the pavement's edge, take a rest, and then walk to the next corner. But, be that as it may, I survived.

At the same time I found a spiritual father – and I really *found* him, having searched for him no more than I had searched for Christ. I went to our only church in Europe which still belonged to the Patriarchate of Moscow[10] – at that time, in 1931, there were only fifty of us there. I arrived at the end of the service (having looked for ages for the church, which was in a cellar), and I was met by a monk – a priest – and something struck me about him. There is a saying on Mount Athos that one cannot give up everything in the world unless one has seen on the face of at least one person the light of eternal life ... And there he was climbing the steps out of the church and I saw the light of eternal life. I went up to him and said, 'I do not know who you are but would you be prepared to be my spiritual father?' I remained in close contact with him till his death, and he really was a very great man: this is the only man whom I have met in my life who had that freedom – genuine freedom and not self-will, which is found in the Gospels, the magisterial freedom of the Gospels. He began somehow to teach me, and having decided to become a monk, I began to prepare for this. I prayed, I fasted, and with this in view I made all possible mistakes.

For example?
I fasted to exhaustion, I prayed till I drove everybody mad at home, and so on. It usually happens that when somebody in the house wants to clamber up into heaven, the other inhabitants become saints because everyone has to have patience with him, to resign themselves to the situation, and to bear everything that the zealot does. I remember once I was praying in my room in the most heightened spiritual state and my grandmother opened the door and said, 'The carrots need peeling!' I jumped up and said, 'Granny, can't you see that I am praying?' And she replied, 'I thought that praying was being in touch with God and learning to love. Here are the carrots and the knife.'

I graduated from the Faculty of Medicine just before the war, in 1939. On the feast of the Beheading of St John the Baptist I asked my spiritual father to receive my monastic vows. There was no time to perform the full ceremony because I had only five days left before I had to join the army. I pronounced my monastic vows and set off for the army, and over five years learned various things: it was excellent training.

What did you learn there?
Obedience, for example. I asked Father Afanasiy: 'I am now joining the army – how will I fulfil my monastic vows and

at the same time obey orders?' He replied, 'It is very simple. Consider everybody who gives you an order as speaking in God's name, and obey it not only outwardly but with all your being. Consider that every sick man that requires help and calls you is your master, and serve him as if you were a slave he had bought.'

Then, life became like that of the holy Fathers. A corporal would come and say, 'Volunteers are needed to dig a trench – you are a volunteer.' Your will becomes completely separated, fully absorbed in the wise and holy will of the corporal. Then he gives you a spade, takes you to the hospital yard and says, 'Dig a trench from the north to the south side.' You happen to know that the officer had said to dig from the east to the west. What does it matter to you? It is your business to dig, and you feel such a sense of freedom that you dig with pleasure: you consider yourself to be doing good, and as it is a cold and bright day it is much more pleasant to dig a trench under the open sky, than to wash up dishes in the kitchen. You dig for three hours and the trench turns out splendidly. The corporal returns and says, 'You fool! You ass! The trench should have been dug from the east to the west.' I could have said to him that he himself had originally made the mistake, but what business was it of mine that he made a mistake? He ordered me to fill up the trench, and having done that I would, most probably, have started digging again, but by that time he had found another 'volunteer', who was given his bit to do.

I was very struck then by that sense of inner freedom which absurd obedience bestows, because if my activity had been defined by my application and if it had been a case of intelligent obedience, I would have queried it at first in order to prove to the corporal that one should dig in a different direction, and the whole episode would have ended in detention in the guard room. At the same time simply because I was absolutely free of my sense of responsibility, life consisted in being absolutely free to respond to everything and to have total inner freedom, the rest being God's will, which found expression through someone else's mistake.

There are other discoveries which pertain to the same period. One evening in the barracks I was sitting and reading and lying next to me was a pencil, sharpened at one end and chewed at the other, and there was nothing tempting about it. And suddenly, looking at it, something inside me said: for the rest of your life you will never be able to say this is my pencil, for you have given up everything that you possess. And (you may well think that what follows is complete fantasy; but then every temptation, every form of attachment, is some form of fantasy) for two or three hours I struggled to say: yes, this pencil is not mine – and thank God for it! For several hours I sat in front of this chewed pencil thinking that I did not know what I would give in order to have the right to say, 'This is my pencil.' In fact to all intents and purposes this *was* my pencil: I used it, I chewed it – and yet it was not mine. And I then felt that not to possess something is one thing – and to be free of objects is something quite different.

A further observation pertaining to those years: that one is not necessarily praised for what one has done and one is also not necessarily blamed for what one has done. At the start of the war I was in a military hospital and I was debarred from the Officer's Mess. For what reason? Because I had been assigned to a ward in which the stove did not work and the orderlies refused to clean it. I took off my uniform, cleaned the stove and brought some coal. Because of this my fellow officers created a great fuss, that I was 'demeaning an officer's dignity'. This is a very small, ridiculous example; and certainly I had been right, for it is much more important that a stove should heat a hospital ward than observing all such matters of rank. On other occasions I was praised and I knew that I was being praised undeservedly. I remember – since we have now arrived at confession – when I was still a little boy I was invited to a certain house, and several of us were playing ball in the dining room, and with this ball we broke a vase. After which we fell silent and my friend's mother praised us for being so quiet, and for behaving so well, and that I was such a model guest. I rushed home afterwards thinking how could I manage to get downstairs before she had spotted the vase. So here is another example for us: I was praised and I was quiet, exceptionally quiet, only unfortunately before this I had managed to break a vase.

During the war there was, however, a measure of danger and therefore the consciousness of being indeed in God's hands was very strong. On the way you make all sorts of discoveries: that you are not all that marvellous, that there are much more important things than you; that there are different levels in all events. There is one level at which you live and feel afraid, and you are overcome by other feelings, and at the same time there exist two other levels: above you there exists the will of God, His vision of history, and below it life goes on, with unnoticed events connected to your existence. I was once lying on the grass on my stomach while being shot at, and at first pressed myself as firmly as possible to the ground, because I felt somehow uneasy, and then I got tired of pressing myself down and I began to look around me: the grass was green, the sky was blue, and two ants were crawling along, dragging a bit of straw, and it became so clear that there was I lying in fear of being shot at, while life went on, the grass was green, ants crawled about. And the world continues. In fact, Man is irrelevant to it – besides which, he makes things worse.

Then there were very simple things which suddenly became very important. When it is a matter of life or death, some questions become totally irrelevant, and in the shadow or life or death a new scale of values is revealed: minor matters acquire some sort of importance, because they are human, and some important things become insignificant, because they are not human. I was studying surgery and it became clear to me that to perform a difficult operation was a matter of technique, whereas to care for the patient was a matter of humanity, and that that moment is the most important and most significant, because any good technician can perform a good technical job, but showing humanity depends on the person and not on technique. The hospital contained 850 beds, so there were rather a lot of severely wounded and dying patients, as we were very near to the front line, and I usually made it a rule to spend their last nights with the dying, whatever section they were in. At such moments your technique is totally irrelevant. You are sitting with a man – a young man, about twenty years old – and he knows that he is dying and he has nobody to talk to. Besides he does not want to talk about life, or death, or anything like that, but about his farm, about his harvest, about his cow. This moment becomes extremely significant, because there will be the inevitable collapse – and *that* is important. You sit there and the man falls asleep, and you sit on and occasionally he simply feels for you: are you there or not? If you are there he can sleep on, and can even die in peace.

I remember one prisoner, a German soldier, who had been wounded in the hand, and the senior surgeon said, 'Cut off his finger' (it was gangrenous). And the German then said, 'I am a watchmaker.' You understand that a watchmaker who loses his index finger is finished as a watchmaker. I then took him into my care, and worked for three weeks on his finger, and my superior laughed at me and said, 'What nonsense, in ten minutes you could have finished off the whole business, and you are working on it for three weeks – what for? There's a war on and you are fussing over a finger!' And I replied, 'Yes, there is a war on, and that is why I am fussing over his finger, because when the war ends, he will return to his own town, either with a finger or without a finger.'

In this context of huge events and very minor ones, it was the interaction between them which played an important part in my life – this may seem strange or even amusing, but that is what I discovered at that time in my life, and found my scale of values in it, because I was never an outstanding surgeon and I never preformed major operations. But I discovered that the essence of life lay in the sphere of human relationships.

Then the war ended and the occupation began, and I was in the French Resistance [*Maquis*] for three years, and then again in the army, and then practised medicine till 1948.

And what did you do in the Resistance?
I did not do anything interesting. It was perhaps the most disgraceful fact of my life that neither during the war, nor during the Resistance movement did I do anything especially interesting or heroic. When I was demobilised, I decided to return to Paris and did so partly legally and partly illegally. I did it legally because I returned with the right papers, and illegally because I had written them myself. It was very amusing. My mother and my grandmother had been evacuated to the Limoges region, and when I was demobilised I went to the Russian Student Christian Movement camp in

Pau – one had to go somewhere. I got there and began to look for my mother and grandmother. I knew that they were there somewhere, as I had received a letter from them three months earlier, which had been forwarded through the army authorities. I found them in a little village: Mother was ill, Grandmother was old, and I decided that we would return to Paris and see what we could do there. My first idea was to join France Libre.[11] However, this proved impossible because by that time the Pyrenees were blockaded. Possibly somebody with more initiative would have managed to get through, but I did not.

We reached a village near the demarcation line of the Occupied Zone, and I went to the town hall. I was then in full army uniform, apart from my jacket, which I had bought in order to hide as much of my army uniform as possible, and I went to the Mayor to explain that I needed a pass. He said to me, 'You know that this is impossible. I am afraid that I would be shot for it.' Nobody was allowed to cross the demarcation line without a German pass. I went on and on persuading him, and finally he said to me, 'You know what we shall do: I will put a piece of paper here on the table, which has to be filled in; and here is the mayor's stamp. You will take it and stamp the paper – and then you will steal it. If you are arrested I will say that you stole them from me.' That was all I needed. I needed papers, and if I had been caught they would not have started asking him, they would in any case imprison me. I filled in the papers and we crossed the line, which also was very amusing. My mother, grandmother and I were in different carriages, not for con- spiratorial reasons but simply because there were no other seats available. In my compartment there were four old French ladies, who were trembling with fear because they were convinced that the Germans would tear them to bits, and a totally drunken French soldier, who shouted the whole time that if a German should appear he would kill him at once: boom, boom, boom. And the old ladies believed it: a German inspector would come in, the soldier would shout, and we would all be shot for it. I was travelling in a certain state of apprehension because under my jacket I was in full army uniform and army personnel were not allowed to enter – or rather, they were allowed to but they would then be immediately taken to prisoner-of-war camps. I decided that I needed to stand up in such a way that the inspector would not look at me below the shoulders, and therefore I suggested to my travelling companions that as I could speak German they should give me their passports and I would deal with the inspector. When the German officer came in, I jumped up, stood right up against him, almost pressing myself against him, so that he would see nothing except my jacket, gave him the papers, explained everything, and he even thanked me for it, and asked me why I spoke German. I said that as a cultured person I had studied in school and of all the languages available had chosen German (which was true: I chose it because I knew it already, and therefore hoped that there would be less work involved – but that is another matter). And so we passed the border.

We then arrived in Paris and settled there. We knew an old French doctor, of pre-war vintage, who was already a member of the French medical Resistance movement, and he recruited me. This meant that I was listed as belonging to the Resistance, and if anybody in the Resistance movement was injured or if medicines were needed, or if someone needed to be visited, they sent for one of these doctors, rather than anyone else. There were cells prepared for the time when Paris would be freed, to which each doctor was previously assigned, so that when the uprising happened everybody would know where to go. But I never got to my cell because a year or two before the uprising I was recruited by the French 'Passive Resistance', and I performed minor surgery in a basement room of the Hotel Dieu hospital. When the uprising began that was where I went: there was a great deal more work there, and I was much more needed. Also, it was very important that there should be people there who could legally ask for new supplies of medicine and for new instruments to be passed on. People came to us from the cells and we handed on to them the government-supplied instruments. Otherwise they could never have got them in such numbers. At one time the French police put me in charge of the ambulance during air raids, and that made it possible for us to drive members of the Resistance to where they were needed.

I also worked in the Broca Hospital and the Germans decided that my department would serve as a specialist diagnostic unit. We were sent the people they wanted to send to hard labour in Germany. The Germans were very afraid of infectious diseases, and so we worked out a complete system so that when X-rays were taken symptoms of tuberculosis would show up on them. This was very easy: we simply drew them onto the X-rays. Everybody who worked there worked as a team. Otherwise it would not have been possible – one nurse, then another, a doctor, and I would start examining a 'patient', would check his X-rays, draw on the glass what needed to be drawn, then would take a film and photograph it and it appeared that he had all the necessary symptoms. Of course this did not last very long. We could not go on indefinitely, and eventually had to leave.

Did you prove to have too many patients?
In fact everybody, everybody – nobody was left out. If it was not tuberculosis it was something else, but for over a year we did not leave anyone out.

For over a year you dealt only with the physically disabled?
Yes. We explained it by saying that we were living in such a time: people did not have enough to eat, young people were not strong. Then the Germans began to get suspicious, and so I changed to doing something else: I began to teach in the Russian school – exchanging one lot of sick people for another!

There is one other interesting discovery from this period of war and occupation. One of the things which we have to struggle with in life, especially as far as prayer is concerned, is the question of time. We do not know, and we have to learn, how to live in the given moment in which we find ourselves. After all, the past is no more, the future has not yet arrived and the only moment you have to live is here and now. And you are not living fully because you are either stuck in the past or you have gone ahead of yourself. I understood something of this through the mercy of God and through the German police. During the occupation I once went down into the Metro and I was stopped and ordered: 'Show your papers!' I showed my papers. My surname is spelt with two 'o's: Bloom. The policeman looks at it and says, 'I am arresting you! You are an Englishman and a spy!' I reply, 'Excuse me, what are you basing this on?' 'You spell your surname with two "o"s.' I reply, 'Exactly – if I were an English spy, I would call myself by anything but an English name.' 'In that case, what are you?' 'I am Russian' (this was during the time that the Soviet army was gradually occupying Germany). He says, 'That can't be true. It's a lie!

Russians' eyes are like this and their cheek-bones like that.' 'Excuse me, you are confusing Russians with Chinese.' 'Oh,' he says, 'maybe. But still – what are your views on the war?' Since I was an officer in the French Resistance, it was clear that in any case I would not be released, and I decided at least to enjoy being under arrest. I replied, 'The war is going splendidly – we are defeating you!' 'Oh, so it means that you are against the Germans?' 'Yes.' 'You know, I am too [this was a French policeman working for the Germans]. Run away as quickly as you can.' That was how it ended, but during those minutes something very interesting happened: suddenly the whole of time, both the past and the future, had got concentrated in that one second in which I was living, because the real past, which had indeed taken place, no longer had any real substance, because I would have been shot for that past; and the past that I was preparing to tell them about in great detail, never had existed. And it appears that there is also no future, because we can only imagine what the future will be as far as we can think of what will happen in a minute. Thinking about all this later I discovered that one can *only* live in the present. It is very easy to pray in this way. It is not difficult to say 'Lord have mercy', but to say 'Lord have mercy' with the knowledge at the back of one's mind that this is only the beginning of an extremely long prayer or even of an entire Vespers is – it seems – much harder.

At that time I had already secretly been a monk for ten years, and it was a *blessed* time, because as Theophan the Recluse says: 'God and the soul – that is a monk's entire being', and indeed there was God and there was a soul, or at least a tiny soul. Whatever there was, I was absolutely protected from people's view of me. As soon as you put on any kind of uniform, be it a military uniform or a cassock, people expect of you a certain form of behaviour, and you somehow adjust to this. Here I was in military uniform, and it meant that people expected of me what they would expect from a military uniform, if I was in a doctor's white coat, people expected of me what they would expect of a doctor; whereas the whole make-up of my inner life remained free, and submitted only to the guidance of my spiritual father.

Here I came to perceive the difference between genuine freedom and irresponsibility in the guise of freedom. Because this was indeed the task before me: to develop the life of the soul. Everything else is of secondary importance.

For example, at one time I was very taken up with the idea of a medical career, and decided to take a special examination in order to obtain a particular qualification. I told my spiritual father this and he looked at me and said, 'You know that this is sheer vanity.' I replied, 'Well if you wish it, I will not take this exam …' 'No,' he replied, 'go and take the exam and fail, so that all can see that you are no good at it.' Such advice, in purely professional terms, is a nonsense – there is no sense in such a judgement. But I am very grateful to him for it. I did indeed sit the exam, got terrible marks because I wrote God knows what even about things I knew; failed the exam, was placed at the bottom of the list which was about a metre long, and everybody said, 'Well, you know, we never thought you were such a block-head.' And I learnt something from this although it sank all my professional plans for the future. But what he taught me at that time he would never have taught me with speeches about humility, because to pass an examination brilliantly, and then humbly say, 'No, God has helped me': that is too easy.

On a previous occasion, when I was working with young people and the work seemed to be going well, Father

Afanasiy called me and said, 'You are succeeding too well, and you are too pleased with yourself, you are becoming a star – drop all this.' I replied, 'All right, what should I do, and do I have to explain my reasons? It would be stupid to say: I want to become a saint and so I won't work any more with young people.' He replied, 'No. Collect some other youth leaders and say to them that you are busy with medicine and you feel more involved in that than in work with young people and you are leaving. If they wax indignant, shrug your shoulders and say, "You know I am making my way in life in my own way, and you are doing it in your ways." But make sure that nobody guesses that you are doing it for the most worthy motives.'

The same thing happened when I took monastic vows. I had already taken monastic vows, but Father Asfanasiy still would not proceed with my clothing as a fully-fledged monk. I kept on asking him to do so, but he said, 'No, you are not yet ready to give yourself over completely.' I said, 'I am ready!' 'No. When you come to me and say, "I have come, do what you will with me, and I am ready here and now not to return home, and never to tell my family what has happened to me, and not to worry about their fate and what will happen to them," then you and I will talk. While you are worrying about your mother or your grandmother, you are not ready to take the full vows – you have not given yourself up to God and prepared yourself for obedience.' I struggled with this for a very long time. I had neither the faith, nor the spirit – I had nothing. It look a very long time to learn that God's call is absolute, that God cannot be bargained with, that every time that I approach God with the question, He replies, 'I am calling you – it is your business to respond unconditionally.' So I struggled at times against God's will, and at other times against my own evil will, until I had understood very clearly that it was time to make a choice: either I must say 'Yes', or I must cease to consider myself a member of the Church, stop going to church, stop taking communion, because there is no point in taking communion and then saying 'No' to God; and there is no point in being a part of the Body of Christ – and the kind of member who refuses to fulfil His will. And – this will probably seem terrible to you – I struggled with this about half a year, and then one day I came to the point that I could struggle no more. I remember I went out of the house in the morning, not knowing what sort of day it would be. I was teaching in a secondary school at the time and during one lesson I suddenly understood that I had to make my decision that very day, then and there. And after the last lesson I went to Father Afanasiy and said, 'I have come.' 'To become a monk?' 'Yes.' At this point he began to ask me the most down to earth questions. 'Well, all right, sit down. Have you any sandals?' 'No.' 'Have you a belt?' 'No.' 'Have you got this?' 'No.' 'All right, we can get that. I will hear your vows in a week's time.' Then we were silent, and I said, 'What should I do now?' I waited to see whether he would say to me, 'Well, you are going to sleep here on the floor and the rest doesn't concern you.' He said, 'Well, now go home.' I replied, 'In what sense, how?' 'Yes, you have renounced your home and your relatives, but now you can show obedience and go back there.' I must say that that was a very difficult moment, but Father Afanasiy would not have accepted any compromise.

Father Afanasiy died three months after I had taken my vows, and for a long time I was at a loss as to what I should do, because after such an experience, finding a spiritual father simply by going through all the possible priests or to imagine having as a spiritual father Stephen, John, Michael or Peter, seemed too absurd. I remember that I sat in my room, I was twenty-seven or twenty-eight years old, and I asked myself, 'What should I do?' And suddenly with complete clarity I heard in my soul: 'Why are you looking for a spiritual father? I am alive.' And on that I stopped searching. After Father Afanasiy's death, in 1949, I became a priest, following the advice of a man whom I trusted very much. He was French and an Orthodox priest. I had met him once before when I was seventeen, on the day I had completed my secondary education and had matriculated. Now I met him in England at an Anglican Orthodox Conference, and he came right up to me and said, 'We need you here. Drop medicine, become a priest and come to England.' I said to him, 'Think about it: are you serious or not? Because if you are serious, I will do as you say.' He said to me that he was serious and I did what he had told me to do, and now I always remind him that he is responsible for all the ill things that I do, and therefore it is his business to pray. He aggravated matters by the fact that after my first lecture in English he came up to me and said, 'Father Anthony, I have never heard anything so boring in my whole life.' I answered, 'What can I do? I do not know English. I had to write my lecture down and read it as best I could.' 'Well then, I forbid you from now on to write down anything or speak from a set of notes.' I countered, 'That will be comical!' And he replied, 'Exactly! At any rate it won't be dull, we will be able to laugh at you.' So from that day on I lecture, speak and preach without any notes – once again, may this rest on his soul.

Church and Society

Chapter 9

❦ ❦

Science and Faith: Education and the Arts

First published in the journal *Art at School* (1993, No. 4).

The question is often put: can a cultured man educated in the sciences, be a believer? Are not the concepts of faith incompatible with the concepts belonging to a scientific education?

Today, science has such an enormous role to play – and rightly so, I am very happy about it – but as a result it seems to us that all questions should be decided in the way that scientific questions are decided. We want to adapt purely scientific methods to subjects to which they are not applicable. After all we do not apply the methods of Physics to Biology, or the methods of Chemistry to History. Why should we then apply the methods of the physical sciences to the sphere of the human soul? I once studied the sciences, including Physics. Any physicist can split up a musical work into its component parts, dissect them mathematically and distort them. That is called 'acoustics': it is not called 'music'. After you have analysed a musical work by the methods of Physics, you have no idea how splendid or how worthless it is, because the perception of beauty in music happens on a different plane.

I must say that a man with limited education finds this much harder to understand than a man with wide scientific knowledge; because Physics and Chemistry at secondary school level are taught as the final and conclusive truth concerning things; whereas the Physics and Chemistry and Biology which are accessible to a scientist who is forever seeking new spheres of knowledge, present themselves completely differently. I graduated in the faculty of Natural Sciences and then Medicine, and therefore I understand these subjects perhaps better than Theology, because I never studied in a theological academy.

I became a believer when I was fourteen or fifteen, and went to university when I was eighteen. The professor of Physics was a member of the Curie family. He was well versed in Physics and could open it up as a mystery and not just as a series of facts. There were other lecturers. They were all non-believers but presented their subjects as discoveries of the secrets of the universe, and I could very easily see how the face of God is reflected in the secret of the universe.

The years which I spent at university studying science, and the ten years that I was a doctor (five years during the war and five after it), I experienced precisely as deeply connected with my faith. I am not speaking now of that side of medical work which expresses or can express Christian love, concern, and compassion. I perceived my scientific work as part of theology, that is an understanding of the works of God, and of God's ways. If one can express this by an analogy, for me it was like the study of the paintings of an artist and a revelation of him through his pictures. To come to religious conclusions through scientific facts is perhaps foolish. When people say in a simplistic way, 'Matter and energy are in fact one and the same thing, and this means that the basis of the whole universe is spiritual', that is a series of leaps that has no justification. But a penetration into the mystery of the created world, a reverential attitude to it and that inexorable scientific honesty which is essential for this, develops, it seems to me, an extremely fruitful scholar of high quality. He stands before the mystery with a living interest, with the wish to penetrate it, and he can put aside his preconceptions, his preference for one theory or another. He is ready to accept objective reality, whatever it may be, and to remain honest to the end. Such a scholar can inject this structure into the whole of his inner life.

Can we combine a secular education and spirituality? If one speaks of a secular education as an education in one or another specific ideology, then there may be a conflict; but if one is speaking of the education of a child simply in the history of a country, in literature, in language, in science, then I can see no conflict. I do not see why, when the depths and riches of the universe open up in front of us, that this should stand in the way of our religious wonder before God.

One must show a child that this whole world is, for us believers, created by God and that it is an open book before us. Instead of setting faith, the teaching of the Church, against the world which surrounds us – literature, art and science – we should show children that through these the mystery of God opens up ever more deeply and widely. God created this world. For Him everything which is the object of our scientific research is part of theology, that is knowledge concerning God. The whole of creation is a kind of introduction to God's creativity.

I also think that it is essential for us to know thoroughly and be acquainted deeply with everything that forms the intellectual, spiritual, historical, and social thinking of humanity – not because in the Gospels there is some

political, or social, or aesthetic doctrine, but because there is
no sphere on to which God's grace does not throw a ray of
light, transforming that which is capable of eternal life, and
withering that for which there is no place in the Kingdom of
God. We have no right not to know by what paths mankind
is moving, because the Christian faith, the biblical tradition
in its entirety, is the only tradition in the world which both
takes history seriously and takes the material world so
seriously that we believe in the resurrection of the dead, the
resurrection of matter, and not only in the eternal life of the
soul. And it is our business to have a deeper understanding
of the world than the world has of itself.

Man must develop himself as much as possible in every
respect: in his mind, in his heart and in all his being to
become as rich an individual as possible. This is not necessary in order to be a Christian. But in order as a Christian to
make a contribution to life, I would say that yes, it is essential. I always say to our young priests in London, 'You
choose whether be a saintly ignoramus or a well-educated
man. But while you are not a saint, please be an educated
man. You will not be able to answer the questions which
people have a right to ask you if you are neither saintly nor
educated.' Suppose a normally educated parishioner says, 'I
have read a book by such and such a writer – what should I
think of him?' and you have never heard of him, while at the
same time everyone else around has for a long time buzzed
about him, what will this parishioner think? What will you
have to give? If you were to ask Seraphim of Sarov the same
question, he of course would not have read the book, but he
would still have answered the question from another source –
but from a lack of education nothing will come. I am not
particularly educated in worldly matters, but experience
shows that sometimes that little that I do know makes it

possible for me to approach people, to whom such an approach is necessary; and if I were to say, 'I do not know. I have never heard of him,' people would simply go away.

I think this applies in the same way to a lay person. One has to decide as quickly as possible to become either a saint or an educated person. Having become a saint, one can forget about education. But until then one cannot simply say that education is worth nothing.

Everything that one sees on earth is God's creation. Everything that exists came out of the hands of God, and if we had sight we would see not only the opaque form of things, but something else as well. There is a marvellous Christmas sermon by Metropolitan Philaret of Moscow,[1] in which he says that if we only knew how to look, we would see on every object, on every person, on everything, the glow of grace; and we do not see it, because we ourselves are blind – not because it is not there. On the other hand, we live in a fallen, disfigured world, where everything is ambiguous; everything can be either a revelation or a deception. Beauty can be a revelation, and it can become an idol or a deception. Love can be a revelation, and it can become an idol or a deception. Even truth can be a revelation or, on the contrary, can freeze the very thing which it is attempting to express. Therefore one has to look at everything with the eyes of an artist or of a saint: there is no other way.

There arises the question of the artist's inspiration and his moral quality. From God's point of view one can see the glow of grace *and* the horror of sin. From the artist's point of view one can see both the one and the other, but the artist cannot make this distinction because that is not his role – otherwise he would speak of sin where one should be speaking of horror, or of sanctity where one should be speaking of

beauty. These are two different callings, which, like everything in life, under the guidance of grace can be full of
grace – or can be quite different.

As far as whether one should engage in creativity – I
consider it impossible to establish a rule. I think that God
leads each one of us in a particular way. If one is to speak of
the expression of one's own being – take, for example, a man
like John of Damascus.[2] He entered a monastery, and he was
a gifted poet and a gifted musician. His father superior considered that this was of no account and set him to heavy, dirty
work. Then, a close friend of John's died, and in spite of all
prohibitions, he poured out his grief and his sorrow in eight
hymns which even today we sing at funerals.[3] And when his
father superior saw and heard this he said, 'I was wrong! Go
on singing.'

Here was a man, who ascetically, by the rules of obedience, should not have written those verses, but his creativity
broke through because it was of his very essence. I know a
case where a confessor forbade a man to express himself in
literature – and the man broke up completely, because he
had no other way to express himself. There are people who
can express themselves fully in prayer, and there are people
who from prayer draw the incentive to express themselves in
another way.

An artist who, from within some experience of life, some
experience of man, some experience of God, would express
himself either in music, or in art, or in literature – such an
artist, it seems to me, can open up spiritual treasures for
others as well. Therefore I think one cannot simply say:
write only ascetic literature and nothing else. Nine out of ten
people will not read your spiritual literature; one has to
come to it. In my generation the works of Dostoevsky
played a colossal role, as did those of a whole lot of other

writers – writers, by the way, who were not necessarily pious or particularly striving in this direction, but simply writers who were deeply versed in human truth, who taught us the truth above anything else, and brought us somewhere new. So I do not think that one can say to people in a wholesale way: stop being creative, but busy yourself with prayer – a man might stop doing the one and not be in a state to do the other.

It seems to me that a painting, as a means to spiritual perception, often puts reality before our eyes which otherwise we would be unable to see. The same applies to literary works, where people are of course brought out in a simplified way. They represent certain types, but however richly they are portrayed, they are simpler than the people one meets in life. Certain details are seen in relief; and a person who in his own life is unable to see these things, having once seen them portrayed by a good writer, begins to see them around him with open eyes. Having looked at a portrait painted by a good artist, one sees the significance of one or another characteristic. And so, looking into life with the help of art, one begins to see things more clearly: both good and evil, but not necessarily with an estimate of its value, because a writer is not obliged to distinguish people as being good or evil.

I belong to an older generation, and therefore I cannot respond to the present forms of music, such as rock music, in the same way that a young man can, but according to my observation rock music is a form of intoxication. One sees young people walking along a street or sitting in the Underground or on a bus with ear-phones on and cassettes which are playing and playing the whole time. They do not experience a moment of silence or quiet, and that, of course, is not healthy.

One can educate a person to take in quiet and silence. I know a teacher of small children, who lets them play, and then periodically suddenly says to them, 'Be quiet! Listen!' And they immediately sit as if under a spell and listen to silence. They experience it, because the noise which they were making has stopped, and silence becomes real. If you have learned to listen to silence, you will, maybe, learn in that silence to hear the Presence. So I do not understand rock music. Its meaning does not reach me, just as jazz did not reach me when I was young. But in everything – be it classical music, or rock – there is a risk that you are not listening to music, but are using it as a means to becoming drunk or stupefied. And in this sense not only music but anything which influences us from outside ourselves can take us out of ourselves and make us drunk. One should not allow this to happen. One has to preserve one's sobriety, because if one loses oneself – in music or anything else – then perhaps later one will not be able to find oneself again.

It seems to me that rock music plays this role for very many people. I see it constantly. But at the same time I know people who listen to classical music for hours and hours simply to forget themselves. They are not listening to music: they are trying to forget their life, their difficulties, their fears. They are waiting for the music to take them out of themselves. They are not taking in the music, but are, as it were, destroying themselves. Therefore whether it is music or anything else which 'takes you out of yourself', you have to know the moment when it is time to say to yourself, 'Enough!'

One of the characteristics of a genuinely healthy spiritual life is temperance. We know in ordinary speech what sobriety means in comparison to drunkenness. One can get drunk in various ways, and not only through wine.

Everything which fascinates us so much that we no longer can remember God or ourselves, nor the basic values of life: this is a form of drunkenness. It has no connection to what I have called inspiration – the inspiration of a scholar, of an artist, to whom God has given the ability to see behind the outward form to that which surrounds it: a certain depth of being, which he can draw out and express in sounds, or lines, or colours so as to make it accessible to the people around it who were blind to it. But when we forget specifically that very meaning which is revealed by them, and create an object of delight out of that which should be the object of contemplation – then we lose our sobriety. In Church life it happens so often and so destructively, when people come to church because of the singing, or because of those emotions which are aroused by the harmony or the mystery of the divine service, when God is no longer in the centre of everything, but only the experience which is the fruit of His presence. The essential feature of Orthodox piety, of Orthodox spirituality, is sobriety, which transfers everything of value and its entire meaning from itself to God.

Chapter 10

❦ ❧

Of Divine Worship and a
Christian Lifestyle

The following are reflections on attending the Fourth Assembly of
the World Council of Churches at Uppsala in 1968. They were first
published in the *Journal of the Moscow Patriarchate* (1968, No. 9).

Metropolitan Anthony tackles the subject of worship and
lifestyle from two angles: the relationship of worship to the way
we live, and the content and languages of the services. The com-
ments he makes on the latter may sound strange to readers in
the West, where there has been so much revision of liturgical
language and practice in recent decades. In Orthodox terms,
however, it is a courageous attempt to address a problem which
is still highly relevant in the Orthodox Church today.

'Orthodoxy' literally means 'right worship', and it is inherent in
Orthodoxy that the services, which are largely unchanged since
the early centuries, play a large part in the spiritual education of
a Christian. Learning about the faith is an integral part of prayer
in church. Although a source of great richness, this presents two
problems for contemporary Orthodoxy. One is that highlighted
here: how can services written more than a thousand years ago
acquire relevance for people in today's society? The other, discussed at some length, is that of language. In the diaspora, though
this is beginning to change, it can be difficult to find services

celebrated in the language of the host country. And in the traditionally Orthodox countries, the forms of Slavonic and Greek language used are not generally those which are easily understood by native speakers today.

In contrast to the Assembly which took place in New Delhi seven years ago and was primarily concerned with questions of faith and order, the Assembly at Uppsala will be remembered as a conference concentrating on the themes of life and Christian work. At Uppsala, the World Council of Churches, that is a considerable part of the Christian world, with the full force of conviction and with the total concern of love and solidarity, turned to contemporary problems: hunger, poverty, lawlessness, discrimination, to all forms of evil caused by humanity's ill-will, or resulting from the grievous, tragic circumstances of life on this earth.

In all the discussions I heard, I was greatly impressed by the sincerity of the people who took part in them. From the very oldest to the very youngest – all with deep sympathy and understanding – wished to take on themselves the responsibility for the world which has been created during two thousand years under the banner of Christ, and into which we Christians have imported so much injustice.

This Christian concern for the present time – and the world is here and now, both to God and to humanity, day by day and millennium by millennium – is not a matter of chance. At the very heart of Christian faith lies the solidarity of God with the fate of the world, and also of Man. It is the solidarity with God, in God, in the Name of God, of a person who believes in Him. Already in the Old Testament, in the Book of Job, a tormented and exhausted Job exclaims: 'Where is that mediator, who will place his hand on me and on my judge?' (Job 9:33). Where is he – he wanted to say –

who will agree to take a step into this tragedy of injustice and deprivation, which would place him in the middle of the conflict? Who will take that step, from which there is no going back, which would make him a participant simultaneously on both sides in this conflict? It is in this that the very essence of the Christian attitude to responsibility and to solidarity lies. A Christian does not take sides. He sees injustice, and he must struggle against it with all his might, but at the same time, injustice must not obscure the person from him. A person behaves badly, but remains a person nevertheless, and one's mission is life must not be to wipe him off the face of the earth, or to move him to one side so that he should leave room for others, but to save him – as was said with tremendous force and with such conviction, born of the sacrifice he had made, by Martin Luther King, whose speech was cited twice at the Assembly.

For a Christian, submission to God and service to Man are one and the same thing. They are two sides of the one coin. We cannot bow down to God, who is love, without love. We cannot acknowledge God, who is love, without embodying this love in our life. We cannot call ourselves the disciples of Christ, who took upon Himself a tragic solidarity with God and with people. Therefore a very important part of the work of the Assembly was the section in which I took part, which was devoted to the worship and veneration of God.

Our discussion on the theme of the service of God showed that two problems now face a Christian's consciousness. The whole subject of divine worship and private prayer is afflicted by two crises: on the one hand, a crisis of faith, and on the other, a crisis in worship of God.

The crisis of faith consists in the fact that in many Western countries, faith in God has been shaken or, more accurately, not so much faith in God, but the concept of God. The so-called 'new' or 'radical' theology has put before Christian eyes an image of God which it is very difficult to honour. We believe in a personal God, in the Living God of the Old and the New Testaments, whereas many now, having passed through the stage of what the Apostle Paul calls the God of philosophers (that is, a God of whom one can think, whom one can imagine), have crossed the frontier and have totally ceased to imagine the God to whom they turn in prayer. That God has become vague. He appears as an object of varying speculation but is not approachable in dialogue. One cannot address oneself to Him. And the result is a severe crisis in the public worship of God, and in personal prayer.

But apart from that, there is another crisis which affects the form of worship in church. In Church worship there are two aspects. On the one hand, Church worship should be an expression of faith, love, hope, and of a living relationship between God and Man. On the other hand, Church worship should be greater than Man and greater than the congregation itself: it should open up a whole world not only of concepts but of experience, which we are given by God Himself. The crisis embraces both these aspects of Church worship.

First of all, those forms of Church worship which we possess, were created in the early centuries of Christianity. They expressed very vividly the religious experience and religious feelings of those people who created them. But centuries have passed. Not only the consciousness, but the attitudes of people, have profoundly altered. And now, many people feel that they cannot pour new wine into old bottles, that they are not capable any more of expressing themselves fully and meaningfully through those forms in which their ancestors expressed themselves to perfection.

Here, language plays a large part. The language of the prayers and the religious ceremonies is that of the epoch in which they were created. We have Slavonic, and the Greeks no longer understand the language of Byzantium.[1] Therefore very many difficulties arise in the path of anyone who wants to experience the words, the images and the expressions of prayer to the full. Very many of the words have lost their meaning. They no longer mean what they meant at the time when these prayers were formulated. And therefore, very often the person praying cannot experience what lies before him, because he does not understand what is being said. If they were simply strange words, he could inquire in order to find out what they meant. However when, for example, these are Slavonic words which have remained in the Russian language but have changed their meaning, sometimes to the point of incomprehensibility, then the person does not even ask the question – and this is worse because he does not understand the real meaning of the words of prayer, and sometimes misunderstands them altogether.

Language is not only words, but also images, experiences, which are connected with the words, and which may at one time be very vivid, but in another time are almost defunct. There are words which belong to a certain period but then fade away and die. There are words which are born and take wing for only one generation, and then are totally forgotten. This is a very serious and important problem, because people often understand the words themselves, but do not understand the associations and the experiences which originally went into them on the part of those who wrote them. They elude people, and the services lose their lustre. It is possible to pour new life into them, in private prayer, in contemplative silence deep within oneself – but it is a new life that bypasses the original words which have lost their meaning.

In this respect, for us, for the Russian Church, the use of Old Slavonic presents a problem – and not only abroad, but even in Russia. And it seems strange to us, living abroad, that our divine services, our wonderful Liturgy, our Vespers, our Matins, all the Easter services and those of Great Lent, can be translated into all the languages of the world except into our native Russian.[2] To some it seems that Slavonic is so close to Russian that there is no need, no point in doing this. To others it seems that the Slavonic language compared to Russian is like poetry in comparison to prose. But that is fair only for those who know Slavonic, and that is far from everyone, that is far from the majority. It is the privilege of a small and constantly diminishing minority of people. And therefore we are confronted with a dual question: the one concerning the use of a living language in place of an ancient one; and the other concerning the modernisation of the text itself, as there are images, pictures, expressions, which no longer express emotion, which at the best leave us indifferent, and in the worst case arouse feelings of bewilderment – we begin to feel uneasy and 'uncomfortable'. This relates not to the content of the service, but only to its form and its expression. If we talk about the essence of individual prayers then, of course, many of them were written in ancient Byzantium and do not find any response in the Slav. Some images which belong to the Old Testament, do not find any response at all in modern man. We are prepared to use some expressions allegorically, but we have no power to use them in a living sense, with living feelings. And we have to think about this, because prayer has to be truthful. It cannot be a convention. It must be the direct, spontaneous expression of a person's experience, both personal and beyond the personal, of the human soul, of the church community. It must not be an archaeological reproduction of something which once had a meaning and has now lost it.

In connection with this, it may be that one should mention the symbolism of divine worship. Our divine worship aims to convey a religious experience, and this experience cannot be conveyed through mental processes alone. It is conveyed not only pictorially and by parables, but also symbolically – that is, through bringing together movement, words and music – and dramatically, as in a performance of events, which penetrates our consciousness better than simply through intellectual narrative. This does not only relate to the Church. There is symbolism in literature, especially in poetry, and in learning; it also exists in the life of politics. There is no sphere in which one or other form of symbolism is not used. Take, for example, a flag. It means 'our Motherland'. It is a symbol. The same can be said about the word 'Motherland'. It is not only a geographical or social concept. In this word is contained a whole world of experience, the whole history, the fate of a whole community, all its mutual hopes, not only of the past, but also of the whole of the future. Such a word is a symbol.

In the Church there are also symbols, and they are used according to the same principles as are all symbols, but they also sometimes lose their lustre. Symbols which had a full and bright meaning at a certain time – because a symbol is not made up, but is extracted from experience – have lost their meaning, have died out, have grown grey. Of course they can be renewed – first of all through sensitivity, because at the heart of every symbolic expression there exists an experience, and this experience belongs to everybody; but on the other hand, one can often find another symbol, a contemporary one, which is intelligible not simply here today and gone tomorrow, but having a lasting meaning, which exactly expresses the same as the previous one, but is easier to understand, and is transparent and glows with meaning.

If we did not have linguistic problems, that is words that we cannot understand, and thoughts and images are no longer comprehensible, if the symbolism of our divine services would become more transparent and more understandable, there would be no problem about the length of the services. We must retain joy in the fact that we are given the chance of being before the face of God, to rejoice, to sing, to weep, to repent, to confess, to live with God – not only before the face of God, as I have just said, but actually with Him. It is given to us to be one single, living body and society, not directed towards God, but living in Him and with Him, who said that we would be his children and He would be our God – with that God, who said to us through the Apostle Paul, that we are no longer strangers to Him, but His own kin, his family, and with that God Who allows us to call Him 'Father' in the full meaning of that word. Then our joy would be transparent and pure. It could not be called the opium which it is accused of being.

If a Church service becomes dark, opaque, beyond our understanding, then an unbeliever has the right to ask what it all means. Is it not a peculiar form of intoxication. Does it not artificially awaken in us experiences relating neither to God nor to people, but only to ourselves, experiences which will last only for as long as the service itself lasts: experiences which have the aim only of delighting us and have no consequences in our lives.

True worship is not like that. True worship and true prayer do not arouse feelings from outside us: they allow our most deep, most genuine feelings to rise to the surface.

And these feelings, once they have come into being, will never die. They have entered our consciousness, have become part of our experience. They will not grow dim because the icon lamp has gone out or because the choir has fallen silent. A whole world of inner life has become active. This does not only bring delight, it brings repentance, an approach to God, and most of all a feeling of deep, steadfast responsibility. These feelings are not centred in themselves, nor in the person who prays, but in God and in our neighbour, and the fruits of this experience must be clear to all. The hallmark of prayer does not lie in whether you have spent Saturday or Sunday at a Church service, but in how you live between the two services, from Saturday to Sunday.[3]

If the religious experience is indeed a true one, its fruits are love, service, responsibility, sacrifice. Then we can speak of the restoration of strength through worship. The services are not deadened by repetition: they become creative work. In ancient times, this was expressed by the creation of forms of worship and ritual. This possibility still exists. The same Holy Spirit, the same Christ, are present in the Church, and our life, as the Apostle Paul says, 'is hid with Christ in God' (Col. 3:3). We are able not only just to repeat what the Fathers of the Church wrote, what they created, but we can learn something more important from them: that passion and that boldness which allowed them, on the basis of the experience of the whole Church, to create forms of prayer expressing that experience. This continues to this day: it is wrong to think that it does not. Throughout the centuries, both in the Orthodox and in other Churches, prayers have been created, entire services, and this creativity has not ceased to this day. *The Journal of the Moscow Patriarchate* has several times printed new forms of service texts to supplement those that already exist. So, on the one hand we must learn the conciliar truth and experience of the Church, and on the other hand we must have passionate spiritual daring which is never satisfied with simple repetition, and which can renew existing prayers, or create new prayers which would correspond as the previous ones did to the spirit and experience of the Church.

I have already said that a prayer is to be judged by its effectiveness and not by the emotions it arouses. These are the words of Theophan the Recluse.[4] On the other hand, the presence of such an attitude must create a whole new system of Christian life. New, not in the sense of being profoundly different to that of past ages, but in the sense that, faced with new problems, a Christian must take up a different position. It was the same in the early centuries. The Fathers of the Church reacted to everything that happened in life. Tertullian[5] said that nothing human is strange to us. And now it is still true that nothing human is strange to us – in any sphere, to any extent, in any sense. At the Assembly a group was formed under the title: 'Of the Christian life style'. It studied the question of what form a Christian life should take – as a way of life, not as a way of thinking, not as an experience, not as an attitude, but as life itself – in our time, in the twentieth century, faced with the whole tragedy which mankind is now experiencing. This group condemned the withdrawal of Christians from the world, which is the opposite to what Christ taught, as both lazy and fearful. He commanded us to be in the world, but not of the world, and our actions are just the opposite: in fact we flee from this world. There should be a detachment from the world, giving us freedom and impartiality, but there should be no estrangement, cowardliness, forgetfulness, or coldness.

At the centre of the conscious life of a contemporary

Christian stand the words 'solidarity' and 'responsibility'. If we claim to be members of Christ's flock, and that we are Christ's people, then we must know how to take up the position which Christ would have taken. That is audacious, but it is so and one cannot escape from it. And so the contemporary life of a Christian does not reject monastic retreat and abdication from the world, just as it cannot reject an individual path taken by a great artist or a composer. But on the whole, our contemporary Christian society is aware that the whole world is one, that there are believers and non-believers, but that the problems of humanity and of the world relate to both, and that we must stand together with all other people of good will and face these problems together, with all the richness of understanding which is given to us. This understanding is not human but Divine. It is given to us not only in the Scriptures but through the experience of the Church. In this way our worship, our veneration, of God, who is love, will blossom into love of humanity. Only when we Christians will understand this, will we become true Christians, and members of a vast, complex, at times tragic, but rich future, full of hope for the human society to which we belong.

Spirituality and Pastoral Care

Chapter 11

❧❦

'Life for Me Is Christ ...'

Address given on being awarded the degree of Doctor of Theology *honoris causa* at the Moscow Theological Academy on 3 February 1983.

Many years ago the Edinburgh Faculty of Theology awarded an honorary degree to one of the most venerable bishops of the Russian Church, Metropolitan Evlogii (Georgievskii). In his speech of acceptance he said the following words, which I would now like to repeat on my own behalf: 'You are bestowing on me a doctorate *honoris causa*, and I accept it *amoris causa*.' It is an honour and also a joyful recognition of the love which links all the members of the Russian Church, making us, living outside the Soviet Union, one with our native Church in our native land.

I will not conceal the fact that receiving this doctorate is a great joy for me – a joy inspired not by the fact that I can set myself above all others, because I know only too well that I am not an academic theologian, and that I did not receive the necessary theological training. But this honorary degree will stand as evidence to the Western Churches that my words are the words of Orthodoxy, coming not from me personally but from the Church as whole.

Ten years ago the Presbyterian Faculty of Theology in

Aberdeen bestowed on me a similar degree 'for preaching the word of God and for a revitalising effect on spiritual life in Great Britain'. I am happy that I can now say that the Russian Church also now recognises my words as being true and representative of the Church. I ask you to convey my deepest gratitude both to His Holiness the Patriarch and to the members of the Academic Council, and to all those whom God has inspired to surround me with such love and to bestow on me such trust.

From my very early years, as soon as I, as a fourteen year old boy, read the Gospels, I felt that there could be no other aim in life except sharing with others that life-transforming joy which had been granted to me in coming to know God and Christ. Then, when still an adolescent, I began to speak about Christ, whether it was appropriate or not – at school, in the Metro, and in our youth camps – how He had revealed Himself to me, as life, as joy, as meaning, as something so totally new that all was renewed. If it had not been inadmissible to apply to myself the words of Holy Scripture, I could have said together with the Apostle Paul: 'Woe to me, if I preach not the Gospel' (1 Cor. 9:16). Woe, because not to share this miracle with those people all over the world who are even now longing – longing for the living Word about God, about Man, about life – would have been a crime before God who had created this miracle. This word of God does not concern that life which we live day by day – a life at times so dull, at times so frightening, and at times so moving, but nevertheless a life limited to this world. It is about life in all its abundance, about eternal life, which throbs in our souls, in our hearts, which illumines our minds and makes of us not only preachers, but also witnesses of God's Kingdom, come in glory, overwhelming our hearts and permeating our being.

At the same time, which of us, priests or students preparing to become priests, can forget Christ's words: 'For by thy words thou shalt be justified, and by thy words thou shalt be condemned' (Matt. 12:37)? When, with the blessing of Metropolitan Eleutherius of Vilnius and Lithuania, I first began, while still a layman, to preach, I asked myself the question: How can I speak of that which I have not yet accomplished: of sanctity, which I have not begun to comprehend, which I can only contemplate with reverence, with trembling and with fear – how can I preach of what I have not practised in life? And then, seeing around me the terrible spiritual hunger of soul and of mind, I remembered the words of St John Climacus,[1] that there are people who can preach the Word of God even if they themselves are unworthy of their own preaching, but at the Last Judgement they will be justified by the witness of those who were renewed by their words, who became new men, and who will say: 'Lord, if he had not preached, I would never have known Your life-giving truth.'

At the same time, when preaching, one has to stand before the judgement of one's own conscience – sober, stern, inexorable – and before the face of Christ, the all-merciful Saviour, who entrusts us with His Holy Word, which – alas! alas! – we carry in vessels of clay. And we should ask ourselves: what does it mean to be a Christian? The answer to this is very simple: the Gospels tell us how we must live, how we must think and feel, in order to be sons and daughters of Christ. But the same Gospels also reveal to us, as do the Fathers of the Church, that it is not enough to follow the commandments if one does not become a different person – a person for whom a commandment no longer appears to be an order from God, but a surge of life: we have to learn to become what the Gospels reveal to us.

Each one of us must steep himself in the Gospels, and find in them those commandments, that call of God, that *plea* of God addressed to us, to which each one of us is capable of responding with his whole life, his mind, his heart, his soul, and with all his strength and all his weakness. We must find those words which are addressed not to each and all of us, but to one's own self personally: those words which burn in one's heart, which enlighten one's mind, which renew one's will and through which God's power flows into us. We have to understand this new dimension of life, which the Gospels, our relationship with Christ, His love for us, and our responding love of Him must create in us. It is a new dimension of God, a new dimension of Man, a new dimension of the world – of the whole cosmos. That is, we have to look deep into life and perceive it as God sees it.

I would like to take as an example the Apostle Paul. You will all remember his audacious words: 'Be ye followers of me, even as I also am of Christ' (1 Cor. 11:1). For a long time I was perplexed as to what he meant by this – how could he say this to us: Imitate me, be like me, as I, it seems I am like Christ? And suddenly it became clear to me that that is *not* what he is saying to us, but that he is reminding us of what happened to him.

You know of his life as a devout Jew, how he persecuted Christ, how he persecuted His disciples, how he used all the power of his passionate soul to destroy the work of Him whom he considered to be a false prophet; and how on the road to Damascus he found himself face to face with Christ, whom he knew only as a crucified criminal and who now revealed Himself to him as his risen Saviour, as God, coming in the flesh to save the world. And then his whole life was transformed, and, as he says, he 'conferred not with flesh and blood: neither went ... up to Jerusalem to them which were apostles before me' (Gal. 1:16–17). What had been revealed to him came directly from God – this new life inspired him to share it with others, and he paid a heavy price for sharing it.

You remember how in his epistles Paul describes his actions. Indeed he could say: 'I bear in my body the marks of the Lord Jesus' (Gal. 6:17). And in this he fulfilled something which we have to imitate: his transformation through repentance, which changed him from being a persecutor into being a disciple, and which enabled him to live a life – not just by word alone, but his whole life – following Christ's call addressed to James and John: 'Are ye able to drink of the cup that I shall drink of, and to be baptised with the baptism that I am baptised with?' (Matt. 20:22). In other words: are you able to endure the horror which awaits me, the terror in the garden of Gethsemane, the week of the Passion, crucifixion, being forsaken by God, the descent into Hell? That is what Paul is calling us to when he says: 'Be ye followers of me even as I also am of Christ': learn from me that heroic transformation, that inspired transformation, which will make new people of you, celestial beings, sent into the world to bear witness of Christ.

And Christ calls each and every one of us and says: 'Follow me'. When Christ was on earth this call was clear, but difficult – oh so difficult! (remember the story of the rich young man) – but at the same time so clear: abandon all your cares, leave everything that you are busy with, and follow Me along the roads of the Holy Land. What does this mean for each one of us? The same: tear yourself away, turn away from everything that makes you a prisoner of corruption, a prisoner of the earth, from everything which keeps you from being free – and follow Me. First, look into the depths of your own life, of your soul, of your heart, of your mind, wherever you can meet Christ the Saviour and the Living God, and God's Kingdom within yourself, and find that Kingdom; and having entered into its life, go out and follow the heroic path of the Apostles. And, finally, bearing within yourself, in your flesh, the death and Passion of our Lord Jesus Christ, His total estrangement from everything that was and remains the cause of sin, of death, of falling away from God and alienation from Him who is dear to you, grow to the extent that you become an icon, an image, a word, signifying the presence of Christ the Saviour.

St Paul says in his Epistle to the Philippians: 'For to me to live is Christ' (1:21). And we may wonder what this could mean. We know that when we love someone or are in the grip of some passion, or if something is so precious to us that we are ready to sacrifice everything for it, it means that that person or that thing becomes our whole life. It could be science, it could be theology, it could be our family, it could be pride – whatever it is, it holds us in its power. Well, it is with the same invincible power that we must be held by Christ. He must be for us, become for us – for the whole of our lives and for every moment of them – the total content, just as the beloved becomes the full content of one's life, and just as a worldly man can devote his whole life till the day of his death to some idea, or some work, to which he has dedicated his life. Everything that is Christ's must be ours, while everything that suggests that He lived in vain, and died in vain, must become not only alien to us, but must horrify us, and then – yes – our life will be Christ.

But how are we to achieve this? Is it possible that it can be done? What gigantic strength is called for to achieve this? Here we must again remember the Apostle Paul, telling us how he prayed to Christ to give him strength, and how

Christ answered him: 'My grace is sufficient for thee: for my strength is made perfect in weakness' (2 Cor. 12:9). One cannot achieve a Christian vocation by human effort alone. Who can, through his own resources, become a living member, a part of Christ's Body, as though a continuation of His earthly Incarnation? Who can by his own strength open himself up to become the pure temple of the Holy Spirit? Who can by his own power become a 'partaker of the divine nature' (2 Peter 1:4)? Who is strong enough to become a son of God as Christ became the Son of God? St Irenaeus of Lyons[2] tells us that the glory of God, the radiance of God, is a man who has reached the full potential of his being, and that when we are united with Christ through the power of the Holy Spirit, both in Christ and in the Holy Spirit, we become one with God's only begotten Son – *God's only begotten Son.* No human effort, no spiritual endeavour can achieve this – but Grace can achieve everything.

The power of God is truly accomplished in weakness, but not in the weakness which continually impedes us from receiving adoption as sons and daughters of Christ:[3] fear, laziness, inertia, sinfulness, that attract us to everything worldly, that removes us from everything heavenly. However, there exists another form of weakness: pliancy, transparency, the weakness into which God can pour His strength, as a sail can be filled with wind and drive the boat forward to wherever the Spirit takes it. We have to *learn* this form of weakness, which makes us completely malleable in God's hands. We have to learn complete transparency, and then God's power will indeed be accomplished in us, in spite of our impotence, in spite of the fact that on one level or another we who preach are sinners, and that salvation is as necessary to us – and maybe even more necessary – than to those to whom we preach life and salvation.

But in the quotation which I mentioned, there are a further few words: 'For to me to live is Christ, *and to die is gain*' (Phil. 1:21). And this is the second strict, sober criterion by which of each of us will be judged: not how we react to death in general, which is a theological concept, but how we react to our *own* death. When I was an adolescent my father said to me: 'Learn to live in such a way that you wait for death as a young man waits for the arrival of his bride.' That is how the Apostle Paul waited for death, because, as he said, while we are in the flesh, we are separated from Christ, but he had 'a desire to depart, and to be with Christ; which is far better' (Phil. 1:23). However deep our experience of prayer may be, however transforming our experience of the sacraments, we are still separated: between Him and us there is a veil, we see things as if 'through a glass darkly' (1 Cor. 13:12) – and how much one wants to break through that glass, to tear that veil asunder as when the veil of the Temple was rent in twain, and to penetrate beyond the veil. Then shall we know even as also we are known by God – these too are the words of the Apostle (1 Cor. 13:12).

If we ask ourselves: 'Are we Christ's?', that question concerns our whole life: what am I prepared to live for, day by day, hour by hour, and for what am I prepared to lay down my life? And similarly, am I prepared to lay it down day by day and hour by hour, renouncing my self day by day and hour by hour, renouncing myself and taking up my cross and following Christ wherever He may lead, not only in His glory but along the road to His crucifixion.

How do we view death, our death, our own death? Do we long for this meeting? Do we see in death only the end of our life, or do we see a door which will open and will admit us into the *fullness* of life? St Paul said that, for him, dying is not to cast off a temporary life, but to be taken in to eternity. Is our faith of that quality? Is it through such a faith that we preach eternity?

But St Paul adds something else, which I will express in my own words. After these words on death he says: 'Nevertheless to abide in the flesh is more needful for you. And having this confidence, I know that I shall abide and continue with you all for your furtherance and joy of faith; that your rejoicing may be more abundant in Jesus Christ for me by my coming to you again' (Phil. 1:24–6). And so he remains alive. Consider what that means: it means that the whole of his life is devoted to Christ. It is his way to the Cross on earth. For him, death is the moment when he achieves access to the blessed life of the risen Christ; and he is ready to renounce this moment in order that the life-giving, transforming and saving words of God can reach others.

Herein lies the third criterion, which I would like to put before you, and which is always standing before me and makes me say: 'God, forgive me! I have not yet begun to become a Christian. Let me grow up – obviously not to the stature of St Paul, but to grow so that my love becomes Thee, and that my hope becomes the encounter, the coming together, and that I should be ready for anything to happen, provided I am serving Thee in the hearts, in the minds, in the destinies, and in the lives of other people.'

Chapter 12

❧ ❦

Freedom and Spiritual Obedience[1]

Talk given in Moscow in June 1988.

We are used to thinking of freedom in two ways – social and political freedom, and freedom in mutual relationships – and to defining freedom as our right to act as we wish. But if we think of the meaning of the word 'freedom' in different languages, when a whole world of completely different and richer meanings opens up, which we can place alongside the concept of obedience. For the most part, however, we place the meanings of freedom and obedience in contrast to each other: either you obey or you are free. In fact, there is between them an organic and very important link. That is why I want to consider the word 'freedom' in different languages: this will open up for us very important depths.

The Latin word *libertas*, which gave us the word 'liberty', and now means, as we use it, social freedoms in our political life – my right to do what I want with myself and with my life – had a judicial meaning. It signified the original social position of a child born of free parents, and not of slaves. But it is clear that to be born with the rights of a free man does not mean to be free or to remain free. If you were born with the rights of a free man but became a slave to your passions, in whatever form, then one can no longer speak of freedom. A person who becomes a drug addict, enslaved to alcohol or some other passion, as described by the Holy Fathers, and known to us simply through experience, is already not free. Therefore freedom in this sense is inseparably linked with discipline. Having been born free, one has to learn to control oneself, and to be one's own master. If I am incapable of following the orders of my conscience or of my convictions, then I am no longer free, whatever my social position might be. As a result of this the two meanings are immediately linked with the understanding of freedom: the ability to control oneself, and that self-discipline which leads to this, which in fact is obedience.

We bring up a child to obey, but obedience can be understood in two ways. It can be understood as training, as in the way a dog is trained. As soon as you say, 'Do this', the dog does it. If you say 'Go!', it goes. If you say 'Run!', it runs. And this, unfortunately, is noticeable in all areas of life, for example in a family where strict parents train their children. I remember two of my contemporaries, who had a very powerful mother. Once somebody asked her how was it that her sons, who were already in their thirties, immediately carried out her orders? With a touchingly surprised look she said, 'I have hands and they have cheeks.' That kind of obedience, obviously, has nothing to do with the education of a free man. It will never lead to freedom: it is enslavement.

But there is an understanding of obedience which is quite different. Reading the lives of the saints, we run into the fact that sometimes an elder would give very strange orders, simply to teach a man to overcome wilfulness. If one stands aside a little from imagining a practice of this kind, or rather from examples of obedience in the Desert Fathers, then it will appear that obedience in fact consists of learning with your whole being – that is, with all your mind, with all your desire, and with all your will – to listen carefully to what the other person is saying. And the aim of that is to outgrow oneself, as a result of listening carefully to the wisdom or experience of another person. And through this to achieve – not stunted adolescence (as in the case of those two men) – but to grow up into mature people who are able to renounce their own will in order to be open to the voice or the example of another person. When this ability to listen was experienced by the Fathers in the Egyptian desert as a means of receiving orders which seemed simply absurd, the aim was certainly not to train people to accept 'What I say, that you will do', but to train them so that at any moment they could forget their own thoughts and carry out what they were told to do, as an education in listening to another's soul, to another's experience, to another's understanding. Such obedience can lead to maturity and to being able to take control of yourself. If I can renounce my thoughts of the present moment, and my emotions of the present moment, because what another person is saying is more important for me than myself, then I free myself from myself by means of self-control. I can empty myself, I can free myself from myself.

So, the first meaning which I mentioned, *libertas*, is the state of a child born free, who can grow into the state of a free citizen, of a person who has such control over himself that he can at any minute control his desires, his thoughts, his will, and even his bodily reactions. Because whatever our thoughts, our feelings or desires might be, if we are physically afraid, if we cannot make our body do one thing or another, then everything can fall apart. You can, having the most worthy feelings, see a group of hooligans attack a man and be too frightened to do anything. Your body is not up to a fight – not because it has not got the strength but because you lack spirit.

In this way obedience and freedom are inseparably tied together. One becomes a precondition of the other. But the final aim of such obedience starts with listening, pondering the thoughts, feelings, and experience of another person. This will teach us such distancing from our preconceived thoughts or from the feelings which control us, that we will then be able to listen to the will of God. Because it goes without saying that to hear an order given by a living person in the flesh is much easier than to understand a word of the Gospels. No sooner do we hear a word from the Gospels, than we immediately know how to find methods of avoiding the uncompromising nature of its demands. Obedience which demands self denial, self-control, has only one aim: to make us able to listen to and to hear the word of the Gospel, that is, Christ's word in the Gospel, or the voice – barely heard, but yet clear and vivid – of the Holy Spirit in our soul. And only such obedience can make us mature people, and not adolescents who require instructions all their lives as to what to do and how to do it.

The other precondition of freedom is discipline. We again wrongly consider that discipline is tantamount to army rules in military conditions, whereas the word is derived from the Latin *discipulus*, which means pupil. Discipline is the condition of a man, who has found a mentor and has submitted himself to this mentor as a pupil, and therefore with his whole soul and with his whole being is listening to everything this mentor may say, not imagining that he can be mistaken in anything, but in order to absorb the whole experience of this mentor and to outgrow himself.

The second meaning of the word 'freedom' we find in Germanic languages. The German *Freiheit* and the English

'Freedom' derive from a Sanskrit word, which as a verb means 'to love' and 'to be loved', and as a noun means 'my loved one'. The ancient intuition of Sanskrit defined freedom as the loving relationship of two people, 'loving' in the deepest sense of the word: I love you enough so as not to change you in any way; I love you so much that you should remain yourself to the end, without my enslaving you in any way, or changing you in order to influence you. It seems to me that this is an intuition of genius, which we sometimes find in words that are so ancient that they almost speak of the birth of an idea through pure experience. Yes, freedom is indeed this, when two people love each other so much, regard each other with such deep respect, that they do not want to cut each other to shreds, or to change each other. They are in a mutually contemplative situation. That is, they look at each other as at an icon (speaking now in Christian language), as a living image of God, which cannot be touched: one can bow before him, he must appear in all his beauty, in all his depth, but he cannot be reformed.

The third word for freedom is the Russian *svoboda*, but here the etymology is much more doubtful. It belongs to the Russian philosopher A. S. Khomiakov[2] and may not be fully authentic. Khomiakov forms the word *svoboda* – 'freedom' – out of 'being oneself'.

Taking all these words, we are indeed born free in the absolute sense of the word. If I do not have control of myself, I cannot give myself to anyone else, neither to God, nor to man. We can obtain strength to give ourselves, in the form of obedience that leads to mutual relationship, to Him who said: 'You are not to be called rabbi, for you have one teacher ... Neither be called masters, for you have one master, the Christ' (Matt. 23:8, 10). This is the relationship of mutual love, when God does not 'break into' our life, when He does not 'tempt' us with promises, when He does not subjugate us with orders, but says to us: 'This is the way to eternal life. I am the way. If you go along this path you will get to the fullness of your being, and then you will become yourself in the full sense of that word, a god–man. You will unite yourself to God's nature, as is spoken by the apostle Peter' (cf. 2 Peter 1:4). When we think about freedom, about obedience, about discipline, we should have these things in mind, so as not to change freedom into arbitrariness, and obedience into slavery, as a result of which we remain for the whole of our lives stunted adolescents, which happens only too often.

I will try to link this theme of freedom very briefly with an idea about spiritual endeavour, *podvig* in Russian.[3] The word *podvig* is connected with the idea of movement. An ascetic is one who does not stay still, but is constantly in a creative state of movement. I do not use the word 'progress', because a man does not move from victory to victory. There is a wonderful letter by Saint Tikhon of Zadonsk,[4] where he says: 'In the Kingdom of God one does not go from victory to victory, but for the most part from defeat to defeat – but those arrive who, after each defeat, instead of sitting down and mourning about it, stand up and go forward ...' A *podvig* consists exactly in this: never to sit down and weep. You can weep along the road, and you can weep when you reach your goal, and fall on your knees before the Saviour and say: 'Forgive me, Lord! To all Your love I replied with a chain of infidelity – but still I came to You, and not to anyone else ...'

If we combine this with what I said about power over oneself, about obedience, about the condition of the pupil as regards his teacher, it becomes clear what a *podvig* consists of. It starts at the moment when we choose our teacher.

Finally this teacher will be God. But before we can say: 'I am in such contact with God, that I can simply hear and act,' there are many intervening stages. The first stage, which goes without saying, is the living Word of God in the Gospels. This word we can hear, but it does not always reach us because we are not always capable of listening. And therefore we, for the most part, need human exhortation, at least an explanation now and then: how to understand this passage and – and this is the most important thing – how to put it into practice; because we either take the most extreme interpretation and are then unable to fulfil something which is beyond our strength, or, on the contrary, we satisfy ourselves with very little and move nowhere.

An important role can be played here by a wise, experienced mentor, who will say: 'This is what the word of God means in the present case. Now let us both think together how you can apply this, how much of it you can fulfil, what you can do as a start.' Because if you start by doing something successfully, the next step will become possible. But if it proves impossible to do anything at all, there will be no second step, and the person will break down. But here you must really know whom you are dealing with, that is, you must know your relationship with the given mentor: is he simply your parish priest who is hearing your confession, or maybe your teacher within certain limits; or you have been assigned an elder, who does not need your explanations, who does not need your confession, who can see you through and through – as St Seraphim of Sarov and Ambrose of Optina[5] saw people. There are plenty of examples both in ancient literature and in the experience of our own days.

Secondly – listen carefully to the Gospels. It seems to me that it is very important to read the Gospels as it were with a free spirit, that is with a readiness to say, 'This I can accept, this I cannot accept. This I can understand, this I do not understand' – and not to try to imagine something which in fact does not exist. I will now explain this a little.

Very often people read the Gospels and mark in them the passages that strike them, as if revealing their own sinfulness or untruthfulness. I think that that serves no useful purpose: it only drives people to despair. When one looks at oneself and thinks: 'I am not all that nice to know', that is already rather bad; but when one looks in the mirror of the Gospels, and it seems that God Himself is saying to you: 'Look how spiritually ugly you are!' – then there is indeed nothing to support you. So my advice is: read the Gospels and mark everything to which you feel affinity. When we read a certain section, we can have three kinds of reaction. There are places which hardly affect us: of course Christ knows best, and therefore He is probably right, but this does not touch me. Mentally it might be acceptable, but it does not disturb me. There are places – if we are absolutely honest – about which we would say: 'Oh no, Lord! Oh no, this is not for me!' I remember one old lady who came to a series of talks I gave on the Beatitudes. When we reached: 'Blessed are you when you are persecuted', she said to me, 'Well, Father Anthony, if you call this being blessed, I will leave you to it. I have suffered enough, I do not want to hunger, or to feel cold, or to be persecuted – enough of that!' She was being honest, but we are not always so honest. We very often behave in exactly this way, but we do not say it to God and we do not say it to ourselves: we only try to edge past such places. So, one has to be honest, and, on the other hand, search for the places which speak of the beauty which is already in us, of things which already exist between God and us. While we are in agreement only to the extent of 'If

God says so, must be true' – it has not yet reached us. But if we can say to God: 'How splendid this is!' – it means, we have met God in this saying, in this image, in this sermon, in this commandment. We can be overcome with joy, delight, and, like the travellers at Emmaus, exclaim: 'Did not our heart burn within us, while he talked to us on the road?' (Luke 24:32). In our terms, this will mean that when we read an extract and can say, 'Lord, how splendid this is! My God, how wonderful this is!' – we have understood something. And if this happens even for a moment we can say: 'I have discovered my kinship with God.' If one thinks of oneself as a very spoilt and damaged icon, it means: 'Here there is a remnant within me, an undamaged remnant of God's image, and I must cherish it as a holy command-ment, for in this I am already in harmony with God. If I break this, I do not only break my relationship to God, but I destroy that which is already godly and holy within me.' And this is the beginning of asceticism, because these little, let us say, stars in the sky must be defended from being destroyed in any way. They are like embers in the hearth which we can put out; and asceticism consists in defending these embers, as it were to feed them, so that the flame will grow, so that the embers will develop into one big flame, possibly a fire.

Whereas if you concentrate only on the bad things which you can find in yourself (even without the Gospels – it is enough to look in a mirror), then life will become a strange exercise, as if it all boils down to clearing the obstacles from a road you do not even mean to walk along. If the aim is to allow one thing or another to grow, of which you have read in the Gospels, you will inevitably bump into some form of resistance, or difficulties, and then you have to combat these difficulties. But do not start by combating those difficulties which do not prevent you from being yourself, because, of course, in Scripture we can find any number of commandments which we do not fulfil, which are not natural to us. That is the asceticism which is accessible to any person. There is no need to be a stylite or to go into seclusion, it is enough to try to be oneself in the best Gospel meaning of the word, following Christ's example. There is a particular spiritual endeavour for every person.

Chapter 13

❧ ❦

Pastoral Concern for Spiritual Life

A talk given at the second International Church Conference, 'Theology and Spirituality' (Moscow, 11–18 May, 1987) during the preparations for the celebration of a thousand years since the conversion of Russia to Christianity. The text was printed in the *Bulletin of the Russian and Western-Europe Patriarchal Exarchate* (No. 117, 1989). Here Metropolitan Anthony discusses the role of the spiritual father (or mother): a key concept in Orthodox spirituality.

The theme of my talk is spirituality and its nurture. I would first like to define the meaning of the word 'spirituality', because usually when we speak of spirituality we are talking of clear expressions of our spiritual life, such as prayer and asceticism as in such books as those of Theophan the Recluse.[1] It seems to me, however, that spirituality consists of whatever is inspired in us by the Holy Spirit. Spirituality is not as we usually define it, but is the expression of the mysterious effect of the Holy Spirit.

This immediately puts us in a very particular position regarding spirituality, because we are not talking of educating a person according to certain principles, and teaching him to develop in prayer or asceticism according to certain stereotyped conventions. Spirituality, in our terms, consists of the fact that the confessor or spiritual father, at whatever stage he finds himself, should be vigilant regarding the work of the Holy Spirit in a person: that He will inspire his actions, that He will protect him against temptations and falling away, against hesitation through lack of faith, so that spiritual activity might appear both much less active and much more significant that we often think.

Before going further, I want to say something about the role of the spiritual father. It is not a concept with a single meaning. I think there are two kinds of confessors.

On the most basic level a confessor is a priest who has been given the grace of priesthood, and who carries within himself not only the right but the strength to perform the Mysteries – the Eucharist, Baptism, anointing with oil, but also the mystery of Confession, that is, the reconciliation of Man with God. The great danger to which a young, inexperienced priest, full of enthusiasm and hope, is subject consists in the fact that sometimes young people leaving theological college imagine that being ordained has also bestowed on them wisdom and experience, and 'the ability to discern spirits'. They become what in the ascetic literature are called 'young elders', that is, while not having yet achieved spiritual maturity, not yet having even that knowledge which gives people personal experience, they think that they have been taught everything that can help them take a repentant sinner by the hand and lead him from earth to heaven.

Unfortunately, this happens all too often and in all countries: a young priest, through the strength of his spirituality, not because he is spiritually experienced and not because God has brought him to this, begins to direct his spiritual children with 'orders': do not do this but do that; do not read this literature; go to church; bow down to the ground. And as a result we get a caricature of spiritual life in his victims, who do everything they are told, doing what the ascetics did – but the latter acted like this on account of their own spiritual experience and not because they were trained animals. And for such a spiritual father it is a catastrophe, because he encroaches on a territory where he has neither the right nor experience to encroach. I insist on this because this is a daily problem for the priesthood.

An elder can only become an elder through the blessing of God. It is a charismatic event, a gift. One cannot learn to be an elder, just as one cannot choose one's own path into genius. We can all wish to be geniuses, but we understand full well that Beethoven or Mozart, Leonardo de Vinci or Rublev were given their genius, which one cannot learn in any school, which one cannot even learn through long experience, but which is a God-given gift of grace.

I insist on this maybe at too great length because it seems to me that this is a vital theme – maybe in Russia more than in the West, because the priest's role in Russia is much more central. Often young priests – young either in age or in their spiritual maturity – 'direct' their spiritual children instead of teaching them how to attain maturity.

To teach people how to mature is to tend them as a gardener tends his flowers and his plants: one has to know the nature of the soil, one has to know the nature of the plant, one has to know the circumstances in which they are placed, both climatic and otherwise, and only then can one be of help. And that is all that one can do – to help this plant to develop in a way that is natural to it through its own being. It is wrong to break a man in order to make him like oneself. One Western spiritual writer said that a spiritual child can only be brought towards himself, and the road into that life is at times a very long one. In the lives of the saints one can see that eminent elders were able to achieve this, just as they could be themselves, but one has to bring to maturity in another person his unique, unrepeatable personality, and to give that person, and another, and a third, the ability to be themselves and not replicas of a given elder, or, even worse, stereotyped caricatures of him.

There is an example of this in the history of the Russian Church – in the meeting of Anthony and Theodosius of the Kievan Caves.[2] Theodosius was taught by Anthony but, in fact, their lives had nothing in common, in the sense that Anthony was a recluse and Theodosius the initiator of communal living. It would seem impossible for Anthony to prepare him to do something which he himself would not do, and bring him up to be the sort of man he did not want to be himself and which God did not call him to be. It seems to me that one has to distinguish very clearly between our wish to make a person to be like oneself and our wish to help him to be like Christ.

Being an elder, as I have said, is a gift of grace, it is a state of spiritual genius, and so none of us can think of behaving as if we were elders. But there is another intermediary sphere – and that is spiritual fatherhood. And again, too often a young – or even a not so young – priest, simply because he is called 'Father So-and-so', imagines that he is not simply a confessor, but indeed a spiritual father, in the sense in which St Paul said 'You have many mentors, but I have brought you to Christ', and the same was said in his time by St Seraphim of Sarov. Spiritual fatherhood consists in the fact that some man – and he may not even be a priest – has brought another to the spiritual life, someone who, having looked at him, as the old saying goes, saw in his eyes and on his face the light of eternal life, and because of this could come up to him and ask him to be his teacher and his guide.

A father is of one blood with his son, and, in the spiritual life, a spiritual father is of one spirit with his pupil and can guide him, because there is between them a true harmony not only of the spirit, but of the soul. You probably remember how, in its time, the Egyptian desert was full of ascetics and spiritual teachers. However, people did not choose a spiritual guide for themselves because of his outstanding fame, did not go to the person of whom most good was spoken, but found for themselves a spiritual guide whom they understood and who understood them.

This is very important, because spiritual obedience does not lie in blindly doing what someone says, who has physical, material or spiritual power of the soul over you. Obedience lies in the fact that the pupil, having found a guide for himself, in whom he believes implicitly, and in whom he sees what he is himself searching for, takes heed not only of his every word, but listens to his tone of voice, and tries to implant in himself the personality of his mentor with all his spiritual experience, to enter into communion with that experience and to outgrow it, becoming a person who has outgrown the stature he could attain through his own efforts. Obedience is first of all striving to listen and to hear not only with one's mind, not only with one's ears, but with one's whole being, with an open heart, with reverential contemplation, the spiritual mystery of another person.

Your spiritual father who bore you, or took you in after your spiritual birth, must act as a father to you. He must have a deep reverence for the way in which the Holy Spirit works in you. The spiritual father, in fact like any conscientious parish priest, must be in a position (and this sometimes requires effort, meditation, and a reverential attitude to the pupil) to see in the man that beauty of God's image, which is never taken away, even if that man is damaged by sin. The spiritual father must see in him an icon, which has suffered from life's circumstances, or from human carelessness, or from blasphemy; he must see in him an icon and venerate what remains in him of that icon, and because of the divine beauty which is in him, must work towards eliminating from him everything that disfigures that image of God. Father Evgraf Kovalevsky,[3] when he was still a layman, once said to me: 'When God looks at a person, He does not see either virtue, which may not exist, or success, which may not have been achieved, but He sees the unshakeable, shining beauty of His own image.' And so, if a spiritual father is not able to see in a person this eternal beauty, or to see in him the beginnings of vocation to become a god–man in Christ's image, then he cannot guide him, because a man is not built up, he is not constructed, but he is helped to grow to the measure of his own calling.

The words 'spiritual obedience' should perhaps be clarified. We usually speak of spiritual obedience as a form of subordination, of dependence, and sometimes even of enslavement to the spiritual father or to the person we call our spiritual father or elder – and this is completely unnecessary and harmful not only to ourselves but to the priest. Spiritual obedience consists exactly of what I have said above: that is, of listening with all the power of one's soul. But this lays equal obligations on the spiritual father and on the disciple, because the spiritual father must listen with all his experience, and with all his being and all his prayers, and – I will go further – with the whole action within him of the grace of the Holy Spirit, to what is brought to pass by the Holy Spirit in the person who has entrusted himself to him. He must know how to follow the action of the Holy Spirit in his disciple. He must revere that which God brings about, and not try to bring the person up either in his own image, or in what he sees as the right way for that person to develop, as a 'sacrifice' to his spiritual guidance.

From both parties this requires humility. We easily expect humility on the part of the spiritual child, but how much humility is needed by the priest or the spiritual father in order never to encroach into the sacred, and in order to relate to the soul of a person in the way that God ordered Moses to relate to the ground which surrounded the burning bush. Every person – potentially or in reality – already is that bush; and everything that surrounds him is holy ground, on which the spiritual father can stand only after he has taken off his shoes. He should never stand on that ground other than as a publican, standing at the entrance to the Temple, and looking in, and knowing that this is the domain of the Living God, a holy place, and he has no right to enter into it unless God Himself orders him to do so, or unless God Himself prompts him as to what he should do or what word he should say.

One of the tasks of the spiritual father lies in bringing up a person in spiritual freedom, in the royal freedom of the children of God. He must not keep him in an infantile state for the whole of his life, so that he will always come running on account of trifles to his spiritual father, but should mature to the extent that he himself can learn to hear what the Holy Spirit says silently in his heart.

Humility can be defined in two ways. In the Russian language, humility is a state of reconciliation, the root of which is *mir* (peace), when a person has become reconciled with God's will, that is, has given himself over absolutely, fully, joyfully, and says: 'Do with me, God, what You will!' As a result he has reconciled himself to all the circumstances of his own life: everything is God's gift, both the good and the terrible. God has called us to be His envoys on earth, and He sends us where there is darkness to be a light, where there is hopelessness to bring hope, where happiness has died that we should bring happiness. And our place is not simply where there is peace, in the church or when a Liturgy is being celebrated, when we are protected by the presence of others, but where we stand by ourselves, like the presence of Christ in the darkness of a disfigured world.

If one thinks of the Latin roots of the word 'humility', then *humilitas* comes from the word *humus*, meaning fertile soil. Think – and Theophan the Recluse has also written of this – what that soil represents: it lies silent, open, defence-less, vulnerable, open to the sky: it receives from the sky both intense heat, and the sun's rays, and rain, and dew, but it receives also that which we call fertilisation – that is manure, refuse, everything that we throw on to it – and what happens? It bears fruit, and the more it experiences what we in our souls call humiliation or insults, the more fruit it bears.

And so to become humble is to open oneself up before God so completely as not in any way to defend ourselves against Him, or against the effect of the Holy Spirit or the positive example of Christ and His teaching. We have to become vulnerable and open ourselves to grace, just as in our sinful state we are vulnerable to hurt inflicted by the hands of men, to sharp words or harsh deeds, and to mockery – and to give ourselves over willingly, giving God the right to do with us whatever He wishes. We have to accept everything, to open ourselves up and then allow the Holy Spirit to vanquish us.

It seems to me that if a spiritual man will learn humility in this sense: to see in another person eternal beauty, and to know his own place (and this place is so splendid, so holy – the place of the friend of the Bridegroom: he is not the Bridegroom, but he is there to safeguard the encounter with the Bridegroom), then the spiritual father can indeed be the companion of his spiritual child, and walk with him step by step, guarding him, supporting him and never encroaching into the realm of the Holy Spirit. And spirituality becomes part of that Spirit and that growth towards sanctity to which each one of us is called, and which each spiritual father must help his spiritual children to achieve.

But where should one look for a spiritual father? The trouble is that one cannot look for elders, even spiritual ones, because we can go round the whole world and not find them; but experience tells us that sometimes God will send the necessary person to us at the right moment, even if only for a short time. And he suddenly becomes nothing other than that which the elders were over a long period of time.

I often think that in some ways my heavenly patron is like Balaam's ass, who began to speak and told the prophet what he could not see for himself, in the sense that so often a person comes to me and I do not know how to respond, and suddenly by chance I will say something, and it will prove to be the right thing. And I think that at such moments God puts the words in your mouth – but to assume that your experience, your knowledge will give you the opportunity always to do this is impossible, and therefore one has very often to remain reverentially silent, and then say, 'You know, I cannot answer you now.' We have a wonderful example in the life of Ambrose of Optina.[4] People came to him asking for advice, and he would make them wait for two or three days. In one case a merchant came, and he said: 'I have to return, my shop is closed and you are not answering me.' And Ambrose replied, 'There is nothing that I can say to you! I asked the Holy Mother of God for a reply and she has remained silent. And I thought to myself that I could say something to you out of my head or out of a book or from stories, but that would be unreal – and so it is that I cannot say anything to you. Pray, and I will pray, that God will put something into my soul, and I will write to you and tell you.' A person will then react to what you do say, when you say it, in a quite different way than when for all life's experiences you have prepared truths, because everyone knows your prepared truths by heart: the only question lies in the fact that a person does not know what applies to him at the present moment.

Now I want to explain that when I spoke of genius, I was not speaking of the priesthood, nor even of the category of spiritual father, but specially and exclusively of elders. And I used the word 'genius', because in living speech it expresses that which one can otherwise call 'grace'. In the life of the world this genius is musical, artistic, mathematical. It is something that we cannot attain through any of our own efforts. Therefore I was not speaking of priests in general, and certainly did not wish to discredit the youngest, simplest, but most sincere, parish priest, who does his holy work, hears people's confessions, sharing with them what he has learnt from the Fathers of the Church, from theologians, and from his own spiritual father and from the prayerful Christian community which surrounds him. This is a very precious thing. But there is something which troubles me a little, and that is that some priests – and the more spiritually uneducated and immature they are – the more easily they think that as soon as they are vested and have put on a stole they will be speaking from God. I remember one highly respected man, whom many people now regard as a great elder, who used to say to me, 'I do not pray any more when people ask me, because after praying I speak for the Holy Spirit, and if then they do not fulfil what I tell them to do, they will be sinning against the Holy Spirit and there will be no pardon for them.' That is what I had in mind; and this of course, thank God, is an extreme example. I feel horrified at the thought that a man can think that if he has said three times, 'Lord, enlighten my mind and suppress any lewd desire,' that his next words will simply be prophetic as if from God.

I think that simple elementary reason plays a part here: one can speak of what one authentically knows. Let us say, taking an example of great magnitude, that the Apostle Paul could say with complete trustworthiness and certainty that Christ had risen, because he had met the living, risen Christ on the road to Damascus; and he spoke of certain other things not from such first-hand experience. Other people also have certain experiences, maybe on a lesser scale, of less power, but of which they can say: 'Yes, I truly know this.'

A priest and a layperson can both speak from Church experience, in which they have participated, even if they do not fully possess it, because having in common with others certain premises of experience, they can listen in to the experiences of others, experiences which have not yet become fully theirs; and when these are needed by others they can say, 'This is the truth, because that is what the Church says, and I know more from the depths of wisdom of Church people than I know from my own experience.' And, finally, there are things of which we can speak simply because the Lord has revealed them to us.

Chapter 14

❧ ❦

Thoughts on the Religious
Upbringing of Children

This text was published in the journal *Talks on Orthodoxy* (1992, Nos. 2–3). The material was collected from various talks.

I am absolutely convinced that anyone can work with children who understands them and can transmit his faith to them – not only intellectual knowledge on religious themes, but the burning of his own heart and an understanding of God's ways. It seems to me that ideally parents should busy themselves with this at home, or it should be done by those people at church who are capable of doing it. There are families in which children are well brought up in Orthodoxy, but in general it is harder for parents than for a priest to teach their child, because a child listens to a priest in a different way. It is true that it is usually difficult for a priest to take on this task because he has services and other duties to attend to.

Thirty-eight years ago we founded a parish school in our church and it has continued to grow since those days. Twice a month after the Liturgy there is a lesson. Then the children are taken to play in a neighbouring park, so that they can get to know each other better. It is very important that they should form a family, which in the future will become the parish community. In the summer we organise a camp for them. We started with a small group, but this year (1987) we will have a hundred children. It may seem like a drop in the ocean, but for us it is a considerable number. The children live together for two weeks. In the mornings and in the evenings there are prayers. There are lessons on matters of faith in groups, and lessons on needlework, as well as sport and excursions. And this develops relationships between the children, which allows them, when they grow up and reach the age of adolescent rebellion against their parents, to share their impressions and to seek advice and help not at school or in the street, but from their camp or Sunday school friends – that is, within Church – and thereby they of course receive completely different types of answers.

Before growing into a Christian a person must first of all be simply a person. If you read in Chapter 25 of the Gospel according to St Matthew, the parable concerning the goats and the sheep, the question is clearly put: 'Were you a humane person, did you grow to the stature of a real man?' Only then can you grow into communion with God. Therefore one has to teach a child truthfulness, loyalty, courage: qualities which will make a real man of him; and of course one has to teach him compassion and love.

If one is to speak of faith, one has to communicate the Living God to children – not rules, not some formal knowledge, but that fire, which Christ brought to the earth so that all nations, or at any rate every believer, should become *a burning bush*, and be a light and source of warmth and a revelation for other people. For this we need to communicate specifically the Living God by the example of our lives. My spiritual father said to me, 'Nobody can leave the world and turn to eternity if he has not seen in the eyes or on the face of at least one man and glow of eternal life.' This is what has to be communicated: the living God, living faith, the reality of God. Everything else will follow.

I am not impressed when children are methodically taught, for example, that the life of Jesus Christ went by in this way or that. Children do not need information, but things which can reach them: they have to have living contact, which can arouse the soul and inspire them. They should not be taught history just as 'History'. Let the stories come in haphazard order – in their time they will find their place.

It is a very precious fact that a child often knows about God and about God's mysteries more than his parents do. The first thing that the parents should learn is that they should not interfere with a child's knowledge, or try to change knowledge born of experience into an intellectual catechism. I do not want to denigrate catechism as such, but it happens that a child knows, and then is forced to express his knowledge in set formulae. And at that moment when instead of him knowing with his whole inner being, he is made to learn some phrase or some image, everything begins to die away.

As I have already said, it seems to me that it is not very helpful for a child to know all the facts from the Gospels as facts. It goes without saying that if you love somebody you want to know what happened to him – but first one has to come to love the person, and then start to collect facts. I remember being taught Religious Knowledge at a Russian school in Paris. The children were told of the life of Our Lord Jesus Christ, and one had to learn either a troparion [hymn], or an extract from the Gospels; and all this 'had to' be done: for all this one got marks as for arithmetic or natural science. And this just destroyed any lively perception one had, for does it really matter in what order things happened?

On the other hand, the facts of the Gospels and the stories about them are so full of interest and beauty, that if the aim is not to learn of this miracle but to have it communicated to one, then something can come of it. In London I worked with children aged between seven and fifteen for six years. There were too few of them to form groups according to age; and it was very difficult to 'teach' them. Therefore we sat round a long table, took a section of the Gospels and discussed it together. At times it would happen that a bright seven-year-old boy could prove to be a much better interlocutor than a fourteen-year-old – and our difficulties were overcome. This depended on their receptivity, on their responses – not only their intellectual responses, but from the whole of their being. So we went through the Sunday Gospels, and the Feast-day Gospels. First I would tell them the Gospel story in as lively and vivid a way as possible, using some phrases from the text but not necessarily reading it all, for often the Gospel text is too smooth and the children's attention wanders. Then we would discuss it and gradually would come to the point of reading the text as it stands in the Gospel. I feel that one has to create a living interest and a living love, and a desire to know what happened later and why.

At other times we discussed moral problems. For instance, one boy broke a window in his home, and we asked him to explain to us why he broke windows in his own home. I am not saying that it is less blameworthy to break a neighbour's windows, but what had put the idea into his head? And a long and lively discussion look place between the children as to why this should happen. And gradually in the course of the discussion, certain phrases from Scripture began to float up, describing or characterising those moods which the children were expressing. These children once told me that it was surprising: everything that we have inside us, both good and evil, can be expressed in the words of the Saviour or of the Apostles. It means everything is there – I am totally in the Gospels, I am totally in the Epistles. Well that, I think, is much more useful than learning things by heart.

Well, that is all my very meagre knowledge about bringing up children. I was not a believing child. God did not exist for me before I was fifteen, and I do not know what one does with children to bring them up to have faith. Therefore I do not work with little children, I only work with children when I can talk with them, that is, between the ages of nine and ten. I only know one thing: one has to pray for a child. A pregnant woman must pray, she must confess, she must take communion, because everything that happens to her also happens to the child which she is expecting. When a child is born one has to pray over him and about him, even if for some reason you are not praying with him. And to pray together, it seems to me that one has to look for prayers (and it is permissible to make them up), which will reach the child – not children in general but the child in question in particular. What he lives by, who he is, how, being himself, he can speak with God – only the parents know this, because they know how their child speaks to them.

Another thing: we manage to make an unpleasant duty of what could be pure joy. Once, on my way to church in Paris, I called on some neighbours, who were getting ready. They had dressed three of their children and the fourth was standing and waiting, but he was not being dressed. He said, 'What about me?' And the father answered, 'You behaved in such a way this week, that church is not the place for you! To go to church is an honour, is a privilege; if during the whole week you behaved unlike a Christian but like a little demon, then sit in eternal darkness, sit at home ...'

We do the opposite. We say, 'Go on, go to church, say you are sorry to the priest ...' And as a result going to church becomes more and more a duty, a mere necessity, even a very bad caricature of the Last Judgement. First a child is told how terrible and frightening it will be for him to confess to sins, and then he is forcibly dragged to church; and I think that is wrong.

In our church in London, children start confessing from the age of seven, sometimes a little younger or a little older, according to when they reach the age when they can judge their own actions. Sometimes a child comes and utters a long list of his sins, and you know that his sins have been noted down by his mother, because she has been irritated in some way by these misdemeanours. And if you ask the child: 'Do you really feel that this is very bad?' He will often look and say: 'No.' 'And why then are you confessing?' 'Mummy said ...'

This is something, I feel, one should not do. One has to wait for the moment when the child already has some sort of moral understanding. At a child's first Confession I do not ask the question of how much he has sinned and how (I am not setting you an example, I am just telling you what I do). I say, for instance: 'Well, you have now become a big boy (or a big girl). Christ has always been a true friend to you; and before you simply accepted this as natural and fitting. Now you have come to the age when you can in your turn become a true friend of His. What do you know about Christ? What draws you to Him?' Mostly a child will speak of this or that, what he likes or what touches him about Christ. I reply, 'It means that you understand Him, you love Him, and can be a true and loyal friend to Him as you can be true and loyal to your friends at school or to your parents. You can, for example, make it a rule for yourself to find a way of giving Him pleasure. How can you give Him pleasure? There are things which you can say or do which may cause Him pain ...'

Sometimes children themselves say something, sometimes they do not. But sometimes you can prompt them: 'For instance, you tell lies? When playing games, do you cheat?'

I never talk about obeying parents at this stage, because parents sometimes use this method to work on a child, using God as a final authority, which will act on him. I try to see that children do not confuse the demands of their parents with their relationship with God. Depending on the child, one can put various questions to him (about lying, for instance) and say: 'Well that is good; please God by telling Him that you will no longer do this or that, or will at least try not to. And if you do, then repent, that is, stop doing it and say "Lord! Forgive me. I proved to be an unworthy friend to You. Let us make up!" And come to Confession, so that a priest can say to you: "Yes, as you have repented and are sorry, I can say to you in God's name that He forgives you for this." But think what a pity it was that such a beautiful friendship should have been broken.'

One has to be sensible with children about fasting,[1] that is, it should not be a case of total and meaningless suffering, but should have an educational quality. It seems to me that it is important for a child to start fasting through some moral impetus. One should suggest to him and give him the chance of denying himself some delicacy or object of greed which he finds pleasing, and not specify particular foods. He should be doing it as much as he can in the knowledge that by doing so he is confirming his devotion to God, and overcoming in himself some negative leanings, is achieving power over himself, self-control, and is learning to manage himself. And one should gradually increase the fast, as far as the child is capable of doing this. It is clear that there is no necessity to eat meat: vegetarians never eat it, and live and flourish, so that it is wrong to say that a child cannot fast without meat. But, on the other hand, one must take into account what a child can do according to the state of his health and his strength.

Chapter 15

❦ ❧

How to Live with Oneself

This talk was given at the annual conference of the Diocese of Sourozh in Effingham, Kent, in 1989. These conferences began in 1975 and continue to the present day, although they now take place in Headington, Oxford. Metropolitan Anthony's last conference address was given in May 2002, the year before he died.

I want to begin by making clear my own understanding of today's subject. What I had in mind when I suggested that we should speak of 'living with oneself', facing oneself, was the fact that, on the one hand, most of us, for most of the time, feel uncomfortable with ourselves: there is a sense of dissatisfaction, there is a sense of failure. On the other hand, when instead of dissatisfaction or failure there is an intense sense of pride and of success, things are perhaps even worse.

There is a saying: that we can give, whether to God or to man, only what we possess. If we have no control over ourselves, if we are not masters of ourselves, then we cannot give ourselves.

So I want to examine a number of ways in which we can discover who we are. When we speak of knowing ourselves,

of discovering ourselves, all too often we speak of discovering what is wrong with us. To me the image that
describes this attitude is something which I saw, a number
of years ago, on a spring day. The air was pure, the sky was
blue, trees were blossoming and the birds were chirruping,
and in the little yard in front of our parish house an old lady
had plunged head long into the dustbin in search of scraps
of letters, because she was dying of curiosity to know who
had written to me. And this to me is really the image of the
way in which many people try to acquire knowledge of self:
by plunging headlong into all the evil-smelling rubbish
which has been collected in the course of one's life, while
above there is spring, there is beauty, there is light. That is
something which, I believe, is encouraged very much by
spiritual writers, by clergy, and by the general attitude of the
Christian: that we should be continuously searching out
evil, searching out sin, trying to find out what is wrong in
order to put it right. I do not believe that one can do that
fruitfully or usefully. And again I will give you an image.

If anyone of us was given an ancient painting, or an icon,
badly damaged by time, by circumstances, by carelessness
or evil intent, we could treat it in two different ways. We
could examine all that had gone wrong and bewail it – and
that would be the end of what we can do. We could on the
contrary look at what is left of the original beauty of the
painting, and having looked at it for a long time very
attentively, having taken in all its beauty, provided we are
capable of doing such kind of work, we could begin to
restore what has been destroyed, by carrying on, as it were,
in the part which had been damaged the beauty which still
had survived.

I think this is a very positive way of dealing with what is
wrong within us, by starting with the beauty that is within

us. Because no Christian can doubt that the image of God, imprinted on us at the act of Creation, cannot be destroyed – it is there. We are like damaged icons – but we still are icons, we are still precious to God. We are still meaningful, significant, to Him, and it is in co-operation with Him that we can do something about this beauty.

I remember a sculptor once said to me: 'Many people imagine that a sculptor looks at a piece of stone, of marble, or of ivory, and thinks what he could project into it and carves it, getting rid of all that does not correspond to his vision. This,' he went on to say, 'is not the case. A real sculptor is one who looks at the material and, looking at it, gradually or suddenly discovers what is hidden within it, and proceeds to disengage the beauty from everything that prevents us, and him, from seeing it. In other words, the statue is already inside the material, the beauty is already there; and the purpose of the exercise is to free it from what separates us from it.' Again, this coincides with a saying of St Ephrem the Syrian:[1] 'When God calls a human being into existence, He puts at the very core of his being all the kingdom of God, and the purpose of life is to dig, to dig incessantly, to dig carefully, to dig with hope and with joy until we come to this hidden treasure and become one with it.'

All this tells us that we have to go on searching for beauty despite the ugliness which we see. We tend to see appearances: we do not see the substance, the essence. When we meet a person – or indeed, when we look at ourselves – what we see is what is damaged, or what is attractive on a superficial level. But it takes a great deal of experience – I am not speaking of time, but of inner experience – to be able to see through the superficial layers of triviality, or ordinariness, or positive ugliness, to the beauty which God sees. I remember Father Evgraph Kovalevsky[2] saying once, 'When God looks at us He does not pay attention to our successes or to our failures, that may or may not exist. What He sees is in the depth of our being, His own Face imprinted in us, His image.'

At times, we do manage to see the beauty – and even that we manage to misinterpret or treat in the wrong way. Several years ago a young woman came to see me. She sat on the sofa in the vestry, her head bent, a bitter and sour expression on her face, and said to me in a sepulchral tone of voice, 'I am a sinner.' I said cheerfully, 'You do not need to tell me that. It is obvious that you are – we all are!' 'Yes,' she said, 'but I am particularly evil.' I said, 'That is pride! But what is particularly wrong with you?' 'Whenever I look at myself in a mirror, I find myself quite lovely.' I said, 'Well, this is quite true – but what is your reaction?' 'Vanity,' she said. I said, 'Oh, if that's all, I can teach you how to deal with it! Put yourself in front of a mirror, take a good look at every single feature, and whenever you find them lovely, say "Oh God, thank you for having created such a lovely thing as my eyes, my eyebrows, my forehead, my nose, my ears – or whatever." And every time you see something lovely, something beautiful, thank God. And gradually you will discover that vanity is pushed out by gratitude. The result of this kind of contemplation will be the moment you look at yourself, you will turn to God in exulting joy and thankfulness. But, add something to it. Take a good look at the sour expression which is on your face at the moment, and say, "Forgive me, God. My only contribution to the beauty which you have created is this horrible expression" – that is the only thing which is truly yours!'

One thing that can help us greatly, and could sober us up

and allow us to understand more truly what and who we are, objectively, soberly, is the reading of the Gospel. If we read the Gospel, there are passages that leave us indifferent. They are true, obviously: if God said so, it cannot be otherwise! – but they do not reach us. Other passages are either too much of a challenge or too strange, too uncomfortable; they represent something which is so at variance with the normality of life that we see around us (life is not normal, but what we see is the norm), that we must be prepared to say to God, 'No, that is not for me.' And in that respect, you admit to God that you are not at one with Him, you do not understand. But there are passages – they may be few, but they are absolutely decisive for our discovery of our true selves – the passages which, the moment we read them, or when we ponder over them, make us exclaim: 'How beautiful! How true! Oh the beauty of that, oh the truth of that!' If we can say that about any parable, any act of Christ, any commandment, about anything which we find in the Gospel, it means that at that particular point – it may be a pin-point, or it may be a vast area (that is to be discovered later) – God and I are of one mind, are of one heart, are in true harmony with each other: I am the like of God, He is like me, there is true kinship between us! And so, I have discovered something of the image of God in me, that is, of my truest self, the self which God has called into existence, unmarred, still whole, or already healed.

That will allow us to start on our struggle for integrity and wholeness, not by any ineffectual effort to reject or to heal what is wrong in us, but by watching over with joy, with tenderness, with a sense of reverence, something which is of God – I was about to say 'which is already God' – in us: visible, a light that pierces the darkness, and which is God Himself.

And then, when we try to overcome our superficial, our social, our distorted self, we have a concrete task: never to mar the beauty which we have become aware of within ourselves. It may be one, two, three, five little points, but these are sacred, and we must protect them as one does with a flame. We prevent the flame from being quenched and gradually help it to set afire all that is around it by protecting it, by acting at one with it, by becoming more and more the person for whom this is his true nature, as distinct from other tendencies and desires within him.

Whenever we discover one of these divine elements in ourselves, we discover simultaneously those things which are in contradiction with it, those things which are incompatible, those things which must go because they are a sacrilege, because they are defacing this image of God, because they are polluting something sacred and holy within us. Then the task becomes concrete, it becomes exciting, because it is not an invented perfection we are pursuing: it is a perfection which we have seen, which is there, which we will try to protect and to nurture. You know what happens when you try to set fire to a heap of wet wood. You try to find a few twigs which are already dry. You set them on fire and they burn. They dry a few twigs around them, which in turn do the same. And if you protect this beginning of a fire, gradually the whole thing will be on fire. In terms of the Scriptures, then, this fire which you started with just a match and a twig may well become the Burning Bush in the desert.

Now, of course, we cannot stop at this. We have also got to try to become aware of other features in us that we can fight as part of the struggle for integrity, for wholeness, for the re-establishment of the image of God in us. We all are aware of a certain number of failings. There is not one of us

does not see that something is wrong with him. To go back
to the example of the girl I mentioned, side by side with her
false humility, there was vanity, there was pride, there was
fear, inexperience of the spiritual life and the mental struggle. Each of us can look at himself or herself, and ask,
'What is wrong with me? What is in me which I perceive as
a disharmony within myself?' We all do that periodically.
All of us go to Confession from time to time, and all of us
bring to Confession one or another characteristic of ours
which we feel is ugly. These characteristics come out in
different situations. They are brought into the open by our
attitude to people around us, our attitude to our own selves.
They are revealed by the awareness which we have of our
attitude to God. The time comes to pray, and we have no
desire to meet God. We can force ourselves to read the
prayers, and we can do that at a very great speed it we know
them by heart, on the assumption that God likes psalms and
therefore He will be pleased to hear one more psalm, or that
these prayers are quite beautiful – they really gushed out
like blood, they burst out like flame from the souls of great
saints. If I repeat them God will probably be pleased, in the
same way in which onlookers enjoy hearing a poetry reading or seeing a Shakespearean play. Well, that is not the way
it works. But when we become aware of this, we can turn to
God and say, 'Shame on me! In response to a real, personal,
deep love which you have demonstrated through the life, the
teaching, the death of the Lord Jesus Christ – in response to
this I say, "Oh no! Not tonight! I have something much
more exciting to do, I have a novel to finish, or, I want to
have a rest! Or, simply, I do not feel like meeting you at all!
Can't we postpone it to a better occasion when I am in the
right mood? Because You are eternal, You can wait."'

Then we can ask ourselves questions about the people

around us. That is what we do in fact when we prepare for Confession: how do we treat all the people around us? At the same time, and in addition to this as a separate exercise, we can ask ourselves questions about our own selves: how do I treat myself? How do I treat my mind, my body, my heart? How do I exercise my will in my actions, in the way in which I relate to people around me? And that is really a lot, because, if we are honest, it provides us with very sad and rich material of wrong, or even of evil.

But if that is not sufficient, we can ask ourselves: What do people think of me? This is a question which we do not like asking. If we ask it, we usually think that those who praise us have a deep and very refined insight, but those who do not, who criticise us or dislike us, must have missed something essential: they must be blind, or they must be really evil – blessed are the pure in heart! Well, it is a very good thing to have a look and ask yourself, what do people think of me? And when you have made a catalogue of what you know people think of you (and you do not know the half of what they think), you must ask yourself a further question, which is very, very important: Are the people who praise me right in their praises? Or are they mistaken because they love me, or are they deceived because I am hypocritical, because I am clever, because I am a liar, or because I can present a front that deceives them? On the other hand, in certain things they may be right in their praise – that can be added to the list of the little pinpoints of the image of God which I have discovered through the Gospel: one more thing which is true, which points to my truer if not truest self.

And then: people criticise me – are they right? Are they wrong? At times people condemn others because they are forthright, because they are truthful, because they are sharp;

at times, they condemn others because they are hypocritical, and slippery, and so forth. Well, ask yourself: what do people think of me, what do they tell me to my face and what do they say behind my back? Gossip reaches one very, very easily! I have received quite a lot of people's opinions about me from people who had no intention of making me share their knowledge of me.

This again adds to your vision of who you are. And when you take stock of all this, you can begin to struggle against those things which are wrong, and reinforce those things which are right. The reinforcing begins really by protection, by creating a hedge, or putting one's hand around the flame so that the wind doesn't blow it out. It may continue by watering and looking after the seed or the little plant as one does in a garden. The fighting against what is wrong begins with asking oneself: I have now seen something wrong in me – how much can I do against it? I remember the first time I went to Confession to Father Afanasiy, a monk of ascetic life, and I thought: 'I will make a confession, and then he will tell me exactly what I should do to right myself – that is the quickest and most direct way.' When I had finished the confession, he said to me: 'This is what you should do. Now stand still, think for a moment, and tell me how much of it you feel you are prepared to do and capable of doing.' I was so bitterly disappointed! And then I discovered that he was right. I would not have been able to cope with the whole problem at once, but I could begin, like a mouse, to nibble at it on its periphery, and destroy the little elements which were not too much for me, waiting until I had gathered more strength and become able to tackle the greater ones.

And so, from the discovery of one's truest, or truer self, to the discovery of ugly elements that prevent us from being what we truly are in essence, we can work out a gradual vision and understanding of who we are at a given moment and move on into the next moment.

Now, a thing which we must avoid is to try to discover more than comes our way. There is a remarkable passage in the writings of John of Kronstadt in which he says that God allows us to see what is wrong with us in one way or another only when He has discovered in us enough faith and enough hope to be capable of receiving this vision, of seeing it; earlier we would be crushed under its weight. So, whenever we see ourselves as more ugly than we saw ourselves yesterday, we can take it that this is a new task which the Lord God is giving us, because now He can trust us more that He did before. Before, I was still too frail, and incapable of facing this. 'Now,' He says, 'you are strong enough to face it – so face it.'

So, all that gradually allows us to see ourselves in a very complex manner and to conduct a struggle on two levels. It helps us to become more and more a Burning Bush and, at the same time, to destroy everything that stands in the way of our integrity and wholeness.

Of course, all this can be done only in the light of God. It is God alone Who can show us our kinship with Him, reveal to us that we are in His likeness, that we are in his image in one way or another. It is only God who can cast a ray of His light and reveal to us the darkness or evil within us. And when we are aware of those things, we can then begin to think of possessing our souls, of taking hold of ourselves, of struggling and conquering. Of course we will not be victorious, but we will stand on God's side and with Him. And then, if we are aware of all that is beautiful and all that is ugly in us, we can gather it all together and give it to God.

To give to God what is beautiful, and true, and whole is

no problem, but what about the things which are not? Those of you who have read the *Diary of a Country Priest* by Georges Bernanos may remember that this young priest speaks to an old countess full of bitterness, full of pride, of arrogance, of disillusionment; and he says to her that the only solution is that she should surrender to God, and she says, 'But I have nothing to surrender, I have nothing but pride, nothing but bitterness, nothing but resentment!' And he says to her 'Yes – give them to God. If you have nothing else to give, hand them over to Him, let Him take possession of them and deal with them' ... We can do nothing of our own accord, with our own strength. Christ says clearly: 'Without me, you can do nothing.' We do not need the kind of strength that we need in order to cope with our material situation in life, because what we have to deal with is beyond that kind of strength. St Paul, knowing what kind of mission awaited him, prayed God to give him strength; and the Lord answered him: 'My grace is sufficient for you, for my power is made perfect in weakness' (2 Cor. 12:9). What kind of weakness? Not sloth, not laziness, not forgetfulness – no! This is the weakness of a child that abandons itself trustfully to the arms of his mother, the frailty of what is transparent, the frailty of what can be filled with a strength from outside as a sail – the frailest part of the vessel – can be filled with wind and carry the heavy burden of the ship across the seas. A surgical glove is the weakest possible thing – and yet it can work miracles if an intelligent, well-trained hand is inside it. That is the kind of weakness in which God can deploy His power. And if we allow Him to do this, then indeed things can happen, because the same Paul, after these words of Christ said: 'And therefore, I shall rejoice in nothing but our weakness, so that all should be of God's power.'

So, this is what I wanted to convey to you. There is no separation between the physical, the psychological and the spiritual, although each of them has got its function and its place. They are interrelated, they penetrate one another. But we have power over the central core – that aspect of our bodies, our feelings and emotions, and of our wills of which we can consciously become aware. If then we open this central core of ourselves to the action of God's power, His grace will overwhelm us, change us, and truly transfigure us.

Notes

❧ ❦

Introduction

1. Archbishop Paul of Finland: 'Suggestions for a solution to the problem of the Orthodox Diaspora'. Reprinted in *Sourozh* No. 91, February 2003, pp. 3–29.

Chapter 1: Encounter

1. I.e. from the German Occupation, in August 1944.
2. Charles Williams, *All Hallows Eve* (NY: Noonday Press, 1981). Charles Williams (1886–1945) was a member of the 'Inklings', the Oxford group of Christian writers that included J. R. R. Tolkien and C. S. Lewis.
3. The Rite of Holy Matrimony in *Service Book of the Holy Orthodox-Catholic Apostolic Church*, compiled and translated by Isabel Hapgood (Englewood, NJ: Antiochan Orthodox Christian Archdiocese, 1983), p. 292.
4. Gabriel Marcel (1889–73): existentialist and personalist French philosopher.
5. Methodius, Bishop of Olympus, was martyred in c. 312.

Chapter 2: We Have to Bring Faith to the World ...

1. See, for example, *Difficulty 41* in *Maximus the Confessor*, ed. Andrew Louth (London: Routledge, 1996), pp. 157–62.
2. Cf. John 18:36.
3. Patriarch Alexis I (Simansky), d. 1970.
4. Cf. Matt. 5:13–14.
5. See Matt. 17; Mark 9.
6. Christian apologist of the early third century; b. probably about

160 at Carthage, d. sometime after 229.

7. Isaac the Syrian (Isaac of Nineveh): a seventh-century monastic, briefly bishop of Nineveh, whose writings have been very influential in Russian spirituality.

8. See Chapter 2, note 1.

9. See Isa. 45:23; cf. Rom 14:11; Phil. 2:10.

10. St Seraphim of Sarov (1759–1833): much-loved Russian saint and monk.

11. The question of human freedom and suffering as explored by Dostoevsky in the tale of the Grand Inquisitor (*The Brothers Karamazov*, 1879, Book II, Part 5, Chapter 5).

12. A reference to Aldous Huxley's *The Doors of Perception* (1954) and *Heaven and Hell* (1956), which described his personal experiments with mescalin and other mind-altering drugs.

13. Sergius of Radonezh: the patron saint of Russia, who founded the Monastery of the Holy Trinity near Moscow in 1334.

14. St John of Kronstadt (1829–1908): the only married priest in the calendar of Russian saints, was widely considered as a saint in his lifetime. He is known as a wonder-worker because of his healing powers, and the icon shows him holding a chalice because he encouraged people to return to the practice of receiving communion at every Liturgy instead of once or twice a year.

15. From a radio broadcast given by Lewis in the 1940s.

16. See Chapter 3, note 5.

17. i.e. Istanbul. Orthodox tend to refer to Istanbul as Constantinople when speaking of its historical and cultural significance for the Orthodox world.

18. First emigration: made up of those Russians who fled immediately after the Revolution of 1917, often referred to as the 'old' or 'white' emigration.

Chapter 3: We Have Something to Say about Man

1. Michael Ramsey (1904–88): Anglican theologian and Archbishop of Canterbury (1961–74).

2. Vladimir Martsinkovsky: writer and evangelist, active in the revival of the Russian Student Christian Movement.

3. Patriarch Tikhon of Moscow (1865–1925): first Patriarch of Moscow following the restoration of the Patriarchate in the

1917–18 Sobor (Council). During the first years of the Bolshevik regime, he was imprisoned on several occasions. He was declared a saint in 1989.

4. See Chapter 3, note 11.

5. Pastor Martin Niemöller (1892–1984): member of the German Evangelical Church, opponent of Hitler and one of the founders of the World Council of Churches.

6. See Chapter 5, note 3.

7. The part of the Russian Church which broke away from the Moscow Patriarchate during the Soviet regime; now known as The Russian Orthodox Church Outside Russia (ROCOR). In 1920, a group of Russian hierarchs, clergy and lay people under the leadership of Metropolitan Anthony of Kiev, left Russia, choosing exile rather than existence under an atheist regime. In the same year, Patriarch Tikhon (see above, note 3) issued a decree (Ukaz 362, 20 Nov. 1920) that the Highest Church Administration in exile should continue to exist until such time as the Russian Church could freely administer itself. There have been a number of appeals for ROCOR to return to canonical communion with the Patriarchate. Discussions are currently underway.

8. The Episcopate of the Russian Orthodox Church, which met on 9–11 October 1989 to celebrate the four-hundredth anniversary of the establishment of the Patriarchate in the Russian Orthodox Church.

9. Orthodoxy resists both the 'vertical' authority structure of Roman Catholicism, and the individualistic approach of Protestantism. According to a conciliar model, all matters of faith and doctrine are decided in council, as a reflection of a Trinitarian understanding of humanity. The paper in question, produced by the Orthodox Church in America, called on the Russian Orthodox Church to return to a more conciliar practice, which had been distorted by increased authoritarianism under the pressure of Soviet persecution.

10. Diocesan Statutes of the Diocese of Sourozh (Oxford: St Stephen's Press, 2001).

11. The Council of 1917–18, consisting of bishops, priests and laity, met to discuss reforms necessary for the Russian Orthodox

NOTES

Church. Because of the Bolshevik Revolution, few of its recom-
mendations were put into practice. See A. Svetozarsky, *The
1917–18 Council of the Russian Orthodox Church* (Oxford: St
Stephen's Press, 2003).

12. I.e. the Orthodox Church in America (OCA), which was granted
autocephaly by Moscow in 1970.

13. I.e. in the early 1950s.

14. After the death of Patriarch Tikhon, Metropolitan Sergius
(Stragorodskii) served as 'deputy locum tenens' of the
Patriarchate from 1927 to 1943, during the time of Stalin's
purges, when literally millions of people, including thousands of
clergy, were imprisoned, exiled and killed. He has been much
criticised for his controversial position as head of a Church that
was simultaneously recognised and persecuted by the State.

15. See Chapter 3, note 8.

16. Mother Maria (Skobstova): born in Russia 1891, died at
Ravensbrück 1945. During the Paris emigration she worked tire-
lessly with people in need, and sheltered many Jews escaping
from the Nazi occupation. She was canonised by the Ecumenical
Patriarchate in May 2004. See *Mother Maria Skobstova:
Essential Writings* (Modern Spiritual Masters Series), trans.
Richard Pevear and Larissa Volkhonsky (Maryknoll, NY: Orbis
Books, 2003); Sergei Hackel, *Pearl of Great Price: the Life of
Mother Maria Skobstova*, (Crestwood, NY: St Vladimir's
Seminary Press, 2003).

17. I.e. the Russian Orthodox Church Outside Russia, or ROCOR.

18. Archbishop Basil (Krivocheine) of Brussels (1900–85): an outstanding scholar, researcher and translator of Patristic literature;
member of the Moscow Patriarchate.

19. Another name for the members of ROCOR, from a synod held at
Karlovats in Yugoslavia.

20. See Chapter 3, note 2.

21. Location of a Conference of the Faith and Order Commission of
the World Council of Churches, held in Lund (Sweden) in 1952.

22. Archbishop Alexis van der Mensbrugghe (1899–1980), who
occupied various sees of the Moscow Patriarchate in Western
Europe and in America: a liturgical scholar and specialist in
canon law.

23. Fr Pavel Florensky (1882–1937): philosopher, theologian, scientist, and art historian who was ordained as a priest in 1911. In 1922, Fr Pavel was silenced, and, after ten years of forced scientific work for the Soviet regime, he was arrested and imprisoned. He was murdered in 1937 by order of the KGB.

24. Leonid Alexandrovich Uspensky (1902–87): iconographer and theologian; author of *The Theology of Icons* (Crestwood, NY: SVS Press, 1992).

25. Andrei Rublev (c. 1370–1430): monk of the Trinity-St Sergius Monastery, whose icon of the Trinity is considered the peak of Russian iconography.

26. Gregory Krug (1909–69): Russian monk and iconographer, who lived and worked in France.

27. Mariamna Fortounatto: iconographer, teacher, and wife of Fr Michael Fortounatto, who is choir director at the Russian Orthodox Cathedral in London.

28. Theophanes the Greek (c. 1340 – c. 1410): invited to Russia as an iconographer in 1395, and very influential in the Novgorod school of icon painting.

29. St Gregory Palamas (1296–1359): Archbishop of Thessaloniki and one of the principal figures of Orthodox mystical theology in the mid-fourteenth century. He practised and defended the hesychast tradition – that of inner prayer and stillness.

30. Leo Tolstoy (1828–1910): author of *War and Peace*, *Anna Karenina*, etc.

31. Eccl. 38:1ff.

Chapter 4: Certain Categories of Our Existence in Creation

1. Archpriest Avvakum Petrovich (1620/21–82): leader of the Old Believers who broke away from the Russian Orthodox Church because of liturgical reforms in the 1650s. Archpriest Avvakum and many others were burned by order of the Tsar for their defence of the old rite. His *Zhitiye* ('Life') is thought to be the first Russian autobiography. The passage referred to here relates to Rublev's icon of the Trinity, itself an image of primordial harmony: the author imagines what the three figures might be saying to each other.

2. See Chapter 7, note 1.

3. Cf. 'The poor man is not the one who has no possessions, but the
   one who has many desires': second sermon on Lazarus and the
   rich man in St John Chrysostom, *On Wealth and Poverty,* translated and edited by Catharine P. Roth (Crestwood, NY: SVS
   Press, 1984), p. 40. St John Chrysostom (c. 350–407) was
   Archbishop of Constantinople from 398, but died in exile. He
   was renowned for his preaching, which earned him the epithet
   'Chrysostom' or 'Goldenmouth'.
4. Martin Buber (1875–1965): Jewish religious philosopher and
   writer, and scholar of Hassidic thought.
5. Alexei Khomiakov (1804–60): writer, philosopher and literary
   critic; key figure in the Slavophile movement which arose in
   response to Westernising tendencies in Russia. Khomiakov held
   that the Church is an organic body characterised by inner
   holiness and in which freedom is combined with unity.
6. Hermas: otherwise unknown author of *The Shepherd*, a second-
   century apocalyptic document. Two main themes are: the
   Church, pre-existent in the mind of God, whose fulfilment will
   signal the end of time; and the necessity for human beings to
   choose between the two angels, or spirits, of good and evil.
7. Voltaire (1694–1778): 'Si Dieu n'existait pas, il faudrait
   l'inventer'. *Épîtres*, xcvi, *A L'Auteur du Livre des Trois
   Imposteurs.*
8. Matt. 5:3–11.
9. 'The soul which is purified by the thought of God in watchful
   vigil night and day is good earth which makes its Lord rejoice by
   yielding a hundredfold'. St Isaac of Nineveh, *On Ascetical Life*
   (Crestwood, NY: SVS Press, 1989), p. 102. Cf. Chapter 5, note 7.
10. Hesychasm, from the Greek *hesychia* ('calm' or 'stillness'): form
    of monastic life focussed on contemplative prayer. Its prac-
    titioners on Mount Athos came under violent attack in the
    fourteenth century, and hesychasm was for a time declared
    heretical. St Gregory Palamas (cf. Chapter 4, note 29) was deeply
    involved in the controversy.
11. 'Lord Jesus Christ, have mercy on me, a sinner.' The practice of
    the Jesus prayer involves the repetition of this phrase many times
    over.
12. 'Let all mortal flesh keep silence and with fear and trembling

stand': from the Prayer of the Cherubic Hymn of the fourth century Liturgy of St James, one of the earliest extant liturgies of the
Christian Church. It is sung at the Byzantine Liturgy on the
morning of Holy Saturday.

13. 'Thou wast transfigured on the mountain, O Christ our God,
showing Thy glory to Thy disciples as far as they were able to
bear it. At the intercession of the Mother of God, make Thine
everlasting light shine forth also upon us sinners. O Giver of
light, glory to Thee.' A troparion is a hymn appointed for a
particular feast.

14. Prince E. N. Troubetskoy (1863–1920): Russian philosopher and
art historian.

15. See Chapter 3, note 3.

16. See Chapter 6, note 23. The Russian word for 'truth', *istina*,
literally means 'that which is'. Florensky argued that truth is
experienced as certitude, and that this is the basis for asserting
that something is true.

17. The Great Canon of St Andrew (660–740) is a penitential hymn
sung in Lent. The full text can be found in *The Lenten Triodion*
translated by Mother Mary and Archimandrite Kallistos Ware
(South Canaan, PA: St Tikhon's Seminary Press, 2001), pp. 378
ff.

18. See Chapter 4, note 29.

19. I.e. in the 1930s.

20. St Basil the Great (329–79): Archbishop of Caesarea in
Cappadocia, theologian and monastic founder.

21. Russian saying.

22. Popular Russian expression for the abstruse and seemingly
irrelevant.

23. I.e. sacraments.

24. A typical Russian dinner opens with salted cucumber and
smoked fish, served with vodka.

25. See note 12.

26. Cf: 'Death in the true sense is separation from God, and "the
sting of death is sin" (1 Cor. 15:56) … Life, in the true sense, is
He who said, "I am the Life" (John 11:25), and who, having
entered death, led back to life him who had died.' *Third Century
on Love*, para. 93, in *The Philokalia*, tr. and ed. Palmer, Sherrard

and Ware (London: Faber and Faber, 1990), p. 81.

27. Praises at Matins for Holy Saturday, First Stasis, verse 3. *The Lenten Triodion*, tr. Mother Mary and Kallistos Ware (South Canaan, PA: St Tikhon's Seminary Press, 2001), p. 623.

28. 'Do not say that God is just ... David may call Him just and fair, but God's own Son has revealed to us that he is before all things good and kind. He is kind to the ungrateful and the wicked (Luke 6:35). How can you call God just when you read the parable of the labourers in the vineyard and their wages ... How can you call God just when you read the parable of the prodigal son who squanders his father's wealth in riotous living, and the moment he displays some nostalgia his father runs to him, throws his arms around his neck and gives him complete power over all his riches? ... Where is God's justice? Here, in the fact that we were sinners and Christ died for us!' (*Ascetical Treatises*, 60).

29. Panikhida: memorial service for the departed, which includes the well-known kontakion, or hymn: 'Give rest, O Christ, to the soul(s) of thy servant(s) with the saints ...' See *Panihkida, or Memorial for the Departed* (Oxford: St Stephen's Press, 2002), p. 28.

30. I.e. Lent.

31. *Endgame*.

32. 'O Lord our God, who hast espoused the Church as a pure Virgin from among the Gentiles ...' *The Rite of Holy Matrimony* in *Service Book of the Holy Orthodox-Catholic Apostolic Church*, compiled and translated by Isabel Hapgood (Englewood, NJ: Antiochan Orthodox Christian Archdiocese, 1983), p. 292.

33. The ceremony of Crowning is central to the Orthodox marriage service.

Chapter 5: The Vocation of Man

1. See Chapter 2, note 2.

2. 'For this reason the human person was introduced last among beings, as a kind of natural bond mediating between the universal poles through their proper parts, and leading into unity in itself those things that are naturally set apart from one another by a great interval.' Maximus the Confessor, *Difficulty 41*, 1305C, in Andrew Louth, *Maximus the Confessor* (London and New York:

Routledge, 1996), p. 157.

3. See Chapter 3, note 8.

4. Cf. 'Thou didst hallow the streams of Jordan [i.e. in being baptised in them – ed.], sending down upon them from heaven thy Holy Spirit … Wherefore, O King who lovest mankind, come thou now and sanctify this water, by the indwelling of thy Holy Spirit'. From the Prayer for the Blessing of the Water in 'The Office of Holy Baptism', *Service Book of the Holy Orthodox-Catholic Apostolic Church*, compiled and translated by Isabel Hapgood (Englewood, NJ: Antiochan Orthodox Christian Archdiocese, 1983), p. 278. Normally the blessing of the water takes place during the service of Baptism itself.

5. 'That He will grant it the grace that all who hear its sound, whether by day or by night, shall be roused to the glorification of His holy name, let us pray to the Lord.' *Great Book of Needs*, vol. 2 (South Canaan, PA: St Tikhon's Seminary Press, 1998) pp. 85–6.

6. Alexey Vasilyevich Koltzov (1809–42)

7. John 6:68.

8. Gen. 5:22–23.

9. 'Then the Lord said, "My spirit shall not abide man for ever, for he is flesh, but his days shall be a hundred and twenty years"' (Gen 6:3).

Chapter 6: Christianity Today

1. Deification: the Orthodox Christian belief that human beings, and indeed the whole of creation, are called to unification with God, as expressed by St Maximus the Confessor, writing in the seventh century: 'God made us so that we might become "partakers of the divine nature" (2 Peter 1:4) through deification by grace and so that we might come to be like Him (cf. 1 John 3:2). It is through deification that all things are reconstituted and achieve their permanence; and it is for its sake that what is not is brought into being and given existence'(42). 'A sure warrant for looking forward with hope to deification of human nature is provided by the incarnation of God, which makes man god to the same degree as God Himself became man. For it is clear that He who became man without sin (cf. Heb. 4:15) will divinise human

nature without changing it into the divine nature, and will raise it up for His own sake to the same degree as He lowered Himself for man's sake. This is what St Paul teaches mystically when he says, "… that in the ages to come He might display the over-flowing richness of His grace" (Eph. 2:7)' (62). Maximus the Confessor, *First Century of Various Texts*, 42 and 62, in Palmer, Sherrard and Ware (tr. and ed.), *The Philokalia*, vol. II, (London: Faber and Faber, 1981), pp. 173, 177f.

2. Nikolai Leskov (1831–95): a Russian novelist and short story writer who often wrote about different forms of popular devotion, including surviving pagan elements.

3. St Maximus the Confessor (580–662) wrote extensively on the close relationship between dogma and prayer. Although he was at first condemned as a heretic for maintaining that Christ had a human as well as a divine will, his teaching was confirmed after his death by the Sixth Ecumenical Council of 680–81.

4. André Lanskoy (1902–76): Russian-born French painter.

5. The Monk Nestor. An historical compilation, *The Tale of By-gone Years*, was the basis of the earliest and most complete written records of ancient Rus': the *Lavrentyesky Spisok*, dating from 1377 (named after the Monk Lawrence who copied it) and the *Ipatsky Spisok*, found at the Ipatsky Monastery. *The Tale of By-gone Years* was long thought to be the work of the Monk Nestor and was known as *The Chronicle of Nestor*. It is now generally thought to be a compilation of many people's work.

6. Cf. John 1:45ff.

7. I.e., at Pentecost.

8. 'For it is just like the way the cutting-edge of a sword plunged in fire becomes burning hot and the heat acquires a cutting-edge (for just as the fire is united to the iron, so also is the burning heat of the fire to the cutting-edge of the iron, and the iron becomes burning hot by its union with the fire, and the fire acquires a cutting-edge by union with the iron). Neither suffers any change by the exchange with the other in union, but each remains unchanged in its own being as it acquires the property of its part-ner in union. So also in the mystery of the divine Incarnation …' *Difficulty* 5 (MPG 1060A), quoted in *Maximus the Confessor*, Andrew Louth (London & New York: Routledge, 1996), p. 178.

9. Rev. 2:17.

10. Nikolai Berdyaev (1874–1948): Russian philosopher who held a chair in the University of Moscow after the 1917 Revolution, but was expelled in 1922, settling first in Berlin and then at Clamart near Paris, where he continued to write and lecture on philosophy and religion.

11. Blaise Pascal (1623–62), author of *Pensées*.

12. 'But I say, that the things which the Gentiles sacrifice, they sacrifice to devils, and not to God: and I would not that ye should have fellowship with devils. Ye cannot drink the cup of the Lord, and the cup of devils: ye cannot be partakers of the Lord's table, and of the table of devils' (1 Cor. 10:20–21).

13. Russian term for a spiritual adviser or elder (often a monastic or hermit).

14. St Silouan of Mount Athos, Russian-born Athonite monk, died 1938. He was canonised by the Ecumenical Patriarchate in 1988.

Chapter 7: The Church Must Be as Powerless as God ...

1. Nil Sorsky (*c*. 1433–1508): Russian saint and the first Russian mystic to write about the contemplative life and to formulate a guide for spiritual perfection.

2. See Chapter 3, note 2.

3. Cf. John 14:6.

4. The Matins of Great Friday, usually held on Thursday evening in parishes, where the story of the crucifixion and death of Christ is told in twelve Gospel readings, interspersed with antiphons (hymns) which meditate on the events described. While these can be sung to the basic Russian chant, choirs tend to use elaborate settings for this service. In particular, the *Exapostilarion* (a hymn read or sung towards the end of Matins) is for this service a reflection on the good thief and is a well-known and loved musical set piece.

5. 'We hymn Thee, we bless Thee, we give thanks to Thee, O Lord, and we pray to Thee, our God'. Hymn sung by the choir either during or immediately before the *Epiclesis*, or the invocation of the Holy Spirit on the bread and wine. See *The Divine Liturgy of St John Chrysostom* (Oxford: St Stephen's Press, 1999), p. 69. The words are usually sung to a composed setting rather than

simple chant.

6. Ibid., p. 70.

Chapter 8: Without Notes

1. An Exarch is a high-ranking bishop with administrative responsibility for a whole region. In 1963, Metropolitan Anthony was appointed Patriarchal Exarch in Western Europe for the Moscow Patriarchate.

2. An exclusive independent girls' school in St Petersburg.

3. Alexander Scriabin (1872–1915), was the half-brother of Metropolitan Anthony's mother.

4. The Curé d'Ars, or John-Marie-Baptiste Vianney, was born in Dardilly in France in 1786. He was ordained priest in 1815 and appointed priest of Ars – a village near Lyons – in 1818. He completely immersed himself in the work of his parish but soon gained a reputation throughout Europe as a confessor and spiritual guide. He also had the gift of healing and of hidden knowledge, but was tormented in life by evil spirits. He gave all he had to the poor and needy and went about in ragged clothes, ate poorly, and slept little. In the twelve months before he died in 1859 he was visited by over one hundred thousand people. He was canonised in 1925 and declared Patron of Parish Clergy in 1929.

5. On Great Friday, according to the practice of the Russian Orthodox Cathedral in London, Vespers is celebrated in the afternoon, with the procession of the Holy Shroud to a specially decorated table in the centre of the church. This is followed in the early evening by Matins, with lamentations over the burial of Christ.

6. Luc de Clapiers, Marquis de Vauvenargues (1715–47): French moralist, author of *Maxims*.

7. The Bolshevik Revolution of 1917.

8. *Chitiya Menei: Lives of the Saints* set out in order through the months of the year.

9. The Valaam monastery, on an island in the lake of Ladoga, in Karelia, dates back to the early tenth century, the very beginning of Christianity in ancient Rus'. In the Russian-Finnish war of 1939–41, the monks were evacuated to Finland, where the 'New

Valaam' monastery still flourishes. Six monks returned to Valaam in 1941, but left in 1944 when the island was finally ceded to the USSR by Finland. Monastic life was resumed at 'Old Valaam' in 1989.

10. The church which Metropolitan Anthony attended remained under the Moscow Patriarchate, as does the Diocese of Sourozh, which he later established in England. In Paris at the time, the largest group maintaining the Russian Orthodox tradition, at the Alexander Nevsky Cathedral in rue Daru, had already placed themselves under the Ecumenical Patriarchate.

11. *France Libre* ('Free French'): a patriotic movement connected with the anti-fascist coalition led by General de Gaulle, with headquarters in London.

Chapter 9: Science and Faith: Education and the Arts

1. Metropolitan Philaret (Drozdov) of Moscow and Kolomna (1782–1867): theologian, political activist, preacher and poet. He was Bishop of Moscow from 1821 until his death, and came to be known as the Metropolitan of All Russia, a 'born Patriarch' of the Russian Church. He is commemorated as a saint (feast day: 1/14 December).

2. St John of Damascus (645–749): poet and theologian, who was a key figure in the iconoclast controversy. See Andrew Louth, *St John Damascene: Tradition and Originality in Byzantine Theology* (Oxford: OUP, 2002).

3. See 'Hymns with their own melody by John the Monk' in *Office for the Burial of the Dead [A Lay Person]* (Oxford: St Stephen's Press, 2004), pp. 60–64. Today the original melodies are lost, but the hymns are sung to traditional chant at Orthodox funerals.

Chapter 10: Of Divine Worship and a Christian Lifestyle

1. In general, services in the Russian Orthodox Church are celebrated in Old Church Slavonic, rather than modern Russian. Some Slavonic words have developed completely different meanings over time.

2. It is still the rule that Church Slavonic is used instead of modern Russian in the Russian Orthodox Church, just as Byzantine Greek is mostly used in Churches of the Greek tradition.

3. In the Orthodox Church, Sundays and Feasts are celebrated with a service the previous evening, followed by a Liturgy in the morning.
4. Theophan the Recluse (1815–94): priest, monk and eventually bishop, whose later years were spent in prayer and seclusion. He was probably the most highly educated of all the Russian monastic authors, and he left behind a substantial body of writings, which are considered by some to be the best expression of the ascetic and spiritual teaching of the Russian Church.
5. See Chapter 5, note 6.

Chapter 11: 'Life for Me Is Christ …'
Biblical quotations in this chapter are from the King James Version.
1. St John Climacus (John of the Ladder): seventh-century monk of Sinai and author of *The Ladder of Divine Ascent*, a classic of Orthodox spirituality.
2. St Irenaeus of Lyons (c. 130–c. 208): great Christian theologian, who developed in particular the themes of Incarnation, and of the living Tradition preserved through the succession of bishops from the Apostles onwards.
3. Cf. Gal. 4:5ff.

Chapter 12: Freedom and Spiritual Obedience
1. The Russian word, *poslushanie*, refers to spiritual obedience as well as to monastic obedience.
2. Khomiakov (see Chapter 8, note 5) was the author of a number of controversial historical and linguistic theories.
3. Literally an heroic feat or exploit, but used to describe any endeavour undertaken for God.
4. St Tikhon of Zadonsk (1724–83): Bishop of Voronezh 1763–68, canonised in 1861. He was one of the models for the Elder Zossima in Dostoevsky's novel *The Brothers Karamazov*, and his spiritual writings were widely studied in seminaries and theological schools throughout Russia.
5. St Ambrose of Optina, a starets of the Optina Hermitage in the province of Kaluga, who was visited by thousands of people seeking spiritual discussion and advice, including Tolstoy and Dostoevsky. Like St Tikhon (see note 4, above) Dostoevsky used

him as a model for the Elder Zossima.

Chapter 13: Pastoral Concern for Spiritual Life
1. See Chapter 13, note 3.
2. Eleventh-century monastics, and founding fathers of Russian monasticism.
3. See Chapter 11, note 2.
4. See Chapter 10, note 5.

Chapter 14: Thoughts on the Religious Upbringing of Children
1. There are extensive rules in Orthodoxy about fasting before Communion, in Advent and Lent, and on Wednesdays and Fridays throughout the year.

Chapter 15: How to Live with Oneself
1. St Ephrem the Syrian (d. 373) expressed his theology mainly as poetry. See Ephrem the Syrian, *Hymns*, tr. Kathleen E. McVey (NY: Paulist Press, Classics of Western Spirituality, 1989).
2. Fr Evgraph Kovalesky (1905–70): priest of the Paris emigration, who joined the Eglise Catholique-Orthodoxe de France, which practises a Western-rite Orthodoxy. Father Evgraph was consecrated in 1964 as Bishop Jean de St Denys, the Eglise Catholique-Orthodoxe de France having left the jurisdiction of the Moscow Patriarchate in 1953. In 1960, they placed themselves under the jurisdiction of ROCOR (se Chapter 3, note 7) and later under that of the Patriarchate of Romania. Since that time, the Patriarchate of Romania has severed all ties with this small group, which continues to exist as an independent entity.